The Garden Butler

GRAHAM HAMILTON

DEDICATION

This is dedicated to Robert Nicholson, who this book is about.

CONTENTS

ACKNOWLEDGMENTS

With thanks to all our family and friends who have supported and encouraged this project. In particular to Nigel Webster for the idea of the title and to David Settle and Pauline Rospigliosi who are always so positive about our adventures and inspire us onwards.

1   LEARNING NEW SKILLS

We decided to leave England for a new life in the Mediterranean sunshine. The plan was simple. I had recently turned fifty and, after twenty-one years of service as head waiter in the House of Lords, taken my civil service pension early, would find some part-time work and write my memoirs of all the personalities and celebrities I had met in service.

We resolved to move from our expensive rented house in Brighton to a place a lot cheaper in the sun. We had been inspired by visits to Southern France and Tuscany but could not afford them. Spain was another country we had enjoyed and, after a lot of searching on the internet, we found a cheap supply of rental properties surrounding another city we love, Málaga.

We flew out to Spain and hired a tiny Smart Car to check out suitable homes. We don't have kids, but do have pets – a dog and two cats - and needed to find somewhere with a garden and maybe a pool, not far from Málaga centre. They are our family. I've had Dickie Dog since he was a puppy and did the wrong thing of buying a dog out of the back of the paper -*The Friday Ad* - without seeing the parents. But when a gypsy woman turned up on my doorstep with a tiny brown and white Staffie in her arms, I couldn't resist. I got Flea, a little black and white cat, as a kitten the year before. She was the last remaining one from a litter of six, being sold in a terrible, run-down pet shop in Brighton. She was covered in fleas and riddled with worms and it seemed like she was going to die; she was so small and dehydrated so I nursed and fed her with a dropper pipette and have now had her for sixteen years. She and Dickie have grown up together. Oliver, named Satan by the animal sanctuary, was Graham's, my partner's, second rescue cat. He has been with us for five years now. The owner of the charity explained that no-one wanted him because he was so aggressive, but Graham saw past that and adopted him. To be honest, Ollie is a bit mad; we call him *Bi-Polar Pussy*. He doesn't really like people and after three weeks of hiding under the bed, he decided he adores Dickie Dog and follows him everywhere, including out on long dog walks.

Graham, is a teacher and always highly organised. He booked an appointment with Ivan, one of the local estate agents, and made of a list of the houses we wanted to see in a town called Alhaurin El Grande. Literally translated this means *The Grand Garden of Allah*. Maybe this was a sign? We both had a strong passion for gardening.

The town was split over a hill with two squares, *plazas*, and two churches. We were told to meet him at one thirty at the Church of Our Lady of Incarnation which had a striking, blue tiled roof.

Everyone is late in Spain by at least half an hour; it seems a matter of cultural politeness. The hot sun, the serene mountain ranges and relaxed people all seem to say: *Hey. Take it easy.* We found it easy to switch to *slow* gear and ordered a couple of beers in a tapas bar by the church. We were the only ones in the square.

At one thirty-two a short, ball of a man with thin black hair and long front teeth, which protruded over his bottom lip, ran into the square and started waving a clipboard at us. He looked like an oversized chipmunk who was acting as an impatient tour guide. 'Please. Coming now,' he said, in a French sounding accent, with his mouth opening and closing as he was chewing gum. 'Following me. *Rapidement.*'

He had parked in a blue bay but didn't want to pay. We gulped down our beers, left a few euros and followed him over to his old, dented, Renault.

2

He was talking on his mobile, in Spanish, making some appointments for other clients and opened a rear door and ushered us in. Whilst still speaking on his phone, he pulled out, in front of a white van, which beeped at him. He ignored it, tore down a busy narrow street, hit the curb and told us he needed to get petrol.

The town was like a living museum. There were rows of small, terraced, town houses, lined with thin pavements of white and pink checquered tiles. Dotted along the buildings were women with skin like raisins scrubbing the steps outside their homes, whilst the men, maybe their husbands, assembled in groups on iron benches, swapping thoughts and stories about their day. Local drivers blocked the road by double-parking directly outside the shops they wanted to enter. Further down the hill, the traffic began to crawl. We were following an old man with a donkey and cart which were transporting crates of tomatoes, wobbling from the uneven gaps in the road between inlaid cobblestones. The tyres of our car rumbled across the pitted surface. I held my shoulder. It reminded me of the pebbled street I had tripped over in Brighton, three months ago, and shattered my humerus complete with its ball and socket joint. A skilled surgeon had stuck it back together with thirteen pins. A follow up x-ray revealed what looked like a game of *Kerplunk* inside, but it was now stronger than ever.

'We're not in Kansas anymore, *Toto*,' Graham said, quietly, staring out of the window.

There was another cart being pulled by a horse which looked like it had died many months ago but was continuing onwards, in automatic motion.

'It looks more like Mexico,' I said, perhaps a bit too loud.

'*Hasta mañana,*' Ivan said, closing the clamshell of his phone. '*Ciao.*' He tossed his mobile onto the passenger chair and then blasted his horn at the horseman, who had pulled up his cart to speak to a neighbour. He drove past him and shook his hand.

3

'*Lo siento.* I'm being sorry about that,' he said to us, turning his head around. 'I'm busy. Very busy. Let us go to the petrol station and there we are speaking about the houses you are wanting to see.'

We proceeded out of the flagstone streets and onto a newly laid road which led westwards, out of the town. A large board announced that the Andalucian government had spent 2.9 million euros on building this highway. From here you could clearly see the jagged mountains of the Sierra Gibralgalia and the green valley of the Guadalhorce, interspersed with the white-washed villages of Cártama, Villafranco and Coín.

At the end of this smooth tarmacked carriageway was a roundabout. There were signs to Marbella, Fuengirola and Mijas. Ivan pointed to this newly formed *rotunda*. 'The locals call this *El Centro del Universo.*'

Graham and I looked at each other and said nothing.

All the petrol stations in Spain have a café in the main building and an adjoining terrace outside. They are more like local community centres than garages. We sat at a small table and ordered three *café con leche*.

Graham took out the house details we had printed off and Ivan stacked them into two piles, declaring them to be *possible* or *gone*. There were only two in the *possible* pile. One was a little brown cottage for five hundred a month and the other was a large white villa for eight hundred. The latter had captured our imagination as there was a video of a dog ambling out of the house, walking across the terrace and having a drink from the pool.

'We like this one,' I pointed, pleased that it was still an option.

Ivan rubbed his chin, and picked at some white stuff, probably gum, lodged between his teeth. 'Only problem is dogs.'

Graham sat forward. 'I did tell you, we've got a dog.'

'He's not the problem.' He held the picture up for us to look at and pointed to a chain link fence at the side of the house. 'The next door peoples are having five dogs. They always are barking.'

We looked at each other and shrugged. 'No we don't want that,' Graham said.

I agreed. 'Eight hundred is too much, anyway.'

Ivan straightened his back, upright. He resembled a Meer Cat surveying the landscape from the sand dunes. 'I like show you Madame Vincent's.' He passed us the details for this one which was still *possible.* 'It's five minutes from here.' He picked up his mobile, dialed another number and spoke to the person on the other end in French.

I remembered the video of the house from the internet. Unlike a lot of Spanish houses, it was painted brown and had a very rustic design with lots of interesting features. All the doors and window frames were dark wood and the light fittings were reclaimed antique lamps, which had been wired into the high ceilings. It must have been a barn conversion.

Ivan took us back towards the town and stopped on the outskirts and pulled onto a long, sloping drive with a high, metal barrier. He jumped out the car and entered a code into a pad, for the solid security gate. Inside was a large tree in front of the end of a tall, dark-red building covered in purple flowering bougainvillea. The driveway was lined with pots of cuttings, mainly lavenders, which had been pruned off last year's plants. A little brown man, wearing frayed shorts and a holey shirt was clipping one of the hedges. '*Buenos tardes,* José,' Ivan shouted. The man waved to him.

Ivan jumped back into the car. 'That's José the gardener and that's the landlady's house. The rental is more up the hill.' He drove off the cemented driveway, past two disused canons which were pointing down towards us and we ascended a gravel track, between fields of ochre dirt with almond and cypress fir trees. The wheels skidded on stones as his car tried to climb. 'You have to be being careful,' Ivan said, embarrassed. 'Madame Vincent is lovely old lady, but she is not liking people making noisy drivings.' The wheels spun around and grabbed the hard surface under the stones and continued to rise up the hill. Near the top, there was a sharp turn to the left with some new chain-link fencing, which defined the boundaries of the rental property. It was very narrow and as he turned he scraped one of the metal posts.

A minute later we saw the house. There was a huge almond tree on a bank to the right of the entrance. Behind this, long wooden beams supported a terracotta roofed veranda along the end of the house. A hunched, bony woman stood underneath, by the front door, with a file of papers in one hand and a gnarled walking stick in the other. '*Bonjour Messieurs,*' she called out to us.

Ivan seemed deferential in her presence, like a proud grandson greeting the matriarch of the family. He spat the chewing gum out into a tissue and put it in his pocket. '*Bonjour Madame Vincent. Ça va?*' He walked forward and kissed the hand which she held out for him.

'*Bien merci, et toi?*' She thrust a big key into the door, turned the heavy locks and forced it open.

It was clear that despite her vintage appearance she was fit and had a physical strength which belied her splintered frame. She put her cane down and held out a hand of lumpy, thin fingers. '*Bonjour. Je suis Isabella Vincent.*'

I received her hand-shake which was strong and vigorous. '*Enchanté, mademoiselle.*'

She giggled and put her hand to her mouth in feigned modesty.

My French wasn't perfect but it was definitely better than my Spanish. '*Je suis, Roberto.*'

She shook Graham's hand but continued talking to me. '*Eh bien. Si vous parlez français Roberto. Merveilleux. Il a été de nombreuses années que personne m'a appelé "mademoiselle." Que pensez-vous de ma charmante petite maison?* '

Oh dear. I heard something about a house.

She laughed and stepped inside. '*Si lo prefieres, hablamos en Español.*'

My blank face met her reassured charm.

'Or we speak in English? You choose Roberto.' She put the papers down on a small wooden table and pulled out a high-backed, chair.

There was something beguiling about the ease and confidence of this grand lady. 'English is good for me.' I blushed.

'Very well,' she said. Ivan rushed forward to help lower her into the seat. 'Please Ivan. You show these gentlemen around. I'm tired today.'

'Of course, Madame.' He put his briefcase down on the table and pulled out his iPad. 'I see you 'ave been changing some of the furniture. I must be making a new video for the website.'

She sighed and brushed a wave of her long white hair from her face. 'If it pleases you.'

Ivan told us to follow him and, simultaneously, he gave his sales speak to us and his digital recorder. 'Janssen's Properties, Alhaurin El Grande, Costa del Sol are pleased to show you this charming country house. This property has telephone line and has rustic character. Fully furnished. With splendid, traditional Spanish table for dining. This is your landlady. Give us a wave.'

She looked mortified and waved him away with a piece of paper in her hand. 'I don't want to be in it,' she snapped.

He realized he had overstepped the mark. 'Just making a joke for you. I am taking it out now.'

She turned away from him and started sorting her documents and muttered, 'It's *Moroccan*, not Spanish.'

He moved the camera off her and scanned the room. 'This property is benefitting from central heating. Kitchen it has shutter. You can close for cooking more private in the kitchen. Lounge area. High ceiling. Wooden beams. Two comfy chairs.' He walked into the narrow hallway and pointed his iPad into the kitchen. 'Country-style kitchen with views backing into lounge.'

The kitchen was tiny and had cupboards with curtains instead of doors. It had a new gas ringed hob and a small grill oven which sat on top of the stone tiled worktop.

'Bathroom opposite with sitting down bath. Wooden beams.'

We squeezed behind Ivan to get into the bathroom. 'What's a *sitting down bath*?' Graham whispered, not wanting to spoil the video commentary.

'That,' I said, pointing to a high walled shower tray behind a plastic curtain.

We could hear Ivan in the room next door. 'Small bedroom, ideal for one bed. Beams. Fitted wardrobe. Radiator. Central heating is with gas.'

Spain can get very cold in the winter and it was unusual to have a house which had proper heating. Usually there is one fireplace in the corner of the lounge which heats a small area.

'This property is located on outskirts of town so you easily walk into town. This next bedroom is having second exit onto the garden. Built in wardrobes. Radiator. Beams.'

This room was even smaller but had a stable door and could possibly accommodate a single bed. A reclaimed, brass oil lantern had been attached to a beam with chains and was hopefully connected to electricity.

We followed him back into the living room where he was careful to keep the camera away from the owner. He tripped up the stairs but carried on without pausing. 'Upstairs you are having big, open space for further bedroom and lounge. This property is fully furnished.'

The mezzanine level, just under the roof timbers, was like its own self-contained studio apartment. There was a double bed under a pitched skylight and a sofa and table on the other side.

'This is charming,' Graham said, leaning out of a small window under the eaves at the far end.

At the other end, over the main living room, was a small raised platform with an armchair and bookcases. I was careful to step up but banged my head on the low ceiling. *Shit* I wanted to yell, but Mrs. Vincent was sat directly below us.

Ivan had gone back down and out into the garden. I rubbed my head and we followed him.

'Outside you are having swimming pool above the property with lovely views over Guadalhorce Valley and forest. Property ideal for one person or couple because of its size. Call me. Janssen's Properties….'

He walked back down to the house and Graham and I took in the views and marveled at the size of the pool. It was longer than the house. An eagle flew up the valley, over the roof and our heads and into the forest.

We decided to take the cottage.

Renting is a much easier process over here. There are no credit checks. You do not need to prove your income, unless you try to rent in one of the busy expat communities on the coast. Most places accept pets. All that is needed is some proof of identity; one month's deposit and rent in advance; to sign an eleven month contract and then make some arrangements for paying the next month's rent. In our case, Isabella lived at the bottom of the drive so we organised to pop in on the first day of each month with the next payment. The only surprise that came with the deal was that we needed to pay fifty euros per month for garden and pool maintenance. Previous tenants had decided to do it themselves and had run the pool dry and blown up the pump. We agreed, for now, but with an option to do it ourselves once we had learned the essential skills.

The agent does take commission. Sometimes this is a separate fee of two weeks rent but with Ivan a percentage was taken out of the first month's rent.

Whilst we were signing the contract, Ivan's phone went off three times. Isabella did seem to like him but was annoyed that he wasn't giving us his full attention. '*Monsieur.* Turn it off,' she ordered him.

He got up from the table, red-faced and went outside. '*Un minute s'il vous plaît Madame.*'

She raised her eyes and continued signing her signature in the corner of each page of the contract. 'Funny little Belgian man,' she said to us. 'Spain is a place for peace, for quiet. Not busy phones.'

We agreed.

We weren't able to move over for a few weeks and she kindly delayed the contract start date for us. We shook hands and the deal was done.

Ivan dropped us back to our car and we thanked him for his

time.

'It's a pleasure for me. You will be happy there,' he said, looking for his next appointment and a new stick of gum. 'What work will you be doing?' he asked us.

We levered ourselves out of the seats and onto the pavement. 'Graham can teach English but it's not easy for me.' I had already decided that I didn't want to go back into kitchen or restaurant work.

'You like gardening?' he asked me.

'I love it.'

'The English are always wanting gardeners here. They are not trusting the Spanish and are wanting the English gardeners.'

Before I could reply, he had clunked the gears into first and was pulling away.

I walked by the side of the car and shouted, 'Thank you.' Gardening could be a good idea.

As we drove back to the airport, I started analysing the prospect of changing my career at fifty and becoming a Mediterranean gardener. We took off from Málaga and I looked out the window over the aqua sea and scorched-brown mountains. The idea took seed and began to root itself in my mind. I kept watering it with glasses of Rioja and became determined that this was what I was going to do.

Graham was drinking some New Zealand Chardonnay and was watching *Elysium* again on his iPad.

'Do you really think I could be become a gardener?' I asked him.

He put his glass down, pulled out a headphone and turned to me. 'Of course. You can do anything once you put your mind to it.' That was easy for him to say.

Learning new things was always difficult for me. 'Like skiing?' I reminded him and chuckled.

'No,' he laughed. 'Hopefully, not like skiing.'

A few years ago, we had hired all the gear and flown out to see one of Graham's best friends, Barbara, who lived in Switzerland. I was eager to get started, so the first night, after a couple of beers, we put on the equipment and skied across a large, snow-covered field, with a slight slope. Graham showed me how to snow-plough and looked like a mini *James Bond* darting through a line of fir trees at the foot of a mountain, shooting away from any hidden baddies. I had a go and it turned out to be easier than I thought.

The next day we tackled one of the nursery slopes which was much steeper, but relatively short. Graham glided down to the bottom, demonstrating the need to go side to side and slowing his movement down by opening and closing the skis. Once again, I followed his instructions and somehow made it safely down. The difficult part was getting back up. I had thought that all the ski lifts would be chairs. This was a metal loop of orange plastic paddles. As it turned, you were supposed to line up straight, next to the contraption, pull the handle up into a horizontal position near your chest and then, assail, effortlessly up the hill.

I got into position, but the snow had turned to ice and I started sliding backwards. I missed the first few handles which shot past me and the kids, who were waiting, started jeering, 'Come on old man.'

Graham was already waiting at the top of the hill. 'Just grab it and hold on,' he shouted.

I grabbed the paddle and it jolted me faster than I had thought. My right leg was thrown high up into the air and the ski flew off my boot, through the air and into a big mound of snow behind me. My glasses, which I was wearing instead of goggles, were flung off my head and onto the floor. My leg came down on the other side of the wire, so that I now had my back to the incline and was travelling up, backwards, but without one ski and my specs. I tried to get off but everything looked blurry and I was being dragged up like a rag doll.

All the children were laughing. 'He looks like Mr. Bean,' one of them said. 'More like your grandad,' another added. I do wear thick glasses and lost all my hair when I was twenty. I'm practically blind without my glasses.

Finally someone hit the emergency button and it ground to a halt. My leg was still stuck, over the wire, as the ski on my other leg kept sliding downwards.

I saw a figure shoot past on my left. 'Just hold on. I'll get your ski.' It was Graham.

Once I had my glasses back on, I could see that about ten children had gathered around to point and laugh. I fell off the wire and landed on my arse. I couldn't get the other ski back on and carried them both back up to the top. My trousers were soaked from the snow.

'I think he's wet himself,' one of the little sods sniggered, skiing smoothly past me.

'Do you want to have another go?' Graham asked, his green eyes sparkling, mischievously. 'We could all do with another laugh.'

'No.' I said. 'I need a drink.' That was the end of my skiing experience.

I looked out of the plane window and saw we were flying over Bilbao, towards the Bay of Biscay. 'I really would like to do be a gardener.'

'Robert, you're looping again,' Graham smiled. He says this when I get stuck on an idea.

'It can't be that difficult, can it? What do I need?'

He paused the film, just before the part where Jodie Foster is killed. 'Well, you need transport to get there.'

'Got that.' I guessed a van would be needed in the future, but our little car would do for now, until I got enough clients.

He closed his iPad and turned towards me. 'And gardening experience.'

'Got that.' I said, proudly.

Despite living in flats for years, my grandparents had shown me how to garden when I was a kid.

In the past three years we had been planting our garden in Brighton and had been very fortunate to have been offered an allotment, up by the race course, where we grew strawberries, raspberries, carrots, cabbages, rhubarb, parsnips, and every type of bean imaginable. My greatest pleasure was growing potatoes.

After planting ten lines of Maris Pipers, John, the retired colonel who had the neighbouring plot, turned up, marched down to where I was standing, folded his arms and sighed.

'What you got in there, lad?' he asked me, leaning forwards to inspect.

I proudly told him. 'Tasty Maris Pipers. Chitted them myself.'

He was not impressed. 'You've put them in wrong. I told you before. You need to mound up the soil above them, to make them grow firmer and stronger.' He tutted, turned away and went back up the hill to his potting shed. 'I'll put the kettle on.'

It was true, he had told me but, somehow, in the excitement

of excavating the troughs, I had forgotten.

Back at the house, I told Graham, 'I'll have to dig them up and plant them again.'

'It's not your fault, Beany,' he told me. 'It's because you were in the *remove* group at school.' He knows it was the *remedial* group but has called it this ever since my mum told him that's what it was. 'I wonder where you get it from?' he added.

We always tease each other. He calls me *Beany* due to my strange brain. It's true, I don't know my times-tables but I can always remember factual stuff like when a song first came out, when decimalisation was introduced, the year the Cold War started and lots of other facts and figures. I don't know why I can't ever remember personal stuff, like my bank account number, but am accurate about tons of unrelated general knowledge that no-one really needs to know. I guess that's why I love politics.

'You should be on *Eggheads,*' he once told me. 'Really. I think you would beat them.'

I generally did when we were sat at home but would be too nervous on the telly.

Graham's brain doesn't work like that. It's the complete opposite. He was a real swat at school, learns academic things at record speed and has never failed anything, apart from a breathalyser test in Swindon ten years ago. He drinks too much, probably because he needs to slow his brain down at times and isn't too good with real life. He hates politics and has terrible general knowledge. However, he does believe that anything is possible. I guess that's what makes him a good teacher. One of his favourite mottos is: *Find out what you what to do in life and then prepare to do it well.* Another is: *The one constant in life is change.* He thinks that he created the latter but I have a sneaky feeling that *Heraclitus,* the ancient Greek philosopher, came up with something very similar.

He also has a good knowledge of gardening, thanks to his parents. When he was seven, his mum ran off with their lodger and they lived in service on large country estates working as housekeeper and gardener. 'Just mound some more soil on top of them. They'll be fine,' he told me.

I followed these instructions and John came down to re-inspect them. 'That's much better, lad.'

It was a hot summer and I kept watering them. Some short green shoots appeared at the tops but then stopped growing and suddenly died.

'I think I should have dug them up and planted them again.' I pointed to the brown, wilted stems on the top of the piles.

Graham laughed. 'Just stick your fork in and see what you've got.'

Hesitantly, I plunged the big metal tool into the soil and dug deep. To my amazement, ten newly formed spuds came to the surface. After repeated digging, we ended up with about three hundred of them.

'That's amazing, don't you think?' I had my arms full of the dirt-covered vegetables. 'It's a miracle really.'

He was bagging them up. 'It's called good gardening and you are good at it, Rob.'

My ears popped as we started our descent over France. 'Do I need anything else?' I was like an eager student asking the teacher how to do well.

'A full driving license.' He chuckled as he spoke these words.

We both knew how difficult that one had been.

I had started learning to drive when I was forty-two and it

took me several tests to pass. I'm usually fearless, but when it comes to tests I am sixteen again, full of nerves and I forget everything.

When we got together, we left our flats in town and moved to a house backing onto the South Downs. It was a beautiful location but miles from Brighton train station and I was still commuting to London for work. The buses were pretty unreliable, so I had no choice but to learn to drive. It wasn't something I had needed before and would have been a lot easier to do in my teens than as a middle-aged man.

The lessons had started in town, as soon as we made our decision to move. My instructor was a hairy, bearded man called Marcus Brown who gave lessons in a large, white people-carrier. He seemed good to start with but kept taking me on the same routes, again and again. We would drive around the more exclusive streets in Hove and he would suddenly tell me to pull over, if he saw any interesting rubbish outside the houses. We did a lot of emergency stops and he would leap out the vehicle, check out the discarded furniture and bric-a-brac and ask me to give him a hand loading it all into the back. I was very eager to get my licence as soon as possible but he would tell me to be patient; it would probably take *at least a year*.

'That's ridiculous,' said Graham, pacing up and down. 'He seems to be stringing you along, Rob. He's like a psychiatrist who doesn't want his patient to be cured, making them come back for as many sessions as he can, to make more money.'

That might be true, or it could have been that I was just a useful driver for his recycling business. We renamed him *Marcus Womble*, in tribute to the t.v. characters in the 1970's children's programme, who were *making good use of the things that* they find. Whatever his motive, it became clear that he had skipped some vital parts to my driving tuition which I kept failing: parallel parking and reversing around a corner. To be fair, it wasn't his fault that I had missed spotting a pedestrian on a crossing on test three and a bus pulling out on the fifth one.

'I'm never going to get this,' I said, looking at my latest failure sheet.

'Of course you will,' Graham said. 'I think it's probably nerves more than anything.'

'You just want someone to drive you back from the pub.'

'Too bloody right,' he said. 'No point having a servant for a partner if they can't drive.' He went into the kitchen to get another glass. 'Go and fetch me another bottle of Ballantine's,' he said, mimicking the often spoken command I had received from Princess Margaret.

'You don't drink whisky,' I reminded him.

'I do now, boy,' he said, with a tied tea-towel on his head, as a makeshift tiara.

Around this time, the Womble decided that he didn't want to teach me anymore. 'I've taught you all I know,' he told me. 'You just need to practice now.'

Graham was scared of my driving but agreed to take me out in his Ford KA at weekends; he needed to prove that you really can do anything if you put your mind to it. The failure sheet for test number six, proved him wrong. I had gone the wrong way down a one-way street.

He was unperturbed. 'You just need to calm those nerves somehow,' he reassured me.

Fortunately the night before my final test, I forgot all about it. We met some friends for drinks in *The Bulldog*, had way too much to drink and were woken by my alarm at ten-thirty the following morning.

'What did you set your alarm for?' Graham said, rubbing his eyes.

'No idea,' I said.

He got up and put the kettle on. 'Oh, shit,' he said, from the kitchen. 'It's your driving test today.'

I had written it on the *Countryfile* calendar.

I pulled the covers back over me and hid under the duvet. The dog and the two cats were still lying at the bottom of the bed, snoring. It was a typical February morning: freezing cold and dark. Heavy drops of rain were bashing the windows and falling in watery snakes down the glass.

'I'll have to cancel,' I mumbled, safely hidden in the cotton cocoon.

Graham had made some strong coffee. 'Nonsense. We've got half an hour. I'll get you down to the test centre by then.' He jumped into the shower.

'I'm too hungover,' I said, burying my head into the pillows. I slowly drifted back into sleep until a sudden draft hit my body and a cold, wet flannel was rubbed over my back.

'Up you get.' He pulled the duvet off the bed and threw it on the floor.

I tried to protest but he persuaded me with a gentle reminder. 'Come on Beany. Today's the day.'

We made it down to Brighton Marina just in time. I swallowed a couple of extra strong mints.

I don't remember the test but the result was undeniable: I had passed!

As we stowed our tables away and made the final descent into Gatwick, I felt so excited about our future plans; we were unstoppable.

Learning to drive in my forties was challenging but it

opened up a whole new world for me. I never thought that I would drive in the U.K., let alone in a Spanish car, on the other side of the road. It was a pity that, a week after our reconnaissance trip, we received a letter from the Spanish authorities.

'I think it might be a letter from the Spanish government, welcoming us to their country,' Graham said proudly, opening the envelope.

It wasn't.

There was a black and white photo of the two of us in the tiny rented Smart Car; my shiny head in perfect focus; with a demand for one hundred euros for driving seventy-two kilometres per hour in a sixty zone.

***

I'm from a little village in Hampshire called Fair Oak and couldn't wait to escape and travel as much as possible. I love food and ceremony. After having served in the Boys' Brigade from 1976 - 1980, I felt that my passport to the world could be in the catering department of the Royal Navy. As soon as I was old enough, I signed up with them and successfully completed ten weeks of arduous training at *HMS Raleigh*, in Plymouth. I hated it. The macho-competitive nature of the place was threatening and it was later explained that we might not get the opportunity to travel for years.

When I left, I went to the local job centre and they signed me up with one of Margaret Thatcher's *Youth Training Schemes*. The wages were low, only twenty-six pounds and fifty pence per week, but the opportunities were great. They were sold to us as an apprenticeship with a guaranteed, permanent job at the end. I was keen to pursue a career in catering and they sent me to the *Fisher's Pond Restaurant* in Colden Common, just outside Eastleigh.

I did six months of service in the kitchens, followed by six months in the restaurant and decided that I much preferred being front of house with the customers. It was here that I first met a tv celebrity, the anchor man news-presenter for Meridian News. The work was hard and I ended up single-handedly running the restaurant. Also I learned the art of silver service, how to fillet a Dover Sole and how to cook Steak Diane and Crêpes Suzette in front of the diners, at the table.

There was a lot of self-training which turned into a real baptism of fire, when I blew up a microwave re-heating vegetables in a metal bowl, and all the customers were evacuated by the fire alarm. There was no real damage and I still believed that I would get a well-paid job at the end of the year. They let me go and took on another cheap apprentice.

The skills I had learned did help me to get another job straight afterwards and to leave home. I worked as a live-in waiter at the Grand Hotel in Winchester. It was owned by a farming family, and part-occupied by a community of permanent residents, who would have been very at home in *Fawlty Towers*. There was a retired wartime nanny who used to ensure all the staff were quiet and in bed, as soon as service was finished, and an old sergeant who used to go out shooting pheasants and bring them around, to the back the door, for the chef. It was very long hours serving breakfast, lunch and dinner, with no weekends off. After paying for my lodgings, there was very little money left.

The only perk was that it was close to the train station and every Monday, on my day off, I would travel up to London and spend the day in the West End.

One week, whilst I was up there, I saw an advert for a live-in waiter for *The Garrick Club* in the back of *The Evening Standard*. I didn't know what a gentleman's club was in those days but, as a young man eager to get up into the city, I didn't care what I did and jumped at the offer of a job with a room included, in the heart of Covent Garden.

I left Winchester on a Sunday afternoon. The train was delayed several times due to broken signals and I arrived at the club late in the evening. As I climbed up the stairs to the main entrance with my suitcase, I could see a warm glow of lights inside, beyond a high-arched doorway. A well-dressed door man, with a face like a bulldog chewing a wasp, stepped outside and stopped me. His long, green trench coat was torn and tatty but made him look official.

'Members, only,' he barked.

I felt my cheeks burn red and pushed the floppy fringe off my face in the hope that he would recognize me as a new recruit. 'But, I. I work here,' I stammered.

He folded his arms over his huge, solid body. 'I don't cares if you's the King of England. You's not coming in 'ere.'

I wanted to tell him that there hadn't been a king of England since George the Sixth died, in nineteen fifty-two, but didn't think that would help.

It had started raining heavily. Just as I was thinking about catching the train home, a large, hunched woman, with a stern face and a manly appearance, stepped outside. 'What's going on out here, Rodney?'

He pointed at me. 'Caught this 'ere fella me lad trying to blag 'is way indoors.'

She pushed past him. 'What's your name, son?'

'Robert,' I said. It sounded more like a squeak than a name and I was embarrassed that I had left my confidence back in Hampshire. I tried not to stare at her short, black hair; it looked like it had been cut around an upturned pudding bowl. She was dressed in a black jumper, with a grey blouse and an old, black skirt and looked more like she was going to a jumble sale than working in an exclusive club.

'Yes, of course,' she said. 'We've been expecting you.' She shook my hand and gave me one of the tightest grips I've ever had.

Rodney softened and lowered his stance. 'That's fine then. In you come.'

His casual tone was met by her stark disapproval. 'Rodney! Rules are rules. Please show Robert around the back to his room.'

'Isn't that your job?' he asked and winked at me, knowingly.

She looked up at the rain-soaked sky. 'I'm not going out in that. I still have the dinner service to clear.'

'I just thought that with the rules being the rules, it were your job, your ladyship, being as you is the 'ousekeeper and all.' He started rocking with gentle laughter.

'Well really, doorman. Kindly show this young man to his room.'

Like an angry duck that had had its feathers ruffled, she waddled back indoors, squawking as she went.

'Come on then, Rob. Follow me.' He led me slowly down the steps, along the front of the building, around the side and then through a dark passageway and into a grimy courtyard, which housed all the rubbish bins and empty bottles. It was filthy and stank of rotting cabbage, urine and fish. There was a small porch over a splintered back door, with a flickering yellow light above. 'I love the rain,' he told me. 'Love to be out in the fresh air.'

'Me too.' I said, wishing I could get inside in the warm and dry.

He rummaged around in his pockets, pulled out a damp pack of cigarettes and, after several attempts to stop the wind blowing out his lighter, lit one. 'Want one?'

'No thanks mate. Trying to give up.'

He took a deep drag and said, 'Yes, course you is.' Whilst we stood under the dripping plastic cover, he told me not to worry about Mary. 'She's a good sort, really. Just needs a good man, is all.'

I agreed.

'Right I'd better get back. Just follow the stairs to the top and find a room that's empty. Good luck me lad and you can always ask me for 'elp in the morning if you needs it.' He unlocked the door, held it open and then locked it behind me. I heard him shout from the other side, 'Go out on the roof. Pucker views!'

It was just as cold inside and just as damp. There was a thin spiral staircase, leading upwards, like a lighthouse, with weak, intermittent bulbs marking the ascent. At the top of the building was a corridor of blue, blistered walls, with doors spaced out on either side. I found an empty room at the end. The door was open and the stained blue carpet from the hallway ran into to the room. It was more like a prison cell than a bedroom. The light didn't work and my mood felt as glum as my accommodation.

A cold wind was blasting in through a rattling sash window. As I went to close it, I remembered where I was: I was in the heart of London! It didn't matter about the room. From this elevated position I could see the glistening city lights urging me to go out and explore. I shoved the window up and noticed that there was a deep, wide parapet that followed the top of the building, like an elevated footpath.

The view from my room was amazing. Beyond the pillars of the members' entrance, I could see the whole of Covent Garden with its covered market, the notorious sleazy streets of Soho to the left, and the glorious, celebrated Royal Opera House to the right. As I climbed out onto the roof, I found there was a large roof terrace with a massive glass atrium in the centre. When you looked down through this, you could see below, into the main foyer which looked like the entrance to a theatre, complete with two ornately carved kiosks with glass domes above their hatches.

From the rear of the building there were amazing views of Trafalgar Square and Nelson's Column. They looked small from here. I could see glimpses of the River Thames and in the far distance the unmistakable clock tower of Big Ben and outline of the Houses of Parliament.

I stayed perched up on the rooftop for hours. Finally, like a damp sparrow, I came down from the skies and back inside to my nest. It was the one and only time I stayed in during the evening.

The next morning I was launched into work by the stampede of men rushing to grab turns in the communal bathroom. There were no female staff living here; they were all placed in a separate house in Baron's Court.

After breakfast, we had to dress for service: black trousers, black shoes, white shirt and a black bow tie and a white jacket that had been so severely starched that you had to smack it against the table to loosen it up. Even when you managed to get your arms inside, the rigid garment made you look like one of The Queen *of Heart's* playing cards in *Alice in Wonderland*.

The stage we were given for service was equally fantastic. The whole building was dimly lit and had the feel of a Victorian Theatre that was on the verge of bankruptcy. However, I gradually realized that the characters and artwork which inhabited this space provided all the colour and charm needed.

The first famous person I saw was Sir Robin Day with one of his distinct bow ties. Rodney caught me stargazing as I walked along the corridor. 'Put your tongue back in your mouth boy,' he chuckled. 'You'll see plenty more of that.'

Before I started the service for breakfast, he asked me to join him outside on the steps and, whilst he had another smoke, he gave me a quick run through of the elite club I had just joined. He explained how the Garrick Club was created as a private gentlemen's club in 1831 and named after David Garrick, the most celebrated actor of that era. It was one of the oldest and most exclusive clubs in the world. It was *the* preferred place where famous actors, theatre critics, Fleet Street journalists, High Court Judges and other distinguished men of London met to talk, drink and smoke in happy company. With such a reputation it had over a thousand cherry-picked members and a waiting list of over seven years.

The Garrick Club was fortunate to have A.A. Milne and his son Christopher Robin as members. Upon the former's death, a quarter of the royalties from the famous *Winnie the Pooh* stories were left to the club and a dining room was named in his honour. This was simply known as *The Milne Room* and there was a little bronze bear on a plinth with a plaque which read: *Winnie the Pooh, 1982.*

The other rooms, almost in deference to their illustrious occupants, were given similarly unimaginative names, based on function.

These included the *Snooker Room*, the *Library* and the *Snug*. Many areas were strictly for men only. The only women that were permitted here were Mary and her team of Irish waitresses. The girls shuffled quietly through each service, whereas matriarchal Mary would chide the members like naughty schoolboys, telling them off for any rude manners or bad language. They seemed to enjoy being mothered by her.

Every effort was made to ensure that the men could enjoy the building in splendid isolation. Female guests were permitted, but only in certain areas, at certain times. The Milne Room was used to entertain ladies at lunch time, whereas the *Coffee Room* –

the main dining room - was only available for them in the evenings. There was also the *Late Night Dining Room* which served post-theatre dinners. Women were also allowed as guests here. It was a favourite haunt for Melvyn Bragg and was one of the more impressive rooms. The huge painting of *The Remains of Baalbek*, in the Beqaa Valley, Lebanon, mounted on the green, stippled walls, gave the space an imperial ambience. It was always the last room to stay open. Last orders for dinner were around nine and patrons could stay as long as they wished.

Also, members could invite guests upstairs into the *Big Lounge*. However, ladies were strictly directed to a separate, rear staircase for access. It had the well-apportioned *Powder Room* for their comfort but they would have to meet their hosts in the foyer or upstairs in the main hallway.

In addition to the people, the rooms were host to an extensive art collection, including a priceless display of Johan Zoffany paintings. Zoffany enjoyed great popularity with his theatrical portraits which depicted many prominent actors and actresses, often in costume; in particular David Garrick as *Hamlet* and *King Lear*. These were displayed in the Coffee Room and were covered in layers of thick tar from years of members' heavy smoking. We often had to take in the humidors of cigars and the room was full of smoke. I didn't smoke but always loved that smell. There was the separate *Smoking Room*, but the men smoked wherever and whenever they wanted, even when Mary acted as matron of this big boys' dormitory and told them not to smoke so much. There was another lady who seemed to be keeping an eye on me. Every time I went into the Milne Room, the huge omnipresent painting of Gladys Cooper at the end of the table, seemed to be looking down on me, in her perfect, beautiful golden dress and sophisticated stance, evaluating my less impressive performance. She must have been over four metres tall.

As well as the art collection there was the *Theatrical Library* and the private *Reading Room* which houses an extensive collection of original and copied books and plays.

There were so many famous characters there; it was like a living Madame Tussaud's. Among these were Sir John Mills, Alec Guinness, Elizabeth Taylor and Richard Burton.

I loved serving these personalities and worked hard. Mary was firm but fair. As the youngest employee, she became my mother hen. She showed me the ropes and took me under her wing. Her most important lesson was how to manage complaints.

'Always do your best.' She usually leaned down when she was advising me. 'You're not always going to please all the people all the time.' She stood back with her hands on her hips. 'If anyone complains, nip it in the bud. Apologise and stamp it out. Otherwise it spreads like a virus and then everyone has summit to moan about.'

It was good advice. By the age of twenty I had become head waiter and was put on the top table of all the major functions. These included Dame Anna Neagle's eightieth luncheon, sponsored by her husband, Desmond Wilcox, in the Milne Room and one of my personal favourites, Sir John Gielgud who hosted private parties in the Coffee Room. I served him many times and often he would stop and chat to me.

I remember one evening when he was sat alone in the Coffee Room, having picked up an award from some local ceremony. It was a Sunday evening and he was sat at the end of the long table. He looked up and said to me, 'I don't like London very much anymore my boy. I used to live just around the corner, in St. Martin's Lane for many years.' He was upset about how commercial the area had become, how busy everyone was and that many areas were now unrecognizable to him. 'One must maintain standards,' he told me.

This was evident at his own, joyous 80th Birthday celebrations in the Coffee Room. He was so happy with the meal and service that he wrote a congratulatory letter of thanks to the staff and left a tip for £120. The gratuity went into the Christmas fund and his letter was posted up onto the members' notice board in the foyer. A theatre critic, who was also the publicity manager for the Old Vic, left an opposing letter saying: 'I don't think Sir John should have left a tip for the servants.' Sir John went over to the notice board one lunchtime, read the letter, his face went crimson with anger and he ripped it up. He nodded at me, winked and left the building. As far as I know, he never came back.

Further to improving my service skills, I acquired some of my own acting talents during my six years there. One of the biggest roles to play was that of a sober waiter after nights of clubbing in the West End. Also you had to assume the part of a social worker, listening to some of the members downloading their failures, disappointments and hopes for new projects. Being a diplomat was also required: some people wanted a lot of attention, some wanted to be left alone and some just seemed to want recognition.

Laurence Olivier came in once, when he was a really old man, with his personal assistant, a woman, and they had drinks upstairs. He had been a member for many years but approached me and asked, 'Excuse me, young man. Can you tell me the way to the main Members' Dining Room?' He was standing directly outside it.

Although it would have been very nice to establish close connections with one of the stars there, that didn't happen. However, I was very fortunate to befriend a very learned and respected theatre critic and writer, Freddie Young (O.B.E.). He recognised my passion for the arts and took me to many performances, where he had been commissioned to write a review. He taught me all he knew about plays and operas, and how to develop a more discerning eye for talent.

Bertram Alfred (Freddie) Young had been the assistant editor and, then, dramatic critic for *Punch*. When I knew him, he was the arts editor for *The Financial Times*. He was not very political and made it his job to outline performances as clearly as possible, describing the impact they had had on him; to help the reader evaluate the potential pleasure or suffering they would gain from the experience.

The first production he took me to was *The Tempest*, at the newly opened Barbican Theatre. It was fantastic and he quickly encouraged me to look beyond first impressions in order to judge the performance. He gave me so many wonderful experiences and I think I gave him the pleasure of my own naive perspective. One grievance that he was known for, in his writing, was his lack of patience with the Royal patronage of the arts. He caused a stir by criticising The Queen for the 'almost complete neglect of the arts by her and her family,' claiming that this was 'bound to have a bad effect on the well-being of the country.' He felt that they should support the splendour of creativity more vehemently than the unveiling of yet another drab plaque or institution.

My first encounter with serving the Royal Family was The Queen Mother. She came to a luncheon as patron of the *Injured Jockey Society*, and Mr. Wilcox, who was then the club's chairman, met her outside from her car. I had a new disc camera which I won from the club's staff Christmas raffle, (as well as a big side of smoked salmon). I took a sneaky photo of her arrival whilst hiding behind one of the huge velvet curtains in the Milne Room. Soon after, she was given special permission to use the main staircase and was shown into the members' bar. An hour later, she came down for lunch which I helped to serve. She only nibbled on some melba toast and hardly ate anything; she only had one or two bites from each course. It was clear that the main purpose of the occasion was socialising rather than eating.

There were twelve people at the meal. Afterwards, as she came out, we three waiting staff were lined up and shook her hand. We all marvelled at how soft her skin was.

Before she left, the patriarch of the Fox acting dynasty,

Robin Fox, introduced himself and invited her into the Snug under the main staircase. 'Oh ma'am, please join us in the holy of holies.' She walked into the small private enclave, laughing like a cheeky schoolgirl. Raymond Huntley, the actor who played the family's solicitor in the television series *Upstairs - Downstairs*, was there and welcomed her in. She was the only female guest that I ever saw who was permitted into that room.

During my six years of service there, the club's income had increased considerably, due to Disney's commercialization of Milne's famous bear. The Theatrical Library and art collection continued to grow and gradually the rooms and paintings were being restored. The menus were extended to include more wild game, and exotic meats and vegetables, though the members generally preferred more basic, comfort foods such as shepherd's pie and bangers and mash.

Unfortunately the conditions for the staff did not change. We still ate overcooked vegetable broths in an unheated room next to the kitchens. My bedroom window continued to rattle with the icy winds and by the time I had paid for my room and board there was little money left for going out.

Six years later, I left for better money and was hired as the wine waiter at L'Epicure Restaurant in Soho. Again, I found the job in *The Evening Standard*, and discovered that it was an eloquent restaurant in Frith Street which served as a venue for fine dining and drinking for many actors and politicians. It wasn't a private members club but there was a private area on the upper level, where ladies provided a discreet massage with a happy ending for paying clients.

The food style reflected the restaurant's passion for alcohol; nearly anything and everything was flambéed. As you entered the restaurant with its burning torches outside, it made you wonder if they were powered by gas or Chablis. As the wine waiter, I attained a lot of knowledge about wine from the deep cellars which ran under the road towards Ketner's. I believe this is now the headquarters for Pizza Express.

One of the more memorable characters who dined here was Frankie Howard. During the staging of *Up Pompeii* he came in many times after performances. Unfortunately the production was panned and he would laugh off the negative reviews with large glasses of vodka, one after another. Other drinking regulars were Derek Jacobi and Francis Bacon. Bacon spent a lot of hours in the *Colony Drinking Club* probably due to the fact that in the nineteen eighties most pubs closed at lunch time.

The biggest spending clients were Margaret Thatcher's preferred PR agency: Saatchi & Saatchi; they spent far more money than any of the others put together. They would often entertain clients there and spend all afternoon drinking vintage port at seventy to a hundred and twenty pounds a bottle, which I would retrieve from the cellars and decant.

I was there three years, earned decent money from the very generous tips and travelled as much as I could in my limited time off. I only had Sundays off and three weeks holidays per year.

It was time to get back to an easier job, with more leave, even if it was less money. I was lucky to find the perfect job, again, in the back of *The Evening Standard*: a service position in central London, a good permanent post with a decent salary and pension, with three months off, due to the annual recess. In many ways it was the top gentlemen's club in the world. With its iconic buildings and political prowess it suddenly became the only job that I wanted: the first waiter for The House of Lords.

2   GETTING THE JOB

There are several ways to travel down to Málaga, but with two cats and a dog we decided the best way was by ferry. All the animals had their PET Passports; customs scanned their identity chips and we took the overnight service from Portsmouth to Bilbao. Flea and Oliver slept comfortably in our pet-friendly cabin and Dickie Dog had a large kennel on the poop deck. His sleep wasn't so good, as curious passengers kept walking through the doggy exercise area and waking them all up.

On the Spanish side we sailed straight into Bilbao. We left the busy port and found empty roads which took us to an overnight stay at the plush Abba Hotel in the cathedral city of Burgos. Despite tuts and frowns from some of the other guests, as we transported the pets with their food and litter trays, in the gold chrome lift, it was a very pleasant stay.

The next day we drove down across the arid Spanish plains to Toledo. The brilliance of the sun continued to rise the further south we headed and so did the heat. Fortunately the car had air-conditioning, whilst the hot winds buffeted the outside of the vehicle.

It was good to arrive safely at our new home the following afternoon.

We drove up towards the solid front gate with a sign that read: *Propiedad Privada. Prohibido el Paso.* As I leapt out and was trying to decipher Isabella's handwriting for the security code, a camera mounted on a pillar above whined as its lens focussed down on me. Before I had entered the code, the gate creaked and started rolling along its metal bar, automatically.

As soon as it was open, we were greeted with a refreshing mist from the spinning irrigation jets and the sweet smell of cut grass that José had made, under the huge carob tree and fruit trees which hid our landlady's house.

We both sighed, happily, and the dog woke up and started yawning.

'It's like another world,' Graham turned and said to me.

I nodded back. 'Sure beats suburbia.'

We continued our ascent up the steep gravel track and found the quaint French-styled cottage at the top of the hill we had rented. Our own irrigation system, on a raised back border containing lantanas, agaves and long stems of purple salvias, was humming away, blissfully.

'Quick, let's get indoors.' Graham said, grabbing one of the cats in its carrying case. 'It must be forty degrees out here.' He fumbled with the key and we entered the little cottage we had seen a month before. 'It's so dark. It's like a cave in here.' The doors, windows and curtains had all been tightly closed but it was a good ten degrees cooler inside. 'It smells stale and musty,' he said, sniffing.

Whilst I carried the stuff in from the car, he busily opened all the windows to let some air in through the fly screens.

On the small, round dining table there was a bunch of fresh cut roses in an old carafe, a blue-glazed bowl with some home-baked cookies, which seemed to have some kind of herbs in them and a bottle of cloudy, home-made wine, with a note.

Dears, when you have settled in come and have tea at the Riad.

'How nice is this?' Graham said, clutching the message. 'Let's have a quick shower and go down.'

'Great idea.' I said. 'It will give the animals a chance to have a look around and settle in.'

An hour later, once we had finished our ablutions and fed the dog and cats, we walked back down the hill.

The heat hit my face like the inside of a dry sauna. 'Crikey. It's even hotter now,' I puffed, with sweat beading on my forehead.

Graham was also starting to sweat. 'You're going to need to get a hat Beany or your skin will blister again and peel off like a swimming cap.'

'Very funny. It's probably even hotter under that nest you call *hair*.'

We arrived at the top of a semi-circular driveway that led to a path under a long canopy of more trees, which gave us some brief, welcome shade as the earthy walls of the main house were slowly revealed to us, in the full glare of the sun.

'Wow!' We both sighed.

High terracotta coloured walls rose up three floors and were framed with a saw-tooth parapet with a few arched, stained-glass windows randomly dotted over the surface.

'I guess this is the front door,' Graham said, standing in front of a pair of high wooden panels, which looked like they belonged more to a barn than someone's home. He knocked twice on the disintegrated wood.

Three minutes passed with no answer.

I wiped the sweat off my head with my hand. 'Ring the bell,' I told him, pointing to a big rusted metal bell with a chain mounted above us.

After another few minutes, a little, inset door within the entrance opened, revealing a dark, sundried man wearing a long white kaftan, which was too big for him and a washed-out, reddish fez.

'*Señores*. Please be welcome. Madame Vincent is expecting you.' He showed us in to a small, dark seating area and told us to take a seat. 'I shall inform the Madame of your arrival,' he continued, shuffling off down a dark corridor.

As we sat on a modest bench, I could hear the distant sound of running water. 'I think they call this the *Setwan.*'

Graham wasn't listening to me. 'His English was pretty good.'

We were both on our own mental journeys.

Memories of my trips to the Medina in Marrakech were flooding back to me. 'It's a reception area to receive guests without disturbing the family inside. Everything is geared for privacy and comfort. It's a sanctuary from the hot, busy world outside.'

'Don't you think he looked familiar?' Graham interrupted my guided information.

'Yes, it's the typical dress of Moroccan servants.'

'No, I mean, really familiar. We've seen him before.'

I scratched my chin. 'No. Don't think so.'

His eyes lit up with a sudden realization. 'It's José. The gardener.'

The vague recollection of the man we had driven past, clipping the bushes, a month ago came to me. 'No it can't be.'

'It is. You know I never forget a face.'

The diminutive man reappeared at the end of the corridor. 'Please follow me.'

We walked along a dimly lit passage, giggling at the unfolding scene and were suddenly silenced as we walked through an arched doorway back into brilliant sunshine. There was an explosion of light and colour as we stepped into a vast, hidden courtyard. In the centre was a square, blue pool, housing a short fountain which trickled gently into the water below.

'Wow,' we said together, breathing deeply inside this hidden oasis. We needed to rub our eyes due to the contrast from dark to light and Graham put his sunglasses back on.

'Rob, smell the air,' he told me.

I inhaled a deep breath through my nostrils and found a blend of jasmine, rose and citrus, which was permeating the air from the rich selection of potted plants and trees inside.

José showed us over to a small iron table with deep, cushioned, chairs. 'Please, sit down. I get now some tea.'

Graham was scanning the courtyard and marvelling at all the intricately decorated surfaces. 'Look at the tiles,' he said, excitedly. 'It's like a mosaic of white, yellow, deep blue and gold pixels.'

The whole surface of the floor was decorated in elaborate patterns, arranged in overlapping squares which gave a three dimensional appearance. Some of this patterning continued up the columns and stopped on the smooth, marble-looking *tadelkat* walls which extended high up, onto two further levels, both defined by carved, wooden lattice screens and arches, with stucco frames of interlocking semi-circles, with more tiling above.

On this level, we could see the windows of elongated rooms, *bayts*, set behind more arches and columns, overlooking the courtyard. Beyond the sound of the running water, I could hear the heavy, repeated sound of someone coughing. Between each cycle was the pained noise of retching from someone who was struggling to breathe.

'Think she maybe smoking too many herbal cigarettes?' Graham suggested, winking at me.

I could see a dim light glowing in one of the rooms. It looked like a sumptuous lounge, with the faint shadow of two figures: one standing upright and another stood, bent over with its head between its knees.

More repeated, rhythmic coughing and, then, suddenly, it stopped.

We both raised our eyes and looked at each other.

'Hope she hasn't died,' Graham said, with his hand over his mouth.

A few minutes of water-trickling silence continued and then two women stepped out into the courtyard, both laughing loudly. Isabella was holding a filled carrier bag.

'Thank you so much, Madame Vincent. I feel so much better now.' There was a large woman, with a purple face and tightly permed, blonde hair. Her voice echoed in the corridor and spilled into the courtyard.

'It's nothing,' Isabella replied, much quieter. 'Just remember, Heather. Two spoonful's of syrup every three hours.' She turned towards a corner of the courtyard and screeched, 'José!'

A few seconds later, the servant hurried out from another hidden corner, tripping over his tunic.

She tried not to laugh. '*Escolta de la señora Heather, y nos trae su té, por favor.*'

He bowed his head. 'Follow me Madame,' he said to Heather.

'And thank you for this,' Isabella said, clutching her bag.

Heather was stroking her throat, confident that her cough had been cured. 'No, thank you. If you ever want any more, or a free trim, just pop into the salon.'

'I will. Thank you dear.'

As the woman followed José back towards the front door, the grand dame of the house dismissed herself, joined us at the table and tucked the bag under her chair.

We duly stood up and tried to shake her hand.

She pushed my hand down. 'So formal gentlemen. We do things differently here.' She offered me her cheek which I kissed and then patted the other one. 'We're in *continental* Europe now.'

Graham moved forward and performed the same ritual.

The old woman looked younger within these walls. Her silver hair had a healthier sheen and fell in a tight plait down her back. Her faded brown eyes had been lifted with ovals of blue eye-shadow and thick mascara had been extended, Egyptian style, beyond the corners of her eyelids. She was wearing a white cotton blouse with a low V-neck and a necklace of turquoise beads. Her baggy Moroccan trousers were in the same marine colour and her feet were covered in white slippers brocaded in gold.

'My apologies for the tea. He will serve us soon.' She looked around for the manservant and we hoped she wouldn't yell his name again.

'Thanks for the biscuits and the wine,' I said, trying not to stare at her theatrical attire.

She tilted her head back and laughed. 'It is not wine. It's, how you say, *repulsive*. In Spanish is, *repelente*. Repellent, I think you say, for the *hormigas*. I forget, in English. My English is so bad now.'

Graham sat bolt upright. 'Nonsense. You are amazing.'

She clasped her hands together, put her head down and giggled like a naughty student and then recomposed herself. 'No, please you must correct my English.'

We agreed to do so.

'Ants!' she cried.

We looked over the floor.

'It is repellent of the ants,' she added.

'Oh,' Graham replied. 'Ant repellent. You made it?'

She pulled her plait over the shoulder and started fiddling with it. 'We make everything here. All *naturel,* all *organique!*'

José reappeared a few minutes later, carrying a big silver tray with a tall, Arabic coffeepot and three glasses. He placed them on the table and poured long streams of hot green liquid, expertly, from standing height. The aroma was earthy and menthol.

'I love mint tea,' I told our hostess.

'How do you say in England? Cheers, gentlemen!' she held up her glass and we clinked them together.

After she had asked us about our journey, she said that she had a business proposition for me. Ivan must have told her about my plans to get into gardening. At the moment José was doing her garden and ours at the cottage, maintaining both the pools and she had a small greenhouse for herbs behind the Riad. He was getting old now, had problems with his cataracts and needed help running things. If I did two hours per week, she would take a hundred euros per month off the rent.

'Also, you can help him with his English and he can help you with your Spanish. What do you think? It's a perfect idea, no?'

I leapt up and shook her hand. 'It's a great idea. Thank you so much.'

Graham looked at me as if to say, *calm down Beany,* but I could tell he was as excited as I was.

'It's my pleasure. Why don't you come down tomorrow morning and José will be happy to show you around.'

As we were finishing our tea, the doorbell rang and, from the edge of the courtyard, I could see the small man scuffling off to answer it.

'Oh my dears, what is the time?'

'It's seven twenty.' Graham showed her his watch.

'That will be Monsieur Shelley.' She stood up and tossed her hair back. 'Terrible problems with *les hémorroïdes*.' She was clutching her tiny bottom and grimacing.

I looked blankly at Graham.

'Hemorrhoids! Piles,' he announced with glad comprehension.

40

She smiled. '*Exactement*. Please excuse me. José will see you out.'

She walked out, as if on air, floating into the recesses of the salon once again.

Graham was leaning over the table, trying to peak into the bag. 'What is it?'

I looked over and caught a glimpse of what looked like pillow fibres. 'I think they're feathers.'

He wasn't satisfied with the response and took a closer look. 'It's hair,' he whispered. 'Human hair.'

After we were shown out and had climbed up the hill, we collapsed laughing at the theatrical scene we had just experienced. We sat on our terrace under the almond tree.

'What do you think is in these?' I asked, bringing out the homemade biscuits.

Graham screwed his nose up, witch-like. 'Essence of José and puppy dog's tails,' he cackled.

'My favourite,' I said.

We ate three each.

The sun was still high in the cloudless sky and the heat was intense. Cicadas buzzed mechanically, like humming electricity pylons, on the nearby trees, whilst a dozen eagles circled on thermals above us.

I was slowly feeling more relaxed than I had felt in years. 'Wow, it's all just so beautiful.'

'You're right. Come and lie down and watch them with me.' Graham tapped the floor and pointed up at the soaring birds.

I knelt down, lay back and saw them rising up into the sky. 'They're amazing.'

We slept soundly that night and the next morning I went down the hill to meet José. As I was approaching the carob tree, I spotted his familiar figure in a pair of denim dungarees, a blue and white checked shirt and a cowboy hat; Omar Sharif had been transformed into John Wayne. He was watering a border of colourful orange and yellow lantana plants.

I wanted to say, *howdy partner,* but greeted him with, '*Buenos Dias.*'

He didn't seem to hear me, so I called out again. He ignored me. Perhaps he had hearing problems, so I walked in front of where he was standing. He continued watering and put his hand up to stop me from talking. '*Espere. Cinco minutos, por favor.*'

Already, I was feeling the limitations of my Spanish and felt that my presence here was, perhaps, unwelcome. When he turned off the hose, I put out my hand to shake his. 'Good to meet you, properly, José.'

'*Encantado,*' he replied, without looking up. His hands were big and rough, from many years of hard work. He tried to shake firmly but his grip was weak and shaky, and he pulled his hand away.

'Lovely lantanas,' I said, pointing at the colourful discs of florets.

He was silent for a moment and then replied, '*Si, señor. Las lantanas son hermosas!*' He nodded slightly, as if in agreement.

'Madame Vincent told me to come, to help you in the garden.'

He looked puzzled and stood silent for a moment, then shrugged. '*Si señor. Señora Vincent. No necesito ninguna ayuda.*'

It sounded like he didn't want any help, but he was probably just being proud. '*Si, Señor.* I *ayuda* you. Shall I help with water?'

'No!' he shouted. He was as surprised as I was at the volume of his refusal and looked embarrassed. '*Not here. I show you.*' He beckoned me to follow him up the garden path, to the back of the riad. His English was better than I had imagined.

As we walked past more groupings of Mediterranean plants, I gave the English name for them. He repeated these and then reciprocated with the name in Spanish; I, dutifully, repeated these back to him.

The high, chain-link fencing was covered by a thick hedge of green bushes with small white, pink and red flowers. I pointed again, 'Oleanders?'

More nodding. 'Ol-y-anders. *Si, si! En Español, las adelfas.*'

As I followed him around to the back, I noticed that his left leg was a bit shorter than the other and he had a limp. Perhaps I could help out with some of the heavy lifting and carrying work?

On the far side of the house was a massive industrial-sized poly-tunnel. It looked more like a facility for a nursery than a private residence. The plastic had been painted white, to reflect the sun and many trees had been planted around the edges to provide lots of needed shade.

Inside there was a thin path in the middle, with rows of different green shrubs either side. There was a network of black plastic pipes placed on the ground for irrigation but a lot of these were broken or disconnected. The plants were generally healthy but the soil was dry and dusty.

He pointed down to the base of the thirsty plants. '*Hay un problema con el agua.*'

'A problem with the water?' I asked him.

'*Si! Si. Dar a todos una bebida.*' He handed me a small, blue watering can that a child might use.

I looked at the tiny vessel and the field of plants before me. It would take me hours. 'Are you joking?' I asked, observing his expression.

His face was blank. '*No entiendo.*' I knew this meant: *I don't understand.* It was one of my favourite phrases. He pointed to a large, metal water butt which had a stopcock for auto-refilling.

He walked me down the length of the enclosure, pointing out

the different sections of herbs. Through further language sharing I discovered hundreds of plants of rosemary *(romero)*, basil *(albahaca)*, thyme *(tomillo)*, mint *(menta)* and many others which I didn't recognise.

At the far end, on the left hand side, there were a few hundred spiky green plants with a heady, earthy smell.

'What's this?' He put his hands behind his head and breathed in deeply. *'Esa es la planta especial, mágica. Medicina.'*

Could it be true that our little old landlady was growing cannabis as an herbal remedy? 'Are you joking?' I repeated, without remembering his previous response.

'No, señor. I'm not joking.' He had understood that time. He walked off, leaving me in contemplation and wonder. In truth, I wasn't that surprised about the plants; Graham's father had used small amount of cannabis to help with his multiple sclerosis. It was just surprising to find so much of it growing here.

Opposite these plants, were a series of large, wooden-framed composting bins, each with a different selection of decaying materials. In one was the hair that Heather had given Isabella yesterday.

I returned to the entrance and began watering. Sure enough, it did take me three hours to water all the thirsty plants. Just as I was finishing, I suddenly stopped and gasped, as I saw a long strip of brown flesh on the floor, winding between the shrubs in the last row, with further coils in the far corner. There was a faint sound of hissing. I don't mind snakes but do have a healthy respect for them. As I crept up, closer, I saw that this was no serpent. It was a long length of garden hose attached to a dripping tap. I turned it on and instantly it spurted out a strong, steady jet of water.

Thanks José, I thought.

As soon as we had the internet connected, I researched plant problems and natural remedies. A lack of magnesium causes yellow leaves and black spot and can be cured by adding rotting leafy vegetables and nuts. This explained the pile of old almonds I had seen in one of the piles. Leaves turning reddish black or with yellow veins need more phosphorus and / or potassium, which can be aided with compost containing banana skins, orange and lemon peel, spinach and tomatoes. A nitrogen shortage causes yellow leaves and leaf drop and this can be cured adding coffee grounds, manure, grass clippings and, of course, hair cuttings.

As I closed my laptop, I realized that, at fifty years of age, I was young again; starting a new career, far from home, with so much to learn.

***

I was invited into the House of Lords for an interview at nine fifteen, a week before the next parliamentary session commenced. The directions were clear but the immense Perpendicular Gothic landscape, set in more than eight acres, was difficult to navigate. It was a cool, misty morning. I walked along the South Bank, where I was living with friends, and could see the honey-coloured limestone building growing through the leaden skies with each step I took. I crossed the Westminster Bridge and was transfixed by the magnificent creation of Sir Charles Barry above me. The structure looked much older than it was. The original Palaces of Westminster were destroyed by fire in 1834 and Barry won the competition to design a grand Gothic palace, where all the previous buildings could be assimilated into one magnificent structure.

Just as I arrived at the base of St. Stephen's Tower, Big Ben began to chime. Like nine sonorous smoke rings of metal, great circles of clanging vibration tore through the heavy air and stopped all the passing pedestrians. We were summoned to stillness. Once the ceremony had finished, I rubbed my ears and searched for *Black Rod's Entrance* which was at the other end of the building.

Once inside, miles of oil-skinned faces, scrutinised my tiny figure from the many rows of gilt-framed portraits. I was met in the *Peers' Dining Room* by a petite, dark-skinned Italian man called Mr. Bibbiani. He was the manager for the Food and Beverage Department and had been brought in to improve service and the menu.

His voice was as cheerful as his smile and he put me quickly at ease by saying, 'Roberto. You are-a, very welcome- a, to our little family-a 'ere in the 'ows of Lords-a.' The soft, high intonation of his engaging accent was instantly reassuring. 'You must call me Meester Bee,' he said.

He pulled two of the high-backed, red leather chairs out from the long, narrow table. They were all embossed with a gold portcullis on their backrests. Five women in black skirts and pink and white striped blouses were dotted along the table, polishing the silver cutlery and refilling the many cruets. They were trying to be inconspicuous but I was aware that they were all watching me with unease. The silver wear gleamed from the place setting in front of me. Every item had been stamped with the portcullis emblem and for a few moments I wondered if I could buy one as a souvenir.

Mr. B pulled his chair beside me. 'I am wanting no more,' he whispered, looking towards one of the waitresses.

I folded my arms. 'Sorry?'

He put his big round face closer to mine. His olive green eyes widened as he spoke. 'It's a time to change. The chefs, they are women. The waiters, they are women. It's no good. In every 'ows you need, 'ow you say, 'armony.'

It was true. With the exception of the doorkeepers and security guards, all the staff I had seen were female.

'You will be our first. Our first man waiter.' He was pleased with this announcement.

It sounded like an honour. 'That would be terrific,' I said.

He seemed so resolute with this plan of campaign that he asked me very few questions and told me to follow him to his office to fill out the paperwork. He did most of the talking and told me about the history of the catering department.

He explained that, previously, fried and grilled plaice were on the menu every day and it was impossible to order healthy or vegetarian options. A big part of his job was keeping the peace between staff and members, and to introduce the changes carefully. Fish had been kept on the menu but had become more varied and flavoursome. Also different varieties of pasta had been made available, alongside staple favourites such as lamb cutlets and fishcakes. The most popular dishes were grilled plaice and bangers and mash.

The kitchen was still in operation on the floor below, as originally designed by Barry. Although this achieved the elimination of unwanted cooking odours, it made it very difficult for the chefs to communicate with the serving staff. Mr. Bibbiani remedied this by placing a chef upstairs who could relay the orders down to the kitchen, in *chef-speak*, to avoid any confusion.

It was no easy task to feed the Lords expediently. There was very limited food storage facilities within the palace and food had to be ordered and delivered daily. In addition to the food preparation, service was a complicated task. The Lords always eat in a rush and the numbers and timings vary hugely depending on the topic for debate. Also, each Lord was able to invite up to four guests per sitting.

Generally, the peak serving time was around 1p.m and the last peers would leave by 2.30pm. During the last hour of service, even when some of the peers were finishing their lunch, the empty tables were cleared away for traditional afternoon tea. This usually consisted of anchovy toast, crumpets, muffins and assorted preserves. Tea was served from 3-5pm. On Tuesdays and Thursdays dinner was served from 6-9pm. I would only have to do one of these. And, on Friday evenings, banquets were served to private clubs, normally with members from the Conservative Party. These were late events but were optional for the staff to cover as overtime.

I told him I was happy to do any overtime that was available.

On our way back through the corridors we were met by a dashing theatrical figure who stopped to talk to Mr. B.

'I need to talk to you about the menu,' this commanding figure said, ignoring me. 'The liver and bacon was awful today.'

'It's not a problem. I'll fix it.' Mr. B pushed me forward and said, 'This is Lord Ampthill, chairman of the refreshment department.' And then, 'My Lord. This is Roberto, our new waiter.'

We shook hands and he waved us good bye as he disappeared through a hidden door, sunk into the wood panelling. As Mr. B escorted me out, my memory banks searched for the details on Lord Ampthill.

Lord Ampthill…George Russell…

I remembered! He was known by the press as *The Sponge Baby*. It had been a landmark paternity case and one of the most sensational divorce proceedings in history. His father had denied intimacy with his mother, Christabel Hart, and had sought to discredit her by citing infidelity and naming two possible lovers. Upon medical examination, Christabel was found to be pregnant but still showed "all the signs of virginity." The conclusion was made that after a failed attempt at intercourse, she had become impregnated after soaking in the same bathwater that her husband had recently vacated. In addition to having his barony restored, George Russell became a highly popular and respected member of *The House*. He was known by the staff as *Uncle Jeffrey*.

My first day of work was three days after the interview. I was shown into the *Cholmondeley Room*, where I was lined up, military style, with the catering squad of women who were being sternly inspected before the day's tour of duty, by a severe Scottish woman in plaid tweed and a shrilled voice. This was Miss McWilliams. She was head of the banqueting department. She had bulging grey eyes which were magnified by her thick glasses and made her look like a tawny owl. As she scoured the room, her head seemed to twist full-circle on her sunken neck.

As she walked past each of the waitresses, she pointed to some article of offending jewellery or make up. 'Now come along girls,' she hooted, her head bobbing backwards and forwards with each step. 'We canny go to service like that. We must all try a wee bit harder.' She pointed to a feathery earring that a girl called Siobhan was wearing. 'We must be dressed for service not a night in a backstreet tavern.'

I wanted to introduce myself and make it known that I wasn't one of the girls. For three months she ignored me and then finally conceded to address us as, *We girls and Robert.*

For my first years of service, I was placed in the *Peers' Dining Room*. It was not an easy room to work in, as the tables were so long and narrow. Convention dictated that as the Lords entered they were supposed to take seats at the end of the room closest to service and to occupy the next available seat to someone already sitting. Generally this worked quite well apart from certain peers who would sit alone, at the far end, in isolation.

A few weeks after my induction, was the biggest annual event in parliament: The State Opening. For the past few days, the whole building had been thrown into nervous excitement, as we hurriedly prepared for Queen Elizabeth's ceremonial visit to open what was to be the next and final session of Margaret Thatcher's government.

There was a lot of preparation to be done in advance of the day. I was lucky as the Peers' Dining Room remained more or less the same. The long table was allocated to Lords and Ladies, who were attending on their own, and an additional officials' table was added to accommodate the Clerks to the Parliament and The Queen's Counsellors (Q.C.s). On the other side, in a separate room, were the Lords in attendance with up to four invited guests. The menu was more or less the same as any other day, although the words *The State Opening of 1989* were embossed across the top of the newly-printed stationery.

Downstairs was an entirely different affair. The Cholmondeley Room and the adjoining function room of the terrace, overlooking the Thames, were transformed into an extravagant buffet, reminiscent of a lavish medieval banquet. I was often asked to help down here and, on this day, was made responsible for carrying in mounds of dressed crab, lobsters, roasted pheasants and partridges, exotic fruits and canapés on huge silver platters. Places here were strictly reserved up six months in advance and many of the Lords made bookings eight months beforehand. This meant that any newly appointed Lords had no chance of entry to that year's event.

As we scurried around the restaurants and rooms, moving and

removing tables, dipping all the silverware and polishing the cutlery, there was a growing buzz of anticipation and the loud hum of conversation amongst the staff as to who would be attending this year. The Queen and the Duke of Edinburgh were a given. But in those early days, before the austerity of Tony Blair's reforms, many other members of the Royal Family would appear and the conversation naturally turned to, 'Will Diana be there?'

On the actual day, all the catering staff had to be in by nine am. This was mostly a security measure, as all the setting up had been done in advance. In fact, at that time, before *9-11*, the security was pretty relaxed. All new members of staff were security checked as standard and issued with a pass. This meant that we could avoid inspection of the security guards at Black Rod's Entrance and scan ourselves in, at one of the other entrances to the building. My favoured point of entry was a hidden corridor from Westminster tube station, which only staff used, once you knew which one to take. This would lead you out onto a terrace beneath the looming figure of Big Ben. I always felt like James Bond reporting for duty but, as I caught the reflection of my small thin figure in the gothic window panes, I realized I was decidedly more double-oh-six and a half than seven.

Once inside, we all stood around like cursors blinking on a computer, awaiting commands and being ordered into service. The one enjoyable moment before the ceremony commenced was the arrival of the sniffer dogs, which were brought in to search the cellars to prevent any modern-day *Gunpowder Plot*. For many years, since Guy Fawkes's failed attempt to blow up parliament and kill the protestant King James I[st], the Yeoman of the Guard were sent down to secure the premises before any arrival of the Sovereign. These had been replaced by the brown and white spaniels. We were supposed to ignore them but, after a while they got to know us, and Bob would leap up at me, cover me with slobber and ask for a piece of shortbread off the table.

Limited amounts of tickets were available for staff to watch the Royal procession. There were four pavement tickets, four for *The Royal Gallery* and a few had the opportunity to go down to *Peers' Courtyard*, where the horses were led in to cool off and the household cavalry were given tea and coffee. Mr. B told me that I probably wouldn't get a ticket as I was new. However, one of the waitresses had seen the assembly so many times that she preferred to sit in the staff canteen and have a smoke, and she gave me her pavement ticket.

I was so excited that I ran down to my locker in the cellars to get my morning coat and left my glasses on the bench.

I couldn't see anything.

I hurried outside where thick lines of people had assembled to see the arrival of the first carriage. My eyes were bleary and I couldn't make out which one it was. I knew from reading history that this must be the one carrying the Imperial State Crown which is brought over from The Tower of London. Since this heavy jewellery is priceless, it is customary and fortunate for the monarch to put it on inside the *Robing Room*.

My frustration increased when the next carriage, presumably carrying The Queen and the Duke of Edinburgh arrived at the *Sovereign's Entrance*, beneath *Victoria Tower*, which contains all our historical, judicial documents. I saw the outlines of two people disappear into the building, towards the Royal staircase.

The first State Opening of the New Houses of Parliament took place on November 11th, 1852. It took twelve years to construct the buildings to Queen Victoria's very exacting specifications and several alterations had to be made. She declared the stairs too steep and unfit; the whole instalment was ripped out and replaced with wider steps carved out of Portland Stone. After these initial problems, the ceremony has always been run through as a set system of procedures and customs, like a well-oiled engine; a machine which I have been very lucky to observe twenty-one times.

Each year, Queen Elizabeth and Prince Philip climb up the steps, lined by the red Yeoman Ushers.

From here The Queen proceeds to the Robing Room which is specially prepared for her. This used to be done by our beloved Rita Bird, head housekeeper for our department. She was well-known for creating a small souvenir concession out of some discarded filing cabinets, under the *Bishops' Staircase*, next to the Peers' Courtyard. She realized that many visitors wanted memorabilia from their visit to the palace and assembled jars of humbugs, (with red lids and the portcullis emblem), chocolates in a burgundy box, and House of Lords branded toffees and tea cups. When she wasn't there selling them, the 'shop' was guarded by a weatherworn statue of King Henry VIIIth who dared anyone to steal from this bounty. Rita said managing the gift shop was far less worrying than the preparations in the Robing Room for Her Majesty's attendance. It was her job to clean and place the Royal hairbrush, polish and shine the tall, lead-crystal mirror and make sure they were always in exactly the same place for Royal use. The Queen would get very upset if anything was at all wrongly placed, as if it were a bad omen for a problematic day. The crown weighs over two pounds and is equivalent to balancing a bag of sugar on your head. So it is never an easy day for Her Majesty.

Rita ensured everything was always in the right place.

From here, The Queen re-joins her husband and they proceed through The Royal Gallery where all the ambassadors and dignitaries are assembled wearing their finery. All the ladies are required to wear hats and curtsy to her majesty. In fact, the event is so savoured by the gentry that many of them are dressed up like museum artefacts, wearing vintage robes and crinoline dresses, expensive fur coats and are decorated with clusters of family jewels, medals, antique rings, necklaces and tiaras.

One year, my favourite waitress, Sandra, and I were asked by one of her ladyships, Lady Biddoff, to look after an emerald encrusted tiara as it was making her head itch. It was worth a couple of hundred thousand pounds. We took it in turns to model it around the kitchen and to make the other members of staff bow and curtsy. We weren't sure where to put it, so we chose the household supplies cupboard and stuffed it under a pile of toilet rolls. Her ladyship was so full of merriment from the buffet that she forgot to ask for it before she left, and we became very worried about being responsible for its safe keeping. A few days later, her valet appeared at the House to take the prize jewels safely home.

When we went back to the cupboard to retrieve the headpiece, it had gone.

'I'm going to have a heart attack,' Sandra gasped, clutching her chest.

I pulled all of the toilet rolls out onto the floor. 'It's not here.'

Sandra emptied all the cleaning products out. 'Oh my God. They'll send us to prison or the Tower.'

'Someone must have taken it.'

'What are we going to do Robert?' She started looking over her shoulder to see if anyone else was about. The corridor was empty.

'It's got to be here somewhere.' I walked over to another cupboard and started searching. 'Perhaps we've got the wrong one.'

It was pointless. There was only one storage place for the toilet rolls and we knew it had gone.

'We'll have to tell Mr. B and pay for it out of our wages.' She put her hands up to her face, trying to hide her despair.

I'm no good at maths but knew one thing for sure. 'Impossible. It would take us a hundred years, Sandra.'

She laughed nervously. 'Maybe I'll get a full house at bingo this week.'

Just as we were beginning to lose hope, we heard footsteps approaching and someone making the noise of a trumpet fanfare. 'Doo dah de doo dah loo. My Lords I am pwoud to pwesent his 'onour, Alfwedo, The Duke of Pamplona.' In walked a familiar, elderly Italian man, with a lisp, who started as a waiter a year after me.

Sandra screamed. 'Alfie. You nearly gave us a heart attack!'

We all laughed, pulled ourselves back together and made Alfredo hand the tiara over to Lady Biddoff's valet. Little did I know then than this happy trio of me, Alfredo and Sandra would continue working together for many years to come.

From the gallery, the Royal couple always continue through to a small, simple room called *The Prince's Chamber* which contains several impressive paintings of King Henry VIIIth and his six wives. This room is like an antechamber adjoining the House of Lords. It's funny to think that directly behind the Royal thrones in the chamber is a cupboard with a carved wooden door which houses an old hoover, a cluttered assortment of cleaning products and several dirty mops and a stained, metal bucket.

The actual speech is over fairly quickly. This is our queue to run back to our departments and prepare for the chaos which inevitably erupts when hundreds of empty stomachs and glasses are waiting to be filled.

The Royals leave, uninterrupted, much faster than they arrive.

After this, herds of gathered assemblies spill out into the corridors and begin hours of short exchanges, as they filter their way through to the feeding stations. Like a pride of lions in a safari park, they greedily descend upon the prey that has been slaughtered and served up for them, under trees of carved stone pillars and canopies of gothic arches.

After the feeding frenzy, we clear the flesh-picked carcasses away and, through fixed grins and looping salutations, we bid them farewell, as they slowly leave the rooms, returning home or commencing the preliminary debate of the speeches in the Commons and the Lords.

When all the visitors have left, Mr. B. assembles all the staff on the terrace for a drink, to toast the success of the day's service and to thank us for our efforts.

3   STRONG WOMEN

I was grateful for the work from Isabella but had to get some more clients to fund our life in Spain. We needed to do some marketing. Graham helped me produce a flyer and we printed off three hundred of these and circulated them in local shops, post boxes and under the windscreen wipers of cars parked up in nearby drinking holes. It took time before there were any calls from these advertisements. The first few phone calls got my heart racing at the prospect of work but turned out to be marketing calls from the classified sections of local papers.

Three weeks later I got my first external client.

A woman introduced herself as Suzie Partridge. She told me she was very busy and had no time. She pronounced it *Part Ridge* with a strong emphasis on the 'r' and was definitely from somewhere in the West Country. 'It says 'ere that you do gard'ning. Are you alright with dogs?' she asked.

'Yes of course,' I said, searching for a pen and paper to take down the details. 'I've got a dog myself.'

She dismissed any interest in my personal information. 'I've got five,' she said. 'Have you got all the tools?'

I looked at Graham's eager face and shrugged. 'I've got some,' I told her. In a bucket by the front door was my current supply of tools: a pair of secateurs, shears, gloves and a rake. We didn't want to spend lots of money until we had tested the market and hoped that most of the customers would have their own.

I heard her breathe out a long sigh on the other end of the phone. 'No matter. I have everything here.' Dogs started barking in the background. 'I've got to go,' she said. I heard a clunk and thought she had hung up. 'I need Tuesdays and Thursdays.'

I scribbled down the days. 'That's fine,' I said quickly, before she disappeared. It was Monday today. 'I'll see you tomorrow. I can be there by ten,' I suggested.

'Oh,' she said. 'I was hoping for nine.'

I crossed out the time. 'That's no problem. See you at nine.'

There was the sound of another phone ringing in the background. 'Got to go,' she said and the line went dead.

Graham was trying to read the details over my shoulder.

'My first client!' I yelled, jumping up, clasping the paper.

He laughed. 'Yes, that's great. She sounds quite a character.'

'You can say that again.'

'I said, *she sounds quite a character.*'

I poked him in the ribs. He takes the piss out of me for repeating myself a lot. I think it's because I'm deaf in one ear, after years of clubbing in London when I was young. Sometimes, I'm not sure if people have heard me, as well as me not hearing them.

'There is one problem,' he said, snatching the paper with his hand, scratching his chin. 'Where does she live?'

I took the paper back and realized that she didn't give me the address. 'Oh shit. She was in such a hurry. I think I'm too scared to call her back.'

We decided to take Dickie and Ollie for a walk in the forest behind the house and hoped that she would realize her mistake and call back.

In August the thermostat outdoors is set to oven-roasting temperatures for most of the month. There is more air in the afternoons, but this is usually a hot wind, *The Terral,* which blows from north to south over Spain and picks up the heat as it crosses the arid plains. Sometimes it is so strong that it rips the parasols out of the sand and bowls them across the beach and into the sea, with sunbathers chasing after them, arms flapping.

Typically, here in the mountains, it is hotter in summer and colder in winter. However, there is a real sense of freedom. The Sierra de Mijas is over ten miles long and stretches from Alhaurin El Grande down to Torremolinos. Its highest point, Pico Mijas is 1,150 metres above sea level. Despite the dry, desert-like, conditions the mountains have a lush, verdant appearance due to the green canopies of the *Pino piñonero*, more commonly known as the Stone or Umbrella Pine. They are green throughout the year.

Their vivid colour belies the crisp, tinder earth beneath. Fire is a constant concern in the summer and helicopters patrol the area, making regular safety inspections. After the burning memory of August two years ago, when fires raged across the neighbouring range of the Sierra Alpujata, from Coín to Marbella, displacing more than five thousand inhabitants and scorching thousands of hectares, the teams are increasingly vigilant. It is everyone's duty to look out for fire. There are now constant updates by watchful expats on social networking sites. This mountain now looks red from the damage; like a huge rock from mars.

Where we walk, we often come across small groups of mountain bikers and a few other walkers, who always exclaim their surprise at seeing our cat. '*El Gato!*' they cry. These never bother him, but occasionally there are packs of *Podenco* racing through the trees which are being trained to flush out *Perdiz.* These birds have long flown from this section of the forest, but the dogs are trained here before hunting commences later in the year, in forests closer to the Málaga.

That day we met six of them. They are small, thin animals with pointed, fox-like faces which have been sandwiched either side by humungous triangular ears. You normally hear them before you see them. A high-pitched series of yelps announce their arrival.

Ollie froze as soon as he heard them. His dark-tabby markings blended perfectly with the dry bark of the trees. They didn't see him, but they certainly found his scent. Just as the pack descended on us, he shot up a tree. They circled the base of the trunk, their front legs reaching up the tree and barked with excitement. He hissed at them, climbed up further onto a branch and began washing his paws. A few minutes later they became bored and ran off, back to their owner. They completely ignored the two of us and Dickie Dog.

'Maybe that was a sign,' Graham said, as we walked back to the house.

Ollie had dropped back down the tree and was rubbing Dickie's face, looking for assurance.

'What do you mean?' I said. 'Are you saying my new customer's going to be a dog?'

He raised his eyes. 'No,' he said. '*Perdiz*, hunting dogs.'

I looked back at him in silence.

He added, '*Perdiz* is the Spanish word for *Partridge*.'

The penny (or should I say *centime*) dropped. I was never going to master the language. We did ten weeks of classes together and I still struggle to say, *Me llamo es Roberto*. Thank heavens Isabella and José were so kind and patient. Apart from them, I decided that it would be better to have English-speaking clients.

On the way back to our cottage, I saw José, below, in Isabella's garden by the lawn, that seemed to be turning yellow. I decided to go down to help him.

He was friendlier today and showed me that some of the irrigation sprinklers had become disconnected or blocked up with dirt and lime scale. I walked around with him, as he took them off, one by one, and we rinsed them in some kind of soapy solution he had mixed up and then blew through them to remove any remaining dirt. In some cases the linking hose had perished and needed to be cut back and re-attached. After we had completed the circuit, he led me into the centre and told me to wait.

'You stay here. No move,' he said. He walked over towards the back of the house and disappeared for a few moments. Suddenly the loop of black plastic heads began to whirr, turning and spitting bubbles of water out of their mouths. Soon they were propelled into fast, frantic motion, spraying full jets of water from the edges, into the centre, and all over me. They blasted my face, my chest and trousers and even my feet. I was drenched.

I could hear a loud braying noise behind me, like a donkey that had woken from a long sleep. It was José. He was rocking from side to side with amusement. 'That's better,' he yelled.

It was such a hot day and the water was so refreshing, that I laughed too. When I came off the lawn, he shook my hand, smiled and said, 'thank you mister Robert.'

Back at our house, I dried myself off and found a text message on my phone. *You forgot to ask me my address!* It said. The expletive was followed by the house number, street and GPS coordinates and a further reminder: *See you at nine.*

Her place didn't look far away on the satnav, but I decided to try and find it the night before to make sure I got there on time. It was located on a lower road heading towards Cártama. Having passed the *Ferreteria,* the local brothel and the dog boarding-kennels, I was directed onto a dirt track from the last exit of a roundabout. The car dropped down into a deep pothole and continued forward. Near the end of the route, the electronic device announced that I had reached my destination. There was no house here; just a fork in the track that went either left or right. Since I was on the right-hand side I went for the road closer to me. The path led through a long grove of olives and I could see the outline of a small white house with the sun setting behind. There was a group of goats nibbling leaves under one of the trees and three chickens pecking around in the gravel at the side of the house. I could hear some dogs barking, which made me think I had found the right house, but nearly every house has a pack of barking dogs in the *campo*. It seemed a staple part of country living.

I decided to leave before any one saw me. The track was very narrow and fell in a steep slope on one side. There was no option but to continue onwards and hopefully find a place to turn around. As I got closer, I saw the silhouette of two figures outside the front door, under a tiled porch way. A man with a black beard and long dark hair was sat in an old cane chair, whilst a woman was bent behind him with a pair of scissors. I heard them singing to each other in Spanish and it looked like she was starting to cut his hair. This was definitely the wrong house.

As I pulled up near the door I called out, '*Excusi. Buenos noches.*'

The man stood up, annoyed that their privacy had been disturbed. He stepped forward and shouted, '*Qué pasa? Qué es lo que quieres?*'

'I'm looking for *Perdiz*. Madame *Perdiz,*' I stuttered. At least some of it was in Spanish. I felt proud of my effort.

He took the scissors from his wife and pointed them at me, shaking his hand. '*Vete a la mierda!*'

I don't know why he thought I was a vet but it was obvious that he wanted me to go. It was only when I turned the car in front of them that I realized why he was so angry. They were both naked. The tyres skidded on the gravel surface and as I pulled away he shook his arm one more time and then sat back down for his trim.

Only in Spain, I thought to myself.

At the end of the driveway, I took the other fork in the road. This led down a more level path and there was a long, thin house with a high chain-linked fence which ran along its entire length, with two small yards either side.

This must be it.

I drove slowly past the building and counted four small dogs in the garden. There was loud music booming from inside the house, the tune and the words sounded English. I reversed the car quietly at the end of the road. The music floated in through my open window. This time I recognised it: *All I Want for Christmas is You.*

The next morning, I parked outside the house at nine o'clock sharp. Suzie would surely be pleased that I had found the house and arrived on time. There wasn't a doorbell on the outside gate but the dogs started jumping up and barking to announce my arrival.

The doors and windows of the house were all tightly sealed; the metal shutters were closed and the garden gate was padlocked. After five minutes, there was still no sign of movement.

'Good dogs,' I said, trying to get her attention. They were fighting with each other to get closer to me. 'Hello,' I called out.

One of the front windows was opened, but the shutter was still down.

'What do you want?' It was the voice I had heard on the phone.

I tried to lean over the gate so that she might see me through the holes in the metal screen. 'It's Robert. The gardener.' It was the first time I had used those words. It sounded good. It flowed more easily than *Head Waiter in the House of Lords* and I felt confident that I certainly looked the part. The students from St. John's - a specialist school in Brighton for young learners with autism - had helped me. Graham used to work there. They have a print shop in Seaford, *Inklusion,* where they do work experience. I had bought a green polo shirt and emailed them the symbol of the portcullis that Graham had modified. There was now a wheelbarrow in place of the crown. They had printed this in white, together with my telephone number and the words *The Garden Butler.* To complete my attire I had a new panama hat, a pair of khaki shorts with plenty of pockets and some brown *Caterpillar* boots.

The shutter graunched as she heaved it up and revealed the window. 'You're early,' she said and leaned out the opening.

'It's nine o'clock.'

'I said *ten.*' She started coughing and put her hand over her mouth. Her short red hair was stuck to the sides of her face. 'It doesn't matter. I was awake anyway.' She withdrew back inside, dropped the blind back down and I heard her yell, 'Just give me a minute.'

Ten minutes later, there was the loud click of a lock being released on the other side of the front door. This was repeated three more times. It was like someone opening up a heavily secured apartment in downtown New York. A stick-thin figure in a red track suit appeared from the cavern. Her hair had been rinsed and spiked up like the comb on a rooster's head. She was fumbling with a thick bunch of keys in one hand and scratching her forehead with the other.

'Come on boys,' she said, gently pulling the dogs back from the gate.

She unlocked the gate and told me to come in.

'What's this one's name?' I said, pointing to a small, black dachshund. They were all jumping up and caught my bare legs with their claws.

She ignored me and pointed onto the road behind me. 'What's that?' she sneered.

It seemed obvious to me that it was a car. I didn't answer.

'Where's your van?'

I bent down to say hello to the dogs. 'Not got one yet. We've only been here a few weeks.'

She was peering through the half-closed gate at my number plate. 'You need a van here. That's no good. If you don't change it to Spanish plates the guard will take it away and crush it.'

Suzie had my attention now. 'How do I do that?'

She tilted her head back as if she was going to crow. 'Go to Jesus in the village, the garage by the *Tabac*. Spanish but speaks good English. He'll sort you out. Got my van from him.' She pointed towards a tarpaulin covered vehicle that was parked up outside a filled shed. It looked like it hadn't been used in years.

I turned my attention back to the dogs. 'Who's this?' I asked, again, pointing to the dachshund that was now licking my boots.

'That's Blitzen.' She closed the gate and locked it behind me.

'And these?' There was a group of three similar looking Pedancos, which were white and sandy coloured.

She dropped the keys on the floor and muttered, 'Prancer, Vixen and Dasher.' She walked back to the house and, in a large kennel, next to the metal bins where she kept their food, was a tired, grey-muzzled German Shepherd who was snoring. 'And that's Comet.'

I bent down to stroke his head. It looked like his star had burnt out many years ago.

The phone started ringing.

'I need to get on,' she said, going back into the house. 'You can start here in the garden.' A new ring tone added to the cacophony that was growing inside. 'There's a brush and dustpan over there.' She pointed to a corner where there was a worn broom and a pan filled with hair and went indoors. The dogs tried to follow her but she pushed them back.

I looked around the garden and soon discovered that there were no plants. It was simply a thin penned area with a long terrace and a small swimming pool at the end. This worried me: I had no experience of pools. The water had turned green and was covered in leaves from the trees in the farmer's field next door. There was no grass, just a brown square of dirt covered in dried dog faeces. The dogs had chewed the bushes which had once been planted by the fence and only hard, yellow stumps of shrubs remained. Discarded pieces of an irrigation system that had once lined the perimeter were dotted around the edges.

It soon became apparent that what Suzie wanted was a cleaner, not a gardener. It turned out that she didn't (or couldn't) swim and she told me to leave the pool. I swept up twenty bags of dog mess whilst the little pack followed me around and offered me brown tennis balls and chewed squeaky toys to throw. I didn't mind. Her animals were one of her greatest passions; she lived alone and needed help to keep things running. It took me two hours to sweep it all up and wash the terrace down. She didn't thank me but must have been pleased since she wanted me every Tuesday and Thursday for two hours per day. Thirty-two euros a week wasn't much, but it was my first paid job over here and it made me feel more confident that I could build up a small business.

On the first Thursday, I decided to appease her indecision by getting there at nine-thirty. She showed me indoors and gave me instructions for cleaning the house. The cleaning part was easy. The difficulty came in the form of the many cats she was hoarding inside. They were not allowed to go outside. She had lost too many on the busy A390 near St. Austell, where she had once lived in Cornwall.

Beyond the front door there was a further screen door, covered in chicken wire.

'Quick,' she told me. 'Shut the door.' It was dark inside due to the shutters being drawn. Whilst the sun blazed outside, the rooms were lit with table lamps and spotlights. The rooms were all closed off, with further double doors. 'They must stay in the rooms they are in,' she said. Suzie directed me into a guest bedroom and gently pushed a large Persian back in with her foot. She explained, 'I won't have any fighting. They prefer it like this.'

This seemed mad but the cats all looked very well and happy enough.

This was the room she used as her office. There was a new Ikea desk in the corner with two cats asleep in the filing trays. Three different coloured phones sat on their cradles whilst their red LED displays blinked the number of messages received.

She saw me looking at the equipment. 'Life insurance, health insurance and funeral plans,' she said, pointing to the relevant handsets. Next to these was a large monitor with a photograph, stuck on the side, of her and a ruddy faced man in wedding clothes. She looked resplendent in her white wedding dress. He had been photo-shopped. His eyes had been cropped out into hollow black holes. The nose had been replaced with a snout and there was a dagger in his neck dripping in blood. 'This is me and Sam,' she said, her eyes lowered to the floor. 'He's no longer with us.'

I tripped over one of the cat baskets and pulled myself back up. 'Oh I am sorry to hear that,' I said.

'Don't be. He took off, a few years ago.' She picked up one of the cats and held it to her face. 'Didn't he, Jake?' She stroked the top of his ginger head and under his chin, and he started to purr. 'Daddy left us, again. He went off with my best friend at work.' Her voice sounded neutral as if she didn't care. 'Silly mummy kept forgetting. That's never going to happen again.'

The room was filled with reminders of her work and personal life. Yellow post-it notes framed the screen with handwritten messages such as: *240 euros today! You are the best. Only the poor are losers. You can do it. My life is up to ME. Today is my creation. Only I can make ME happy.* There were also several framed prints with similar sounding mottos. The most blatant one was a full-sized poster in typescript with a smiley face hovering over a table laden with coins. It read: *I make money. That's what I do.'*

On the floor there were boxes of old photographs of her past. Some of the photos had been ripped in half and now spilled over the floor for the cats to use as extra bedding.

The main bedroom was similar but contained three large, red, metal cabinets. These were stuffed with invoices and receipts. Again, all the cats in that room looked healthy and ran up to see her.

The area that had the biggest impact was the lounge. From each corner of the room, semicircles of red ribbon had been hung, supporting hundreds of cards. A large plastic snowman took centre stage on a coffee table and there was a huge, fifty inch screen that was partly obscured by the laden branches of a tall, artificial tree, covered in ornaments.

I knelt down to admire the two stuffed reindeer toys next to the table. 'I see you love Christmas,' I said.

Suzie picked up another cat, a Persian Blue. 'We used to. Not anymore! We hate it, now, don't we Portia?' The cat licked her fingers as she rubbed under its chin. 'That's when he left us; my works' Christmas party.' She put the cat down, next to two others, on the red velour sofa. 'Mummy makes sure that we never forget what nasty daddy did to us, doesn't she darlings?'

I saw about eighteen cats but there were probably more. All the felines looked healthy and in good condition with a clean supply of water and cat food in the corner of each room. The litter trays were emptied daily and sprayed with a lemon-scented bleach. There was no cat-smell in any of these rooms.

She led me through another set of double doors into the kitchen. This was where she really needed my help. There were piles of unwashed pots, pans, plates and cat dishes on every surface. The sink was junked with dirty bowls and there were a dozen black plastic bags, filled with used litter and empty cans. It smelled like rotting fish and ammonia. The cats were not allowed in here.

'You can start in here,' she said, taking a shopping list off the notice board. 'I've got to go out for a couple of hours. You'll find all the cleaning stuff under the sink.'

I started pulling the dishes out the sink and ran some hot water. 'No problem,' I said.

She grabbed her cycle helmet from a hook by the front door. 'Don't let the dogs inside and make sure all my babies stay in their rooms.'

The stacks of bowls were starting to sway. I made smaller piles. 'No problem.'

After I heard her shout at the dogs to get back, and the clank of the padlock as she re-locked the gates, I sighed at the mad house I had entered. I knew that places like this existed but this was the first time I had been in one.

Nearly all the cookware and crockery were red. I wasn't sure if this was a deliberate attempt to extend the non-Christmas cheer or if she simply liked the colour. In fact I had never seen such an assemblage of crimson since I had left *The Lords* three years ago.

As I started scrubbing the encrusted dishes in the hot soapy water, my mind travelled back to another unusual Christmas story.

***

The Palace of Westminster is clearly divided into its two houses by their own unique carpets and upholstery. *The Commons* is like a green meadow, whereas *The Lords* resembles fields of poppies.

Within our department was the House of Lords gift shop. This had evolved from the successful series of cabinets which Rita had managed into a highly profitable gift shop. Sales were managed through a hatch by a new, dedicated member of staff, Victoria. It now had many different lines of portcullis-embossed merchandise. On one occasion, back in 1999, when I was walking past the shop, a familiar face was stood outside, scratching her coiffured head and ringing the bell for attention.

It was my job to stand in if Victoria had gone on a break. I opened the side door and appeared at the hatch. 'Can I help you Lady Thatcher?'

Her bright, blue-grey eyes twinkled at me as she put her handbag up onto the counter. She was wearing her pearls over a sea-blue blouse and a matching jacket with a sparkling silver brooch. She always looked immaculate.

'I've come for my order,' she said, producing a paper slip from her bag.

I looked down the list and saw that there were a number of Christmas items. 'I'm sorry, Lady Thatcher. We don't have these items in yet. Do you have another one perhaps? Another list?'

She looked up at me. 'Another one? No, indeed. I need *these* things today.'

It wasn't the first time she had seemed confused. 'I'm sorry but we won't have those things for another three months. We're still selling things for this summer.'

She looked at me again. She blinked and added, 'Quite right, quite right, young man. Well make sure you have them ready for me please.' Despite the strength of her appearance there was a feminine weakness in her manner. They all worked such long hours and gave so much of their lives in service that it seemed inevitable that their minds could get over-worked and muddled. It wasn't a wasted trip, however.

'I'll take a bottle of your best Scotch,' she said, smiling. 'I'm sure you must have that.' She looked like a little girl at the greengrocers, asking for a treat. 'Medicinal purposes,' she added.

She thanked me and went off with her purchase.

I had met her many times before, and she usually used my name, but this time she didn't remember me. It was becoming increasingly clear to those of us that worked there that her mind was gradually slipping away.

On an earlier occasion, in 1991, not long after she had been forced to step down from office, she was far more lucid and chatty.

I had started a new hobby of collecting autobiographies of the many people who visited the House. Sandra, who was always looking out for new opportunities when we were working, suggested that I should get all the authors to sign their books, when they came to visit. She said it would top up my pension. I didn't care about any monetary gain; it gave me a great chance to meet these wonderful characters and have a quick conversation about some of the work they had done.

Sandra could talk to them all without needing an excuse. She was fearless and had recently won her own, long battle against breast cancer. She was proud of the reconstructive surgery and would say to any of the members, 'You can feel them if you like.' Some of them did and others would talk about the skills of the doctor and the NHS and show their admiration for her courage and cheerfulness.

'She's hanging outside the ladies,' Sandra said to me on one occasion. She was rushing back to the kitchen with a stack of plates.

'Who is?' I said.

'Thatcher.' Her wide mouth grinned from under her short bob. 'Her ladies have been drinking too much of the vino and she's waiting for them outside the bogs.'

Lady Thatcher had been hosting one of her lunches, for well-heeled American ladies, in the Cholmondeley Room. They had finished their luncheon and she was escorting them into the Peers'

Courtyard.

'Thanks Sandra,' I said, brushing my morning jacket down. 'I like the blonde by the way.'

Ever since her hair had regrown, she had experimented with different colours, despite warnings from the doctors that it might fall out again. 'They say blondes have more fun and I'm determined to find out,' she winked. 'Now get going. I'll cover for you.'

I ran down to my locker. I had a couple of her books in there and picked up *Ten Years at Number Ten*. She wouldn't stay there for long, so I hurried back and caught my breath before I approached her. 'Lady Thatcher. Would you be kind enough to sign this book for me?'

'Do you have a pen?' she said and put out her hand to receive the book.

As I was searching my pockets for a pen, she flicked through the photographs inside.

She was absorbed by the colour photographs and seemed to have been transported back into the memories they had captured. 'I like this book,' she said as she turned the pages over.

I found a pen and tried to present it to her but she continued to flick through the leaves.

She stopped towards the back of the book and looked at a picture of her and Ronald Regan dancing in the White House. 'Always good on his feet,' she said, with a gentle sigh. She took the pen and signed the front of the book.

'Thank-you, Lady Thatcher,' I said. I needed to hurry back to service.

'No, thank-you, Robert,' she said. 'Thank *you* for asking.'

I couldn't find a reply. I was humbled by her kindness and also the fact she had remembered my name.

There was a kind and considerate side to this woman that not all people saw. I remember another occasion, later, in 2001. She and Dennis had been attending a reception in the Cholmondeley Room and she came up to me and whispered, 'Dennis and I don't want to be at this thing. Is there another way out?' She checked the corridor to see if anyone was looking.

'Follow me,' I said and led them both into the kitchens.

She poked her husband's shoulder and said, 'Come on Dennis. Let's go.' He was quite fragile, so they walked through slowly and caught the attention of some of the surprised kitchen staff.

One of our new kitchen porters looked up from the washing-up and dropped one of the saucepans. 'Hello, Missis Thatcher,' he said.

The exit door was in sight, but she stopped and turned back to him. 'Hello. How are you today?' Dennis was trying to lead her on, but she stood still.

'I'm doing fine, Missis Thatcher,' he said, drying his hands on his apron.

'Where are you from?' she asked.

'I'm Thomas,' he said, putting his hand out. 'I'm from Nigeria.'

She shook his hand. 'We were in Nigeria three of four years ago, weren't we Dennis?'

He nodded without answer.

'Lovely country,' she said and waved to all the staff, as her and Dennis dashed out through the back the door.

***

There was a crash back in Suzie Partridge's kitchen. One of her cats had squeezed through the double doors, jumped up on the side to lick some of the cat bowls and knocked the stack over. Fortunately they were plastic, so they bounced on the floor and the frisky feline fled back into the living room.

I continued to go round to Suzie's for a couple of months. I never did any gardening. I did a lot of cleaning and sometimes just did some pet sitting whilst she was out on her bike shopping or looking for a new house. The naked farmer next door had started letting his dogs run down the side of their shared fence and this caused a lot problems with her animals. They would all bark and growl at each other through the fence and he refused to keep his in.

Every time she saw me, she would make some jibe about the car.

She added that she still thought I needed a van and asked if I wanted to buy hers. It needed some work doing to get it running again but I could have it for two thousand euros.

I told her, *thanks*, but *no thanks*.

One of the last days I saw her was removal day. It was many miles from where she lived at the moment. She had hired some local people to move the furniture a few days before and asked me to transport her pets. It took several hours and several trips to get the cats into their carrying cases and I thought the civil guard would stop me with five dogs in the car, with one on the dashboard and another leaning out of the window.

When we arrived, I heard the phones ringing from a back room and I noticed that a series of double doors had already been installed. The living room was large and uncluttered, apart from a glittering tree which had been put up, next to a closed window.

4 SOAP AND KIDS

One week after her move, Suzie told me she wouldn't need my services any more. With this sudden departure of my first client, I needed to resume my marketing efforts. Graham changed the flyers by taking off *cleaning services*. I didn't mind doing it if I had to, but my real passion was gardening.

We printed off two hundred of these and widened our scope by targeting the post boxes on nearby urbanizations and swanky villas. Nearly every house had at least two dogs so, by the time we had finished, the valley was resonating with an un-conducted orchestra of barking hounds.

Our other targets were customers of some of the local drinking holes. There were a few bars on the outskirts of Alhaurin which the ex-pats favoured. Below the town was the popular, though unglamorous, pub called *El Oro de Tontos*. It looked like a disused petrol station, made up of a couple of white building blocks, which had been stacked one on top of another. Inside there was a growing crowd of people who had stopped by to take advantage of one of the many social groups or simply to refuel their beer-empty stomachs. It had a large community notice board and a small stage area.

We asked a man with long, ripped-looking hair if it was alright to put up a flyer. He looked like an ageing Rock star. He was clad in black denim jeans and jacket, and was wearing a pair of Jesus sandals. He was wandering around aimlessly, humming to himself and looking for something. Perhaps he had lost his guitar? 'Of course,' he said, still drifting around the room. 'It's your noticeboard.'

There were a lot of business cards and flyers pinned to the board and it was difficult to make ours stand out. In the centre of the board was a big A4 poster of a woman in ball gown; *An Evening with Polly*

Perkins, the announcement read, complete with the date and time.

It turned out that the man who okayed our leaflet was Derek, the owner. He had a lot of links with the world of t.v., particularly with actors who worked in the English soaps.

'A lot of them have places around here,' Derek explained, pushing back his long, grey fringe, which had an orange-stained patch in the middle. A gold Rolex flashed past his tanned, wrinkled face. He pulled out a yellow metal case and a shiny, polished wooden instrument. Ceremoniously, he pinched out some tobacco from the case, made a small nest of leaves in the bowl at the end, scored a match down the side of the bar and lit his pipe. We must have looked shocked, although it wasn't the first time we had seen people smoking indoors in Spain. A chuckle rose up, somewhere deep, below his swollen belly. 'My place, my rules.'

'How come they live here?' I asked. It seemed an unlikely place for t.v. stars to hang out. Maybe it reminded them of the pubs where they had delivered their lines?

He blew out a long flume of earthy smoke. It was sickly-sweet smelling like burning hay. This was a smell I loved; it was classically smooth and exuded an air of relaxation.

'*Eldorado,*' Derek said. His voice was as deep and thick as his breath. He walked over to the bar, invited us for a drink, pulled up three stools and ordered some brandies. The barman poured three half-measures and this unhappy boss told him off and demanded that he fill up the glasses. He took another drag and puffed it out along the bar.

'That was the BBC drama that flopped, wasn't it?' Graham asked. He put his hand over his mouth and stifled a cough.

'That's right,' he said. He pointed to another board filled with photographs. He was in most of them and I recognised some of the stars from *EastEnders, Emmerdale* and *Corrie.* 'The set is just a mile from here, near Coín.' He pointed to a dog-eared photograph of a white-washed Spanish village. 'A few of the cast and crew bought property out here on the back of the promise of lots of work.'

The cogs of my factual mind started whirring. 'It was the biggest BBC financial failure ever,' I said. 'The set alone cost over two million pounds and that was back in 1991.'

Graham nudged me. 'Here he goes. The Egghead of the Costa Del Sol.'

Derek took another puff. 'We could do with him on our quiz night.'

The problem is, once I have an audience, I find it impossible to switch the *off* button. With writing it's easier; there's always the *delete* key. So with his encouragement I downloaded all the facts that were stored in my cerebral files.

I told them about how the BBC had been under pressure to increase viewer numbers, to justify the licence fee. Sure, they had *EastEnders,* but what they needed was another corner-stone soap opera to rival ITV. The creators of *Albert Square* were drafted in to save the day. In November 1991, Tony Holland was engaged as the creator with his former colleague, Julia Smith, as producer. He had an excellent idea for a script called *Little England,* where a group of expats would live in a safe fort away from the siege of the native Spanish inhabitants.

'Fill it up,' Derek shouted and banged his empty glass on the bar. 'Sounds a bit like this place. All our customers are English.'

As he said this, a group of elderly, cockney ladies, in shiny tracksuits, bashed through the front door, in single file, carrying their *Nike* sports bags and water bottles. 'High, Derry,' they yelled to our host. It was like a steady stream of blue rinse, babbling over a bed of marble, on the stained floor.

'Hello dear ladies. Come for your aerobics?'

One of the women stopped their flow and shouted, 'No. We've got Zumba with Christine.' She pointed at his pipe. 'You should put that out and join us.'

He coughed and waved the smoke away from his face. 'I'm sixty-nine, Kathy,' he said.

She pushed the girls onwards. 'I know. Too young for us lot.'

Graham gulped his drink down and ordered another. 'It's a bit like *Cocoon* in here,' he said to me.

Derek stood up and waved them off. Once they had left he turned and said, 'More like *Invasion of the Body Snatchers.*' More gold bling bounced on his wrists as his hand flapped from side to side. 'Go on Rob, tell us more about *Eldorado.*'

I found the pause mark in my story and continued to explain how the BBC directors forced Julia to change the whole nature of the drama. The economic barriers of Europe were being pulled down and she was told to bring the non-English characters to the forefront. They were to be given an equal amount of dialogue as the rest of the characters. Unfortunately, the decision was made for them to deliver their lines in their native languages, without any subtitles for the poor, confused British audience. Viewers switched off in their millions. The new BBC Controller at the time, Alan Yentob, decided that the long-term damage to the BBC's brand would be greater than the loss of the ten million pounds spent, if the programme continued, and decided to axe it. The last episode of Eldorado was aired on July the ninth, in 1993.

Derek finished his drink, turned to Graham and said, 'You're right. He is an Egghead. We need him on the team.' He excused himself saying that he had a staff meeting. Two minutes later, the barman gave us the bill. It was only eighteen euros but it felt like we had been stung by this clever business bee.

'If he'd been in charge of Eldorado it would never have gone bust,' Graham chuckled.

We were grateful for the opportunity to meet some other English people and handed out some business cards and put flyers on all the customers' windscreens, under the wiper blades. It was seven in the evening and the temperature was still high in the thirties. As September drew closer, the sun began setting further to the west; away from the mountain peaks and closer to the sea.

In addition to the cards and flyers, we placed advertisements in two of the widely distributed expat papers: *The Sur* and *The Sentinella.*

The phone remained silent and it seemed that this whole idea of reinventing myself at fifty as a gardener had gone pear-shaped.

'It will happen,' Graham said, ever the optimist. 'Use the time to learn more about the plants out here.'

As I sat out on our terrace, reading *Garden Plants for Mediterranean Climates,* there was a loud roar of a motorbike at the end of the driveway. The gate creaked open and the rhythmic crunching of advancing footsteps on gravel grew louder. It was ten o'clock on Monday morning, which meant it had to be José. I picked up my book and took it indoors.

Graham was studying the Cambridge examination details which he needed to give to his students. 'How come you've come in?'

'It's raining,' I said. Since we only have about five days of rain throughout the year, he knew this was a joke. 'No. José is on site.'

'There can't be many gardeners in the world who have little work and have a private gardener to do their own.'

I felt like sulking. 'Very funny. You know it was part of our rental agreement. Besides, I do some work with him but still don't know how to do the pools yet.'

Graham went into the back bedroom to do some photocopying. 'Then give him a drink and get him to show you *Beany,*' he said.

Offering him a drink was a good idea. He accepted the cold beer gladly and I remembered to ask, '*Qué tal?*'

He told me he was fine but pointed to the pool. '*Está nublado,*' he growled, in his deep, rasping voice.

'*Qué?*'

'*Nublado. Nublado!*' He pointed at the water that was milky-coloured and up at the one thin puff of cloud in the sky.

'Oh, cloudy,' I realized. '*Sí señor. Entiendo.*'

He scratched his black-grey beard and climbed up the rocks, like a weathered Spanish goat, to the little pump house above. The filter was running so he turned the motor off and brought down a tub of *Chloro en Polvo*.

I knew some of the basics of pool maintenance after watching some *YouTube* videos. 'Chlorine tablet?'

He had worked out what I meant. 'Chlorine, *si*. Tablet, *no*. *Es Polvo*.' He took a plastic cup and filled it with smooth, white powder. Then, he walked slowly around the outside of the pool and poured a thin white line of the treatment around the pool edge. Once he had completed the circumference, he put the pump back on and said, '*Qué necesita más tiempo. Más tiempo.*'

After that, he left the pump running for twenty-four hours and came back the next morning to switch it off. I went back up with another beer for the inspection.

'*Gracias*,' he said, gulping it down as if it was chilled water. '*Lo ves. Está claro ahora.*'

It was true. There was a bit of powder left on the floor but the water was clear.

'That's great,' Graham said, when I went back to the house. 'Free tuition and we can add *Pool Maintenance* to your flyers now.'

During the first few months in our new home, José gave me many more tips in the gardens. The intense heat dries everything out and there is a constant, seasonal schedule of maintenance. Things that went wrong or needed doing in our garden, inevitably needed to be done in everyone else's.

Three weeks after our advertising blitz, I got a call from a warm sounding woman called Janet who had moved over ten years ago from the East Midlands with her husband John.

'The hedging needs a chopping.' There was a baby crying in the background. 'Stop that scratin,' she yelled, with her hand over the mouth piece. She gave me the address and directions and, at the end of the call, she added, 'We'll see you tomorra afternoon.' The baby was bawling louder than Drew Barrymore being knifed in *Scream*. Janet had to go and hung up.

There was no need to check my diary but I was concerned that I wouldn't have the right tools. It would be hard to cut a lawn without a mower but I had a pair of shears for the hedge.

It probably sounds mad that we didn't buy all the tools before starting the business. Truth was, we had very little money in the bank and didn't know if the business would take off.

Janet's garden was only a couple of miles away. Initially the directions were easy to follow. I drove down towards Coín, past the ceramics factory and turned right by the chicken farm. Once again, the smooth, tarmacked road changed into an unsealed, pitted track. It had such a deep camber on the right-hand side, I heard the wheel arch graunch against the stony bank. I followed the *left, then right*, but should have realized that when she said *go past the big white house*, I would get into difficulty. There were dozens of big white houses. Just as the car dropped into another gulley, I saw a huge, plain house on the corner. On the opposite side of the road were a long line of overgrown fir trees. Their branches were forced up against the chain link fencing and their heavy tops were arching into the garden behind. Was this the hedge that needed *a chopping*?

I drove up to a rusted automatic gate that was closed. Through the railings I could see two parked cars with UK number plates so I got out and looked for the buzzer. There was no need. Three dogs had spotted me and lunged down towards the entrance. There were two young Alsatians barking and gnashing their sharp teeth and an old Corgi, sucking its gums, which was trotting behind them.

'Hello, there.' I said with my most confident voice; demonstrating my experienced dog-handling capabilities. They continued to growl.

'Ey up mi duk,' a tall woman, at the top of driveway called. She had a big glass of wine in one hand and waved with the other. Her hair was piled into a high nest on her head and she was wearing a short summer dress with a small flower print and a low, brocaded collar.

I waved, uncertain I had found the right house. 'Janet?'

'Yes, mi duk. Who'd you think it was? Dusty Springfield? There's a lot of fellas reckon she looks like me.'

Not anymore, I wanted to say. The cogs had started turning. Dusty Springfield, (1939-1999). English pop singer and record producer. *The* blue-eyed soul singer. The woman with that distinct, deep, soulful sound of the sixties.

The gate crunched and gradually opened, its buckled frame grated against the metal groove and made a terrible rubbing noise. My new client started singing in an equally painful voice.

'*You don't have to say you love me. Just be close at hand,*' she sang, raising her arms in the air, swaying the emptied glass.

The dogs ran past me and tried to escape through the open gate. I felt an urge to run out with them but called them back in, as the gate automatically started closing. The corgi nearly got its head stuck in the gap, but I pulled him in just before he got squashed.

Their owner was undisturbed by their attempt to leave. '*You don't have to stay forever. I will understand.*' She beckoned me to join her on the small terrace beside the kitchen.

I brushed the paw prints and scratch marks off my legs and walked up the driveway. In my head I had the words to another of her idol's songs. *I just don't know what to do with myself.* This was accompanied by, *Should I stay or I should I go now.* I sincerely hoped that me and this woman wouldn't *Clash.*

'I'm mashing. Fancy a cuppa?' she asked and disappeared inside.

I waited on the terrace and played with the dogs. The house was a simple design; it looked identical to any bog-standard bungalow you could find anywhere in the U.K.

The location was fantastic. From the front, the garden and buildings were hidden by the high line of coniferous trees. There was a pool and hot-tub area tucked behind the end of the house and the back garden had views across open fields to the mountains on the horizon. An eagle flew overhead and called out to two more which were riding high on the thermals.

Janet gave me a mug and told me she would show me around. She had decided against tea for herself and refilled her glass. I noticed that she had beautiful blue eyes, deeply set in pools of wrinkles and framed by very long lashes, thickly lined with mascara. Her hair had been washed and set but was decidedly more rust coloured than peroxide blonde. She looked like an old Barbie doll that had been left out too long in the sun.

'I like your nails,' I said, as she gave me the tea. She had long, porcelain talons which had been intricately painted in individual white and blue patterns; they would have looked more at home on expensive crockery than someone's hands. 'Are you going out somewhere nice?' I asked her.

She held her hands up in front of her face and splayed her fingers open. 'They are good-uns, aren't they?' The dogs followed her around the garden but respected their mistress. They didn't jump up at her.

Janet showed me the trees which all needed to be cut down by half but it was important that no-one could see in. There was no way my shears would get through that lot. There was half an acre of lawn at the front which had been dug up by the dogs and was littered with dried faeces. 'I only picked this up last week,' she said, embarrassed. 'It's amazing how much mess they make.'

'No problem. I'll clear it up.' It would take me a day to pick it all up and give me an opportunity to buy a saw for the trees. There were also dozens of half-chewed sticks and plastic toys and pipes littering the floor. The bigger Alsatian bounded behind me and bent my leg forward as he shoved past.

'Toby,' Janet yelled. 'Bad boy.' She turned back to face me. 'Sorry Rob. Are you alright?' She pointed to a small scratch that was beading red spots on the surface.

'It's fine, Janet.' I picked up some half eaten insulating cable with wires hanging out and threw it across the garden. Both the young dogs ran after it, whilst the small sandy one came up and licked my leg. 'This one's taken care of it.'

She smiled. 'That's Shorty. Toby and Oscar pick on you, don't they sweed- art?' She scooped the little mutt up in her arms and cradled him with his belly in the air. 'You're mummy's special boy, aren't you short-stuff?' She blew a raspberry on his tummy.

As we walked along the pool, Janet pointed to the water. 'It's suddenly gone cloudy.'

I grinned at the milky pond. 'That's no problem. I know just how to sort that out.'

'I don't know why it's gone like that,' she said, stroking her chin.

'It's the sun,' I told her. 'It just needs a bit more chlorine and we probably need to set the timer to come on for longer.' I smiled, knowingly. It was good to feel informed.

The sun does so much damage over here; it dries everything out. Plants have to be continually water fed through complex irrigation systems. Trees need to be continually drip fed at regular intervals, whereas grasses and shrubs need a powerful saturation a few times a day. Plants are not the only victims of the scorching conditions. People, cars and anything that contains oils are also vulnerable. It is very common to see paint peeling off cars; sunbeds and awnings which are split and have been sucked dry; and the burnt, dehydrated husks of bodies walking on beaches and terraces that have been drained of fluid, like heavily microwaved potatoes which have kept their jackets but lost their flesh.

The solar temptress first seduces you, then she drains you dry.

We walked along a deep, raised border which the dogs had attacked and she told me about some of the new plants she wanted to put in. Behind a high stone wall was another overgrown section of garden. It was surprising to see that in this heat, long tendrils of ivy had claimed the entire rear wall. There was a huge pile of cuttings which were ready to be burnt.

'I suppose you're waiting for the permit season,' I said,

remembering some of José's words.

'What?'

'The bonfire season.'

She stepped over some discarded tools on the ground. 'Oh my days,' she gasped. 'We don't worry 'bout stuff like that. My John's just been busy.'

John was her husband who was down on the coast doing electrical work. They were both on their second marriages. Her first partner was violent and used to hit her; his was unfaithful and went off his with his best mate.

'We are so lucky,' she added. 'Lucky to have found each other at our time in life.' Her smile looked genuine and she was proud that she had a man that was hard working. He was good with business and good with his hands, she said with a cheeky wink.

I wondered why he didn't do the garden but she explained that he was always working during the week and that they enjoyed their weekends together.

'We go to *Tontos* every Sunday,' Janet said. 'That's where we found out about you.' She stepped over more machinery and walked past a tractor, an open-backed truck and another car.

'Did you get one of my flyers?'

'No, Derek told us about you.' She walked over to a long metal freight container. 'This is John's pride and joy.'

I was grateful that, despite charging us for the drinks, Derek had been kind enough to mention us to his customers. Janet grabbed a hammer and hit the metal bar on the door which released the levers. Inside was every tool imaginable. There were hedge trimmers, strimmers, three lawn mowers, a *Karcher* machine, electric saws, a cement mixer and lots of other items which I had no idea what they did. 'Wow, it's like *Raiders of the Lost Ark* in here.'

'Use anything you need,' she said.

'That's great. Are you sure?' My voice echoed inside this metal cavern.

'Cors-u-can.' She checked her watch. 'Oh my Lord. Is that the time? I've gotta go and see to Eleanor. I'll see you in a tad.' She shot out of the container and ran back to the house. She must have meant the baby I had heard crying yesterday. Perhaps she was baby-sitting her grand-daughter?

I dragged a bucket of tools over towards the front gates and started with the tall cypress trees, planted either side. They must have been fifteen feet high. Before I started attacking these green monsters, I stood back, gauged a bit over half, cut a small chip in the first one and made that my bench mark. Unfortunately, I had cut the first two a bit short and started higher up on the others; I realized that I could always take more off if she wanted but couldn't put any back on.

It was nearly 2 pm. and the heat of the sun seared on the back of my neck. Unfortunately, I had left my hat in the back of the car but felt sure I would be fine for a bit. I had no covering to protect my head so I climbed into the foliage and used the branches as shade.

The big dogs wrestled for a while over an old car battery, then bullied Shorty and eventually collapsed by the side of the house. I could hear Janet singing again and the baby was laughing now.

After two hours, I had sawn down about half the hedge. The wood was tough and had scored cuts and blisters across my hands. Janet came back out and asked if I wanted a cold drink. I would have loved a beer but had decided it was best not to drink in front of the clients and asked for a Coke. I was going to gulp it down whilst I carried on working, but she had cleaned off one of the patio tables near the kitchen, poured the drinks and put out some biscuits. She definitely wanted a bit of a chat.

She told me about how she had met John. He had come over to check her plumbing in her house, back in Leicester, and had never left. They had been together over fifteen years and she had never been so happy. She wasn't wearing the same dress as before; she now had on a low, blood-red halter neck top and tight, curvy denim shorts.

'We 'ave so much in common,' she said, combing her big hair with her long finger nails. It looked higher than before. I felt an urge to get my secateurs out and trim it back down. The low neckline of her dress was swollen with the swell of her large buxom breasts. 'Love the heat.' She patted her neck. 'It's unusual for us to be wearing threads.'

'Threads?'

She winked one of those heavily mascaraed eyes at me. Had she put more make-up on? There seemed to be a thin black line at the outer edge of each one giving her an exotic look. Janet stroked one of her ear lobes as she sipped her wine. 'Duds. Clothes, darling.' She was definitely flirting with me.

It had been years since a woman had done this and, to be honest, I was enjoying the attention. I was pleased she had her clothes on though.

'That's why John let the trees grow so high.'

I choked on my Coke. 'Oh I see.'

She purred. 'I don't mind if the neighbours watch, but he likes to keep it private.'

It was time for a change of subject before my face became the same colour as her top. 'What did you do before moving to Spain?'

She took another sip and placed her glass on the table. 'Piss and piles,' she yelled.

I was speechless and now redder than a sundried tomato.

'Just teasing,' she giggled. 'Well, sorta.' She topped her glass up with the half-empty bottle in the cooler. 'Home care. I used to be a pediatric nurse but I look after the old 'uns now. I fly back home every other month just for a couple of weeks. It fits in with Eleanor and the money's good.'

Shorty had climbed under the table and was licking one of my hands. He was happy, hiding away from the other two, so I took care not to give him away.

'You got any kids?' Janet asked.

'No. My partner's called Graham,' I explained.

She lit up a cigarette. 'I didn't want to be rude, but I had a feeling you might be, you know, that way. You can still have kids. Look at Elton and David Furnish.'

This was a subject which came up quite often now. We had rehearsed our response to this. 'Graham says it's me. He reckons I fire blanks.'

She laughed. 'No , really. A lot of guys are having kids now.'

'Too much responsibility,' I said. I had finished the Coke and accepted the offer of a beer. 'I think if we were going to have kids we would adopt.'

She liked this answer and was nodding vehemently. 'Too right, too right.'

'There are so many unwanted kids already,' I added.

'That's why we got Eleanor,' she told me, wiping a small tear from her eye. 'They are a lot of work, but worth every minute.' Janet recomposed herself and gently pulled out a long lash which had slipped into her eye. She placed it on the back of her hand, closed her eyes, blew and made a silent wish. 'Yes, it's gone,' she said. 'That means it'll come true. I can't tell you what it was but I can tell you it was for you and Graham.' She grinned like a child who had opened their favourite Christmas present.

'Thank, you.' I said. I hoped that I wouldn't go home and find Graham pregnant.

'So, what did you do in the U.K?' Janet asked.

I told her that I had always been in service and about the magnificent building and some of the Prime Ministers.

She stood up and walked into the kitchen. 'Let me get you that beer.' I heard the tinny clink of metal as she got more drinks out of the fridge. She reappeared with a six pack of cans and another bottle of wine. 'Not really into politics. Any famous people?'

I tried to think of the stories which she might find more entertaining. 'I met Simon Cowell a few times.'

'Yes,' she shrieked, banging her glass on the table. 'Go on.'

***

One of the best events we hosted each year was for *The Children of Courage Awards*. It was set up in 1973 and is sponsored by *Woman's Own* magazine. Since then it has been an annual celebration and recognition of some of our children's greatest acts of heroism in fighting pain, hardship, disabilities and looking after others. After the awards ceremony in Westminster Abbey, the children are chaperoned across the road and led into the House via Black Rod's Entrance.

For many years our beloved pastry chef, June, transformed the Cholmondeley Room into a sweet-toothed paradise. It made the witch's house in *Hansel and Gretel* look dull. In place of the usual mounds of cheeses, lobsters, crabs and game birds were castles of decorated sponge cake, towers of assorted jellies and ice-creams, mountains of cream-topped desserts and enough chocolate to put *Willy Wonka* out of business. The children ran from table to table helping themselves to an endless supply of sugar and playing with the many helium balloons strung up next to each table. It was great to hear laughter and cheer echoing through the great halls instead of conversations of business and political debate.

In addition to the children were many famous celebrities. Some were yearly regulars and others were making guest appearances to represent patronage of their own children's charities, and perhaps win credit towards the next *New Year's Honour's List* or, at least, a mention in tomorrow's tabloids. Some of my notable favourites were June Whitfield and Tony Hart. There were always some members of *EastEnders* and occasionally the lovely Amanda Barry. In some cases they seemed the same as their public personas but Simon Cowell was completely different to what I was expecting. He had loads of time for the kids. In fact, he was happier sat talking and listening to them than being in adult company.

A big white screen and camera had been set up in the corner of the room so that the children could request photographs with some of their favourites. The person they most wanted to be seen with was Simon Cowell. He spent hours tirelessly smiling and posing for their souvenirs. Also, he made sure that the *X-Factor* finalists were always invited so that the kids could meet their popstar heroes.

There was magic in the room at those lunches. The pastry chef had been told that she could never have children but, after one of these events, soon after her fiftieth birthday, June fell pregnant and had the first of two beautiful children. Unfortunately cancer claimed her some years later but she had been ecstatically proud and happy to have experienced motherhood.

***

'I met Bet Lynch in Mercadona, buying some melons,' Janet said.

I managed to suppress the tear that had formed from the memory of June. 'Yes. Derek told me about *Eldorado* and said there's quite a lot of them out here.'

'Sure ees, mi duk.' Her eyes looked shiny and there was a slight smudge of mascara in the corner of one of them. 'They all come to *Tontos*. June Brown is always in there and Claire King was in last week.' She refilled her glass. 'I'm surprised he told you about *Eldorado.*'

I finished my beer. 'I thought everybody knew.'

'Naughty Derek. It's true. We put in an offer to buy the village.' She was pushing her boobs back under their cover. 'Yep, it was gonna be a naturist haven.' She hadn't struck me as being a wildlife lover. 'A place to kick back, take it all off and let it all hang out.'

'I'd better get on with the hedges,' I said, realizing my mistake and blushing again. There was still the area next to the sun loungers to clear.

'I think I should check with John what height he wants those ones,' she said. 'He won't want to give the neighbours an eyeful,' she giggled. 'Me, I think it's just what this place needs.'

I was sure she was going to tear her top off any minute. 'I'll start cleaning up the grass, if you like.' A lot of the dogs' mess had turned into powder and needed lifting off the dying grass.

'I'm so sorry about that. You shouldn't have to do that.' She stood up, looking at the mess. 'Let me clear this table and I'll give you a hand.'

I tried to stop her. The idea of her dirtying those perfectly manicured hands seemed like blasphemy. There was no need to worry. She carefully covered them with a pair of white leather driving gloves. She un-wrapped a new silver trowel and got stuck in.

In two hours she told me all about her care work, her wedding, her abuse from the first husband who had locked her in the house for six days and big plans she had for Eleanor's birthday party. 'Perhaps you could serve us the drinks, if you still do that kind of thing?'

Yes, I thought. *Provided you all keep your clothes on.* 'It would be my pleasure,' I said.

5   SMOKEY BAKING

The gardening work continued at Janet and John's and seemed permanent now. I did four hours every Friday. It was great to have my first regular contract and hopefully they would recommend me to their neighbours and to other customers of *Tontos*. They told me that eight euros per hour was too cheap and increased it to ten.

It is cheap to live in Spain, but not free. Our rent was only five hundred euros per month, as we took on the pool and garden maintenance, but electricity and petrol are expensive. Despite the news stories saying that unleaded and diesel was coming down, we didn't see any decrease over here.

I needed to get some more hours.

We took some flyers to the English bar at the other end of town, *The Fox and Ferret*. The owners were a couple from Shirley, near Southampton, where I grew up. They introduced us to some of their locals and pointed out a small exotic woman, with dark skin and silky black hair. She was hosting a business lunch for some new clients and dashed around the table in a red jacket and skirt, edged in a thick band of cream. She looked efficient and in control, like a senior air stewardess for Virgin Airlines.

'Robert, this is Alhaurin's most glamorous lady,' the landlord said. 'This is Sheba, from Persia.'

'Ssh, Mick, darling. You are so naughty with Sheba,' she purred, like a pedigree cat receiving the attention she naturally commanded. 'I need two more bottles of Verdejo and a good Rioja.'

He jotted them down on her bill and handed my leaflet over to her. 'This is Rob. He's looking for gardening work. Sheba knows everyone. She'll sort you out.' He left the bar and went in search of the wine.

Sheba held my leaflet at the edge, as if it was a piece of dirty toilet paper. She took her gold rimmed glasses, which were hanging around her neck, placed them on the end of her small, rounded nose and read through my sales pitch. 'That's a load of rubbish,' she said, looking up and dropping it onto the bar.

'Really? I thought it covered what it needed to,' I said. I felt like a student, who had handed in a crap piece of homework and was being told off by teacher for a severe lack of effort.

She stared at me, awaiting further explanation. She oozed charisma and despite her advancing years was still a beautiful woman with admirable strength. The Persian Empire collapsed centuries ago and emerged as modern Iran, but this woman was solid and steadfast and would remain in power here for many years. 'What is it that you do? Who is Robert?' she asked and dropped her Armani glasses back on her neck. She looked more Italian than Middle Eastern.

I told her about my job in London, the gardening work I was doing and why we had moved over to Spain.

'Where are you living?' she asked.

'You might not know it. It's a small brown house on the edge of town near *El Postillon.*'

She sighed. 'Isabella's,' she exclaimed. 'Of course I know it. She's a great friend of mine. How much are you paying?'

'Five hundred a month.' I decided not to tell her about the extra fifty we had been paying for José the gardener.

Sheba took a thin silver case out of her Gucci handbag, flipped it open and handed me a thick embossed card. The words were printed in gold typescript and read: *Alhaurin Dreams.* I wanted to find out where she had got this printed but she was continuing with the interrogation.

'I normally do Isabella's house. You should have come to me.'

She took a silver compact mirror out and checked her face. Unhappy with her lips, she retrieved an orange-brown lipstick and recoated them. 'Who did you use?'

I could smell roses as she reapplied it. 'Ivan.'

She put the lid back on and tossed it in her bag. 'That rogue. He doesn't pay his taxes. I've been doing her house for years.' I thought she might explode with rage.

Sorry. I didn't know, I wanted to say.

'No matter. It's a dump. You won't stay. Too cold in winter and too dark. It's got no lounge.' She took a final look in her mirror, clamped it shut and put it away. 'You come to Sheba next time.'

One of the chairs was under the stairs, so she was right about the living room. There were radiators in every room, so we were confident it would be warm.

'Of course we will,' I surrendered.

She turned around, picked up my *rubbish* flyer and walked back to her clients. Detention was over; class was dismissed.

I got a call from her four days later, just as I was approaching the checkout in *Mercadona* with a full trolley.

'You come now, darling. I have *The Boys* in the office. We will go for lunch and talk business.'

I'm not too good at the networking side of the business. My brain doesn't think like that. It keeps things simple and factual. 'I can't Sheba. I'm at the checkout.'

There were a series of angry tuts on the other end. 'You come now or Sheba will not be happy.'

'My ice-cream will melt,' I said. The person behind me was trying to push past in the queue. He only had three onions so I let him go. Food shopping was boring enough without leaving it all there and having to do it again. 'Please can you give them my number?'

More tuts and the phone went dead.

I told Graham about my failed business call. He just laughed. 'We're never going to be rich at this rate. I'd better get some more teaching hours before the bank gives us a call.'

'At least we've got food in the fridge.' I had emptied the bags and packed the stuff away in our tiny kitchen.

The phone rang.

'Guess that's the bank now,' Graham said, marking some English essays.

'He-llo,' a voice puffed down the line. It sounded like the person had been out running or I was receiving my first heavy-breather call. The panting continued. 'Hello. Is that Robert? Robert the Gardener?'

'Yes. It's Robert the gardener.' It still sounded good to say those words.

'Simon eya. Got yaw number frum Sheba.' He paused. His breath still rattled on the other end and he skipped words to make himself heard. 'She's a good friend of yourn?' There was definitely a strong northern accent, as well as the breathing problems. Maybe from Birmingham?

I wanted to say *I think she's a good friend of everyone's,* but didn't. 'Yes,' I replied.

'Big garden here and some acres.'

'Oh, yes.' This was sounding promising.

'Got a strimmer?' There was a croaky cough coming through the ear piece as he cleared his throat. 'I've got ten acres need clearing. Soon as. Needs a decent strimmer. Metal blade. You got one?'

It would have taken a year to clear it with my shears and I couldn't find a solution. 'Yes, well no. Not at the moment.' I find it impossible to lie.

'Alroit then. Not to worry.' With one final cough he hung up.

Graham was twitching in the background. He had passed me a note which I read now. *Buy a strimmer.*

'It's no good. I think he wanted me to do it tomorrow.'

He looked up at me with that frown he gives me when I'm procrastinating. 'Well go and buy one then, Beany. Call him back now, before he gets someone else and tell him, *Yes. Of course I've got one.*'

'Where from?'

'Mmm. I guess you could try the *Panaderia.*'

'Very funny. That's the bread shop, isn't it?'

'Well done Beany. Your Spanish is really coming on.'

'*Pisso, Offo,* you square-bodied creature.' I threw my baseball cap at him.

He caught it, threw it back and it landed on my head. 'Goal!' He yelled. 'How about the *Ferreteria* at the end of the road?' It was close to our house but a bit expensive. 'Or Leroy Merlin?' Graham added. 'But he speaks really good English in the Ferreteria.'

'True. And at least it's probably open,' I said.

We had driven down to Ikea a few weeks ago, on a Tuesday, and the whole retail park had been closed for another *Fiesta.* There are so many celebrations here. Some are local to the towns, some to the province of Andalucía and a few are national for the whole of Spain.

I was worried that if I tried to use Spanish I would end up buying the wrong thing. 'Shall I get an electric one? Like we had the in U.K.?'

Graham thought for a minute. 'You need one with a strong blade like we had but it's probably best to get a petrol one. The weeds might be miles from the house and you'll have more freedom. You should be able to get one for about two hundred.'

I agreed and decided I'd call Simon back and as soon as I had managed to buy one.

Ferreterias are a staple part of the Spanish shopping experience. They are as integral as the hardware stores you find in the UK but are usually five times as big. They contain all the bits and pieces you could ever want for the next DIY task.

Carlos was very helpful and had one sturdy machine available which was displayed on a rack. I saw a price tag for two hundred and thirty nine euros. It was the only one that looked industrial and came with a metal blade. He took it off the rack, found a copy of the instruction manual in his filing cabinet and bagged up the head, the metal blade and a reel of plastic cord. '*Eso es trescientos veintinueve. Por favor.*'

I handed him five fifty euro notes. It was slightly over budget but I would have spent the extra euros on petrol going down to the coast and felt proud of my purchase.

'*No señor. Tres cientos veintinueve. Three* hundred and twenty nine.'

I pointed to the label. 'It says two-three-nine,' I said. Someone must have changed it. It now clearly read three-two-nine. The problem is, I know I'm dyslexic and sometimes read things around the wrong way. I handed over the extra *dinero* and consoled myself that I would soon pay it off with all the work I would get.

Graham's reaction was not surprising. 'So you've bought a second hand strimmer, with no box, for over three hundred euros. They see you coming, don't they?'

When we first got together, he discovered that I had three life assurance policies and two endowments to pay off one mortgage. I don't know what happens. I just smile and agree to what they say. 'It's got a three month guarantee,' I told him.

We decided to test the machine and switch the heads over from the cord one to the metal blade. The tiny metal pin for holding the locking mechanism was missing so I had to pop back down to *Carlos* who smiled and gave me one for free. I also needed to buy some oil and a plastic petrol can which were another twenty euros.

'*Gracias, señor.*' I said, with a good Spanish accent.

'No problem, *señor*. You come again soon.'

After a few more setbacks we changed the blade, filled it up with fuel, pulled the starter cable and the machine roared into action. Its hungry metal blades would tear through the toughest of weeds, bring them down to the floor and make them eat dirt. I was ready for battle.

Simon's house was set on a slope on the other side of town. He lived with his old friend and business partner, Steve. They had grown up together in Dudley, on the outskirts of Birmingham. They had been to school together, been best men for each other, helped each other through their divorces, worked together and now lived together, albeit in separate ends of the house.

I had been told to look for *Villa Rosa*. It was *The big red 'owse on the hill*. The area was decidedly upmarket. Instead of the regimented, white, terraced town-houses in the centre of Alhaurin, there were huge independent villas which had all been personalised to match their owners' tastes. Gone were the fundamental white square *casas*. Here architects and designers had been given a free hand and open wallets to create fantasies in brick and plaster. At the bottom of the hill there was a cream, French styled house with four turrets and rows of green framed windows with matching shutters. On the other side it looked like the QE2 had run aground: a long house with lines of glass-sliding doors, joined externally by a boardwalk of balconies, edged in glass and steel tubing. Further up was a mock Tudor mansion which looked like it had been airlifted from Surrey and dropped in a field, bordered with palm trees.

At the top of the hill I found *Villa Rosa*. I was expecting a big house in pillar-box red covered in roses. What greeted me was a large, Italian villa painted in flamingo-pink with white, shuttered windows. It was like something out of a Barbara Cartland novel.

There was a double entrance shielded by high gates made from white iron railings. I pressed the buzzer and the gate started humming and slid open to let me in. As I drove along the gravel track I saw a short pole on the terracotta roof with the Union Jack hanging lifeless from the top. In the gardens, there were a series of white marble statues encircled by box hedging and patio roses. It was a private display of *Michelangelo* figures – *David, Bacchus* and *Madonna of Bruges*. They looked down at me and grimaced at my gardening clothes. Three white arches had been installed at the front of the building and were covered in white flowering jasmine. I stepped out the car and inhaled the heavy honey-sweet scent. I could hear water running from a fountain at the side of the house and was embarrassed to disturb this man-made paradise. I pressed the doorbell and a series of loud *ding-dongs,* scaling up and down, erupted from inside. Just as the door opened I heard a woman screaming.

A big round figure appeared in the doorway shrouded in smoke from his lit cigar. His thin black hair looked like it had been cut with secateurs, but this was compensated by his attire; it was classic and looked expensive. Ralph Lauren was clearly his favourite designer. He was wearing a tight, orange polo shirt with a dark blue emblem and slim-fit, dark-blue chinos which needed taking up and letting out at the waist. His neck was covered with an orange, paisley silk scarf.

The screaming continued behind me.

'Is she alright?' I asked.

The man coughed and waved me inside. 'Who?'

The distress was getting louder and seemed to be coming closer. It sounded like *Al-Al-Aaaal.* I pointed to the wailing.

'That's alroight. It's just Percy. He's our resident guard dawg.'

Moments later a white peacock appeared, trailing his elongated feathers like a bridal train.

Simon introduced himself and led us through the living room, past a formal dining room and into a small kitchen at the back.

A thin, yellow-skinned man with fine ginger hair was wiping the white marble worktops down. His clothes were clean but tired. He was wearing cut-off jeans and a bleached, holey t-shirt. 'You always make such a mess when you're baken,' he said, squirting more cleaning fluid over the surface.

Simon shrugged. 'You won't be complainen when you're eating cake for your tea. Steve, this is Bob. He's come to do the strimming.'

He stopped wiping for a second and shook my hand with his wet bony fingers. 'I normally does it myself but I've got na time.'

Simon looked up at the floral kitchen clock with its Roman numerals. 'Oh damn it. Should have got it out foiv minute ago.'

'Simon! You're not supposed to be smoking in here.' Steve squawked, waving his arms through the thick smoke and opening the window.

He ignored him, held the cigar between his thick lips, grabbed a rose-patterned oven glove and plundered the oven for his treasure. 'Thank 'eavens. They look perfect.' He pulled out two golden discs of sponge and placed them on the cooling rack.

Steve was still waving his arms, as he dried a stack of plates with a *Bake-Off* tea towel. 'Thought you were making chocolate cake.'

'No cocoa powder. I've made The Queen of Baking's own speciality.' He bowed to a framed picture of Mary Berry, hung above the cooker. 'Victoria sponge.'

Steve threw the towel into the washing machine. 'You made that last week.' His frayed denim shorts had dropped slightly below his skinny waist. He pulled them up, tightened his belt and hurried off saying he had too much to do.

Simon showed me out of a backdoor, into a conservatory. The cane table and chairs were immaculately clean and a few emptied ashtrays were dotted around the area. There was a thin film of brown on the window panes at the top and a bitter-sweet scent of burnt oak hung in the air. This was their smoking den. He led me through another door and into the garden. The back walls were also pink.

Three Alsatians started barking from behind white trellised panels at the far end of the candy-floss building. They pounded their big black and brown paws against the fragile fencing, making it sway and it looked like the partition would yield and topple forward any minute.

'Calm down boys,' Simon shouted at them. 'They're rescue dogs. Got another comen on Fridoy.' His face looked redder outside. He explained that the orchard was behind the swimming pool and he just wanted the weeds strimmed between the trees and left on the ground for mulch. I could bring my tools through the side gate next to a greenhouse, where Percy normally lived. 'I'll leave you ter it. I've got loads of paperwerk to do and I can't stand the heat in the day.'

Despite it being October, the sun was still bright in the day and the rains had not yet arrived. I had been so keen to get my strimmer up and running that I had forgotten the protective goggles which Carlos had put in the bag and had left my straw hat at home. Still, it was autumn now so surely the power would have gone out of the sun? I was wrong. It was around twenty-five degrees and after half an hour of strimming my shirt was dripping in sweat. The fruit on the trees were at different stages of maturity. The apples were nearly ready but the oranges, limes and lemons only had small green buds, waiting for more water and cooler temperatures to grow and ripen. José had taught me that it's important to clear the soil around the base of the trees. You need to ensure that any precious water soaks directly into the roots and is not stolen by weeds or grasses. The best type of watering for citrus is a very slow, regular drip. This can be best achieved by digging around the root ball and laying out lengths of irrigation pipes, with small plastic side shoots, which are placed about a foot from the trunk, and set to come on early morning or late evening by a timer. It is advisable to water in the mornings as late-afternoon and evening spraying can attract mosquitos.

My *Stihl* strimmer tore through the high canes of weeds. It mashed up the coarse yellow rods into little sticks in seconds. My glasses soon got covered in sprayed splinters and dust, and I had to keep stopping to wipe them off. It was a heavy machine which was supported by shoulder straps and two bicycle-like handle bars either side. I was worried that my pinned shoulder would ache but it held firm and seemed stronger than the other one. After a while, your brain can become mesmerized with the whirring of the device. Like driving a fast sports car, you become caught up in the power of the engine and have to check yourself that you are still in control and not being driven by the machine.

Occasionally, I put the blade too close to a tree and made a nick in the trunk. The other mistake I made was ripping through a black hose which was exposed on the ground. It's not much of a problem; you just need to carry some spare jubilee clips and plastic joiners in case.

After two hours, I saw Simon waving me up to the conservatory. There was a clean, freshly-ironed cloth on the table and many pieces of a Royal Albert Old Country Rose tea set, which had been arranged in symmetrical patterns, to accompany the elevated centre piece of the Victoria sponge, set on a crystal cake stand.

'Bob, come and join us for a cuppa and a slice,' Simon bellowed from an armchair near the doorway.

I left my grass covered strimmer on the floor and stepped inside.

Steve was still flitting, like a bee with ADHD between flower heads, backwards and forwards into the kitchen. He carried in some silver tea spoons, decided they were dirty, polished them with a clean towel and brought them back out. 'You might want to wash your hands,' he told me. 'You can use the sink in the utility through there.'

Simon let the dogs out into the garden and they started pawing the glass trying to get in for cake.

'Did you have to let them out?' Steve snapped. 'They're marking the windows. I only did them yesterdoy.'

'Oh, stop your fussen. You be mother. Pour us some tea and cut us some cake.'

Steve put the tea towel back in the kitchen and brought in a long, silver knife. 'I have to do everything around here.' He poured tea into the cups and handed them out on saucers. He cut a wafer-thin slice and handed it to me.

Simon heaved himself out of the chair. 'That's not a slice. Give him a decent bit. He's like you; bag of bones. He needs feeden' up.' He took the plate off me, cut out a sixth and handed it back. 'Sorry about that,' he said. He did the same for Steve and handed it to him.

He frowned. 'That's too much fer me.'

'Ah go on with you. Cake is good for you.' He cut a bigger slice for himself and took a big bite. 'That's a good bake. Even if I do says so, moyself.' Crumbs of cake and a blob of strawberry jam fell from his mouth. 'Any sugar for yer tea?' he asked me.

'No thanks,' I said, swallowing a mouthful.

'Yer like me,' he chuckled. 'Sweet enough.'

Steve sighed. 'More like: *fat* enough,' he grumbled.

'Do you want another bit Bob?'

I'm not keen on being called Bob, but had decided to let it go. 'No, that was great thanks.'

Steve tidied the plates away and Simon walked over to a pile of papers which were stacked on a bookcase behind us. 'It's a good cake. That will last us the rest of the week, that will.' He sat back down and asked how many hours I was looking for.

I told him the truth. I only had a few hours and needed as many as possible. It was clear that I needed to get more tools and eventually I would need to take a leap of faith and buy a van for the business.

He explained that him and Steve ran a cleaning business and a few of their clients had pools and gardens. Steve had been doing the gardens but with all the airport *meet and greets*, a new contract with a large holiday company and supervising the team of cleaners, he was always running out of time.

Steve heard part of the conversation from inside the kitchen. He shouted from the sink, 'Simon. I told you. I'm fine.'

'Ignore him,' Simon told me. He also explained that they had been running the business for years and that he found it difficult to trust anyone. The last gardener had been Spanish, left the grass clippings in black bags by the front door, like a welcome gift for the guests, stopped showing up, but kept demanding money. It had been very stressful. 'People take advantage of us. I always keep a thousand euros in the top drawer of my desk.' He pointed to the office area which was behind the conservatory. 'Not only that. There was an elderly couple who lived on the other side of town. They were from Brum. We did everything together – meals out, holidays, dog walks. A couple of years ago they had legal problems with their villa. The kitchen extension didn't have planning permission and they had to pay compensation to the local council or they were going to rip it down.'

'It seems like a lot of people have problems with houses out here,' I said.

He pulled himself up in the chair. 'It's Spain, isn't it? Tell me Bob do you like Spain?'

This was an easy question for me. 'I love it.'

He started coughing. 'So does Steve. I bloody hate it.' He wiped his mouth. 'Too bloody hot, same weather every day and everyone's trying to rip you off.'

I thought of my recent strimmer purchase. 'We are renting. I think that's easier.'

'Us too. This place is nineteen fifty a month. It's a lot but there's a laundry in the basement for the business. I've kept my place in the U.K. and I will go back, even if he doesn't.' He looked over towards the kitchen. 'Well, these friends of ours asked if they could borrow the money from me. It was twelve thousand euros.' His face was getting redder as he recalled the details. Small beads of sweat were bubbling up on his forehead. 'I'm such a bloody idiot. Was even paying for all our meals and holidays that year. They never offered to pay me a penny back. Steve and I went round to see them, to see if we could agree on something every month. They told us they couldn't afford anything. But there was a brand new car, straight out the showroom, tucked round the side of the 'owse. Bastards.' He started fighting for breath and his red colour had now gone grey.

Steve had heard him gasping and came into the room. 'Simon. Where's your inhaler?'

His chest was heaving in slow, deep rises and his skin was turning blue. 'By my bed,' he managed to utter.

Steve ran back inside and reappeared a minute later, pushed the plastic tube into his mouth and depressed the *release* button.

Five minutes later, Simon was back to normal. He picked up some files with customer details on the sheets of paper and seduced me with promises of six gardens, with pool maintenance in the summer, which would net me around fourteen hundred euros a month.

'Yes I'm up for that,' I said. I relished the thought of having some extra money every month. We could go out to nice restaurants again and take a trip over to Morocco.

'Let's celebrate,' Simon cheered. 'Steve. Get the cigars.'

Steve glared at him. He gave a look as if to say: *do you think you should be smoking with your asthma?*

I hadn't had a cigar for years. Graham doesn't smoke and there's not normally an opportunity for it. There's nothing like it. Soon the air in the conservatory turned thick and blue. It became heavily scented with a sweet-sickly smell, with a slight bitter after taste at the back of the throat. Three lit orange pokers glowed through the fumes. Once they found out where I used to work, they asked me what atmosphere was like in *The Lords*.

So many memories. 'It was a lot better before the smoking ban,' I said.

'That's why *I* like Spain. No one gives a shit over here,' **Steve smiled. The smoking had relaxed him and made him friendlier. 'And it's so much cheaper.'**

It felt like, in the back of this house in Andalucia, they had created their own private Gentlemen's Club.

***

Smoking dens always me think about my six years at *The Garrick Club* and of looking after Lord Wakeham in *The Lords*. He was one of the biggest personalities in Westminster. He never remembered my name but used to call me *Our Own Little Elton John*. I don't think I actually looked like the music legend, apart from wearing colourful glasses and having a round, balding head.

Lord Wakeham always looked distinguished. In the years I knew him, his thick wave of black hair got shorter and greyer and he always strode, with a slight limp, around the building with a cigar in his mouth; even, sometimes, after the smoking ban in 2007. The Lords was very much a private members club and it was not surprising that they felt the laws which were passed inside their chambers were designed for the world outside and didn't apply there.

During the year that I joined in 1989, Lord Wakeham was appointed as Energy Secretary in Thatcher's government and was responsible for the creation of plans to privatise electricity. He had also been Leader of the House of Commons. He was responsible for the televising of Parliament which a lot of the members, including Thatcher, were against. A clever decision was made to pilot the broadcasts from the Lords before the Commons. These debates were long-winded and less likely to attract public attention. The funny thing I remember was that when the broadcasts began, long queues began to form outside the toilets. When we were serving, it was obvious that a lot of the peers, including the men, had bought new business clothes, designer fragrances (as if that mattered) and had applied makeup to cover skin blemishes and pale complexions. Some were better at it than others; some looked youthful and healthy; some looked like they were about to stage a performance of *A Midsummer Night's Dream* or host their own drag show. Whilst they were eating, the usual discourse on political topics changed to recommendations for good tailors and hairdressers.

Lord Wakeham seemed a bit like *Puck* – slightly mischievous, quick-witted and responsible for setting in motion some large events which caused others to squirm and think on their feet.

He was a survivor, literally and politically. His first wife, Roberta, was killed in the tragic bombing of *The Grand Hotel*, in Brighton, in 1984. He was trapped in the rubble for over seven hours and suffered serious crush injuries to his legs. He married his secretary, Alison Ward, a year later.

In his years as a director of Enron, from 1994 until its liquidation in 2001, he hosted many corporate functions in the Atlee Room, where I served. At the end of the meal he would summon me over. 'Elton, bring round the humidor if you please.'

I retrieved the large wooden box from the cellar and handed out the expensive cigars. Unlike their English counterparts, these American men radiated the style and sophistication that only money can buy. They were immaculately presented in Alexander Price suits, like models from a *GQ* magazine. Their watches cost more than the flat I had recently bought in Shepherds Bush.

Lord Wakeham was in happy company. Unlike a lot of the hosts, he was usually the last to leave and embraced the thick, blue smoke and celebrated company.

As he left, he called me over. 'Elton. Thanks for looking after us this evening.' He gave me a cigar but suggested it may be best to have it after my shift, although he didn't mind.

'Pleasure my Lord. Thank you.' I tucked my treasure into the jacket pocket of my morning suit. I would enjoy it on the Embankment before catching the tube home.

Before he left, he pulled me aside for a private word. 'All those men you saw today. All millionaires. All have their own jets.' It was clear that he had high hopes that England would follow these American moguls into sweet energy success. Alas, it was not to be. I guess those planes had been too expensive to keep in the air, even for energy magnates. Enron collapsed in 2001. Coincidentally, or incidentally, his role as chairman of the Press Complaints Commission also ended in that year. However, he was attributed with successfully protecting the princes from unwanted media attention after Diana's death.

Lord Wakeham, in true survivor style, stepped out of his Conservative Party, albeit momentarily, and made headway in Tony Blair's government. In 1999 He was appointed to head a Royal

Commission on the Reform of The House of Lords. *The Wakeham Report* was commissioned by the Prime Minister to make the Lords more accountable to the electorate. It was the beginning of the mass extermination of the hereditary peers within the House. This may have been a good prospect for the government, but would turn out to be a loss of job satisfaction and benefits for me and my team.

***

'Bob, there really is as much work as you want next summer and there will be lots of painting work in the winter if you want it,' Simon assured me.

I left the pink palace feeling very optimistic about the earning potential of my new profession. Simon asked me to go back for another two hours the following day and the same ceremony recommenced with afternoon tea and cigars. The Victoria sponge had already been finished and there was a half-eaten chocolate cake in its place.

6   GO WITH THE FLOW

Not far from the cottage is the local *Centro de Buddhismo Moderno*, the Buddhist centre. Graham had gotten into meditation when we were in Brighton. He's not too good with real life and, after a tragic accident which resulted in the death of one of his nephews, he had propped himself up with beer, wine and made close friends with Mr. Daniels; firstly with the company of Coke, and then just the two of them. The relationship was harmless enough at first but then turned into an unhappy dependency and he had to go for a short spell into rehab to break the connection.

For several months he took classes in meditation at the Kadampa Centre in Hove. I was worried that he might get absorbed into some kind of cult following but, in fact, his spirit (rather than his glass) increased in measure and he seemed to find a new strength, threw out the boxes of anti-depressants our local GP had prescribed and has never taken them again.

It turned out, by fluke, that the Buddhist headquarters for Spain were ten minutes from our rental property. It was a renovated hotel with a pool with ten acres of well-clipped gardens. There was a resident monk from Yorkshire who many years ago had swapped his wacky-backy for an orange cloak, spoke perfect Spanish and English and was now high on the teachings of Buddha instead of herbal inhalations.

I thought it may be a good place to do some networking with the visitors for some gardening work.

One of the new recruits was a short, round woman who introduced herself in a very loud and high-pitched voice as *Zany Zelda,* over coffee and biscuits during the meditation break. She was complaining because she was expecting a women-only session and to have the teachings from the local nun and not our little Yoda-looking fellow.

Zelda was wrapped in a tight, tie-dyed purple dress and a pale blue cardigan which looked like it had been pulled off the knitting needles before it had been finished. Her hair was a bob-cut of violet which framed her red-lipped, smiling face.

'I need some help setting up a Zen garden,' she told me. She must have noticed a bewildered look on my face. 'Have you got experience of that?'

I stopped scratching my chin and nodded. 'Yes, Giselda. That's no problem.'

'No, not *Gizelda*, just Zelda. I gave up the Jiz years ago.' She chuckled, coughed and pushed a whole chocolate digestive between crumbling rows of yellow teeth. She dismissed my apology with her free hand. 'But first, I need roses.' She coughed again, spraying brown crumbs down her front. She picked them off and put them back in her mouth. 'Fields of roses.'

Graham had been watching her in silence; bewitched. 'Rhodes?' he suddenly asked.

'No,' I told him. 'Roses.'

She wiped her chin. 'He's right Robert. I'm just like the great dame herself. Zandra Rhodes. In fact, we could have been related.' She clutched the long strand of wooden beads that fell across her wrinkled neck, in her fingers.

'Shouldn't it be pink?' Graham asked, pointing to her hair.

I nudged him in the ribs. 'It's purple pink, isn't it Zelda?' I didn't want to lose this potential customer.

She didn't answer me and turned away from him, winked and said quietly to me, 'I'm sensing a weak blue aura from that one. He has a blockage in the fifth chakra. It is impairing his communication skills.'

Unlikely, I thought. Graham rarely suffered with making his point clear.

Graham raised his eyes and spoke to the monk about the meditation.

Zelda explained to me how she used to live in Byron Bay, in Australia and her husband, Jerry, had gone off with her neighbour. 'I'm done with men,' she announced, pulling the cardigan more tightly around her. 'You gays are alright but normal men just think with their dicks and chase the next piece of fresh skirt available.' Two small tears had formed in the corner of her dark brown eyes. 'I say *fresh*. The *Sheila* he ran off with was the local bike. Most of the town had ridden her. She had flat tyres and a few hundred miles on her clock.'

I put my hand over my mouth, trying not to laugh.

A tear tumbled down her face and lodged in a wrinkle under her eye. 'I take care of myself these days. It's time we women looked after ourselves and that's what I'm doing. We girls need to stick together, don't you think?' She growled the words in a low rasping sound and coughed again. She shook one of her sponge fingers towards me.

Graham was miming, *Sisters are doing it for themselves,* behind her and swaying as if he was back in Brighton, performing in the Gospel choir.

'You're so right,' I said, trying to ignore him.

She folded her arms and grabbed her elbows in, tightly. 'Can you come and plant the roses this Thursday?' she asked. Her voice had climbed back higher, from tenor to alto and was softer.

'It should be okay. I'll just need to check the diary.' There was no need. I still had a lot of free days in the week, but I always thought it sounded more professional. 'I pulled out my thin *Agenda Escola* . It was a cheap school journal Graham had bought from one of the local Chinese Bazaar shops in town. I held the opened diary to my chest to conceal the empty pages. 'Yes, that's fine.' I pulled the thin pencil out the side pocket. 'What's the address.?'

'Here you go my lovely.' Zelda seemed to be using her fingers to retrieve more fallen crumbs from her breasts, but magically plucked a business card from the nest at the top of her dress. The card was purple and had a watermark of the female Buddha *Tara* with gold lettering embossed across its face. It read: *Concordia. Meditation, Reiki and Yoga Classes for Women with Mistress Zelda Dove*. In very small print was her address and telephone number.

'What a lovely name,' I said.

She pointed to the top line. 'Yes, *Con-cor-dia*. It means goddess of harmony and agreement.'

I nodded. 'That's lovely, but I meant your name.'

'It should say "*Master*." But I am my own special creation.' She rubbed her eye. 'Shall we say twelve?'

I made a note of it on the empty page.

'I have a class at ten. You could come and join us if you want.'

Graham moved forward. 'That might be fun, can I come?'

She pulled back. 'Actually, I've just remembered I've got a couple of girls coming from Monda. We're full.'

I held my fading smile. 'That's perfect. I'll see you at twelve.'

She started walking away. 'Great. You can't miss it. Just look for two massive palms on the road towards Coín.' She shuffled away, swaying her arms side-to-side to help propel herself forwards.

Graham leaned over and read the card. 'Zelda Dove? More like Miss Mallard. Why did she run off? Was it because your prices are too high?'

I pushed him. 'No, it was you. I think you reminded her of her ex.'

'Not likely,' he said. 'There's probably a sale on boxes of

chocolate HobNobs in town.'

We drove home and I searched online for tips on planting roses and establishing a Zen Garden.

Thank God for the internet. Through sites like *Wikipedia, How-to, YouTube* and the *RHS plant guide,* I became a horticultural expert at the click of a button. My mobile didn't have internet access, so sometimes the information took time to retrieve. I could delay the clients by saying, 'I need to look back through my notes on that.'

Another invaluable tool was *Google Translate.* This was essential for ordering tools at the ferreteria when Carlos was not around. Also José would write down instructions for me in Spanish and Graham would help me decipher his doctor-style handwriting. We would work together like *Robert Langdon* to crack the *José Gomez Code.* Many times I would follow José around the garden, watching him carefully when we were working together. He was always pleased with the offer of a drink and now seemed glad of an extra pair of hands.

Many people put their pools into *winter-mode* in November. It's still hot enough to sit and eat outside but the water drops to around 18 degrees which is too cold for many. This is a simple procedure; just give the pool a final clean, backwash and rinse, and get an *invierno,* winter, floating tablet dispenser from your local ferreteria. They usually cost around eighteen euros. Pierce some holes in the sides and leave it in the water for the whole winter with the pump turned off. You can't swim once this has been done but it gradually releases sufficient chemicals to keep the pool clean for the whole winter.

I tried to do this for Janet and John on one of my weekly visits. I now worked for them every Friday from ten 'til two.

'Poor babby Eleanor was shivering after her swim yesterday, Rob,' Janet told me, puffing on a cigarette. At least I think that's what she said. I was so busy admiring the white leather cat suit she had squeezed into, that the words disappeared over the top of my head. The golden zipper gleamed in the bright sunshine and the reflection dazzled my eyes.

I could see the silhouette of her body jiggling from side to side. 'I see you like my *Onezee*,' she said. 'It's fabulous, isn't it? I always thought there should be baby grows for grown-ups. Why should Eleanor have all the fun? Bought this thing in Camden Market a few year' ago. It's like a second skin.'

The leather was wrinkled and had dried out in the sun. The sheen had gone off the surface and rings of brown, crumpled suede, like a well-used sofa, had appeared at the knees and elbows. 'It sure is something,' I agreed.

The dogs had followed her out onto the grass. Toby and Oscar had their jaws clamped over either end of an old piece of hosepipe and were growling, whilst tugging each other around. Shorty had quietly walked up behind his mistress, grabbed her foot and was writhing up and down again her leather-clad leg.

'Shorty, put mummy down,' she cackled. 'He always loves it when I wear this.'

I stifled a laugh and told her, 'I'll go and start on the pool.'

She was walking off with the dog still locked onto her leg. 'That would be fine pet, but canny give John a hand at the back first? He's having a bonfire. I'll get us some drinks.'

I hadn't met John before. I found him near the tool cave, on top of the huge mound of dry cuttings I had made over the weeks before. It was as high as the back wall and he had climbed up with a red plastic fuel can and was dousing the pile with petrol. He was a tall, brown figure with dark hair spilling down his face. He was wearing a pair of silver *Police* sunglasses which were being swallowed up by the sides of his beard and the long fringe which fell over his face. The only clothes he had on were a pair of denim cut-offs and some leather sandals. It was clear that the rest of his body was covered in hair too. Like a wild yeti that was making his bed in the Himalayas, he was raking and thumping the pile down into a flat top with his feet.

'Hi there. Need a hand?' I yelled up to him.

He ignored me and continued to circle, pulling any loose

branches back on top of the heap. 'Alright mate,' he suddenly called. 'Didn't see ya there. Ya must be Rob.' He leaped off the stack, scratched his legs and landed down beside me. He threw the emptied petrol can by the tool store and shook my hand firmly. His hands were rough with many old cuts and grazes, not from doing the garden but from years of hard manual work. I had a quick look at my own hands. They were starting to show their own scars of labour and beginning to look impressive.

Under the mane of hair was a warm, lined face with shiny grey eyes. His teeth must have been polished or replaced as they were whiter than white and perfectly aligned. On close inspection he was a handsome man; more *Barry Gibb* from the *Bee Gees* than *Bigfoot*.

'Do you want some help?'

He shook his head and a small hidden earphone dropped out from where he had been listening to his iPod. 'What did you say?' His accent was a lot softer than Janet's.

I repeated myself once again and he directed me to a further mound of clippings on the other side. Those weren't there a couple of days ago and I hadn't made them. He must have done them himself, probably earlier this morning. I was impressed by the extent of his efforts. Most people left the work up to me. At the same time I was secretly embarrassed that he had created the same mass of debris which had taken me two weeks to do. Probably mine was more and had started to rot down in the heap.

As I loaded armfuls of cuttings into one of the wheelbarrows, he told me how happy he was living in the sun and starting his life over with Janet. A police helicopter thundered overhead and then disappeared like an angry hornet on the blue horizon.

'Just as well I decided to get me permit this year,' he said. 'They'll charge you for anything they can over here and they are very serious about fire, with good reason I suppose.' He unloaded the barrow and tossed the branches high on top of the pile.

'Janet's a really nice woman,' I said. 'You're lucky.'

He grabbed the rake off me and growled, 'You keep your hands off her mate. She's mine.'

My face flushed red. 'No, I didn't mean that.'

He laughed, deep and loud. 'Only kidding mate. I know you like sticking your dick into other holes.'

I returned his joking with smiles and yet my face still felt like it was going darker.

Once the barrow was empty he poured more petrol around the base. 'Actually, I envy you gay guys.'

I threw a final armful onto the mound. 'Why?'

'No nagging. No demands for new clothes and none of that baby shit.'

'Yes, but you're lucky to have Eleanor though.' I raked up the twigs we had dropped in transit.

'Have you met *it* yet?'

I was puzzled by his apparent lack of affection. 'No, not yet.'

'Well you will and then maybees you won't think me so lucky.' With that, he lit a match and tossed it onto the pile. There was an enormous bang and the blasting air pushed me back by a foot. 'Shit!' he yelled. The fire erupted into a high, burning inferno within seconds.

My ears were ringing and my heart was racing with sudden terror. 'Shit,' I echoed, stunned. I felt lucky to be alive and wondered if this was what it was like to be near a bomb going off.

'Sorry about that,' John said, pacing round the bonfire, checking the damage. The fire hissed and crackled as the huge orange flames devoured the fuel beneath it. 'It should calm down in a minute.'

It didn't.

A sudden northerly breeze fanned the flames higher until they met a row of six palm trees I had trimmed back a few weeks ago. Like a line of roman candles, they exploded, one by one, into blazes.

John had run over to one of the outbuildings. He pulled a length of hosepipe out of the door, turned the water on and passed it to me. 'Here, Rob. Grab this and aim for the top of the trees.'

I did as I was told and he dashed off to get more water and call Janet for help.

Within minutes the trees were stripped into burning, blackened poles. I felt the irrigation sprinklers come on at my feet which helped to dampen the grass but couldn't save the trees. My own flesh felt like it was burning from the intense heat.

'You bloody idiot,' I heard Janet screech at John, as they both ran through the yard with buckets they had filled from the pool. She was still wearing that jumpsuit and looked far too glamorous to be doing this burden.

'Here, you take the hose,' I said and took the buckets from her.

'Cheers love,' she sighed.

John and I tried our best, ferrying water in buckets out of the pool, either in our hands or with the wheelbarrow.

After a few trips, Janet said, 'It's no use boys. We've lost them.'

It was true. The line of trees were now scorched pillars of black; the fire was beginning to die down because it was running out of fuel.

'Who's for a beer?' John asked, rubbing the sweat off his face.

Janet tossed the hose onto the floor and said, 'Count me in. Rob? You'll stay and have a beer wit' us?'

'Absolutely.'

She brushed her dirty hands on her legs, on the white leather that was now covered in black and brown marks. 'Give us a hand pet. Let's pull a few chairs off the terrace and sit and enjoy the heat.'

For about an hour we sat in reverent silence, drinking beers, watching the fire devouring its meal. The intended bonfire had shrunk into a low, burning pile and the trees were thin columns of acrid-smelling charcoal.

John threw an empty can onto the floor and said, 'Never liked those trees, anyway.'

Janet laughed. 'No, too bloody tall and blocked out the afternoon sun.' She finished her beer and pulled out a pack of cigarettes. 'Anyone for a smoke?'

John stood up and kissed her. 'That's what I love about you,' he said.

She kissed him back and I knew it was time to leave. As I left, I heard the long rip of a zipper as the couple started to undress.

When I walked past the pool it was clear that it needed more than switching to winter-mode. There were about twenty discarded containers from the firefighting and the water had turned brown and cloudy.

The next day, I was back at Simon and Steve's pink palace, harvesting their olives. There were only thirty trees in the orchard but it was hard physical work. You place a thin circle of fine netting around the base of the tree and then thwack the branches with plastic rakes and long wooden canes. There are electrical methods but for this number of trees the hand method is more cost effective and should produce better oil.

The north winds were increasingly strong but not cold; the temperature was still eighteen degrees in the sun, but the autumn breezes can cause a lot of root damage to plants and shrubs, especially if the soil is dry and hard. It's a good idea to trim back roses and ornamental grasses. I cut the last blooms from Simon's borders and carried them into the conservatory.

Simon clapped his hands in cheer and took a rose-patterned jug down from the pine dresser and filled it with water. Again, the tap pressure was too high and half of it sprayed over his lilac shirt. 'Don't tell Steve,' he laughed. 'Would you loike a piece of me coffee cake? It was a fresh bake yesterday morning.'

I put the flowers on the draining board and rinsed my hands. 'That would be great. Cheers.'

He gave me a large chunk of cake. It was the last remaining slice.

'What about you?' I asked.

'No worries,' he smiled and tapped the oven door. There was another one inside baking. 'Orange Madeira this time.' He inhaled the citrus odours escaping from the door, licked his lips and rubbed his stomach. 'What you doin' next Tuesday? Are you free?'

I didn't answer for a few moments, trying to remember what day it was today. I remembered that Zelda's was Thursday and Janet and John's on Friday. 'Yes, that's fine. Why?'

He sat down on one of the kitchen chairs. 'We really need a hand over at the Snipes'. He was thumbing through a rolodex that had been placed in the middle of the table. 'N, O, P, Q, R, arr here we go, Snipes. Here's the address. It's over by Cala de Mijas. You know it? Steve can meet you there at ten.' As he passed me the card for me to copy down the information, the door chimes erupted into their melodious mayhem. 'That will be Fernando, me personal trainer.'

This was my cue to leave, so I gulped down the cake and brushed past a handsome, young Spanish guy, with pecs the size of dinner plates, who was taking some exercise mats out the back of his Black Jeep. '*Buenos Tardes*,' he said and winked one of his dark, black eyes.

'I'm in eya Fernando. I'm just getten changed into summat more comfortable.'

It seemed like everyone was at it over here. I guess it was the warm climate.

Things were very different over at Zelda's: Thursday, soon came around and it was time to boot up the satnav and try to find this next new client's garden. Our little yellow car was now full of tools and I had to wind down one of the rear windows to fit in some of the longer handled appliances.

I had bought a second-hand rotavator and a basic electric lawn mower; I would have preferred a petrol one, but couldn't afford one. Besides, I already had a long extension cable and most of the gardens had external power outlets, which they were happy for me to use. A lot of them were surprised that I had brought my own tools and, like Janet and John, were very keen to offer me theirs to use. This seemed beneficial until I thought, *what happens if I break them?* Also, I had become confident and comfortable in using my own.

After following the lower road from Alhaurin towards Villafranco and looping around the same series of mini roundabouts three times I found *The Twins*, a pair of majestic Canary Palms, *Phoenix Canariensis,* towering over a sharp, gated driveway on the right and pulled in. A strong westerly wind was rushing through their two hundred feet high branches, making an eerie whistling sound. I saw a pair of high, metal gates, covered in rotting rush matting which was flapping up and down.

Beyond the gates were three large country houses, *cortijos* set on individual plots of farmland. There was only one button for the gate. I pressed it and a loud horn blasted through the peaceful interior, like a disgruntled truck driver trying to wake up one of his sleeping neighbours.

There was no answer and I was afraid to press it again.

Ten minutes later an elderly white-bearded man, who could have been the Mario Brothers' grandfather, appeared from the driveway of the first house and let me in. I asked him where Zelda lived. He shrugged and pointed to a long l-shaped bungalow behind his olive orchard.

As I drove into her entrance, she appeared in a long white dress and cardigan, with hair that looked even more violet in the bright sunlight than before.

'G'day. Howzit going?' she cried and directed me to a small

space, edged with overgrown oleanders next to an old wooden shed. 'Was it easy to find us?'

I looked around to see who else was with her, but she was alone. 'Yes. No problem,' I said. 'So where are the roses going in?' I opened the boot and began pulling out the tools. I'm not too good with small talk and am eager to get started.

She put her hands together, as if she was preparing to pray. 'Slowly. Slowly. The universe is not meant to be rushed through.' She smiled and took some deep breaths. 'Can you smell the jasmine?'

There was a thick odour, like a cat had sprayed up the side of the shed. 'Yes,' I said.

'Come 'n' see,' she said, walking to the far side of the timber construction. 'I'm so rapt with this.' She pointed to a dwarf clump of green leaves with dark red stems and long white trumpet flowers. It was certainly a jasmine; it said so, on the fifteen euro price tag from the garden centre and was still in its plastic pot. 'What d'you think?'

'Very nice,' I said. 'But we need to plant it into the ground to let it get established so it climbs over the shed.'

She was nodding but then grimaced at my last word. 'This is no shed.' She pulled the warped door open to reveal an unexpected sight. 'This is the meditation 'n' healing chamber.' She walked inside. 'I just finished painting it yesterday.'

It was too late to apologise so I decided to go with dumbstruck praise. 'Wow, it's amazing.' Essentially it was a garden shed that had been freshly painted in a lilac wash. There were eight framed certificates on the left-hand wall, an Ikea bookshelf on the end panel, with more Buddhism and Healing books than you would find in the Spiritual section in Waterstones, a chakra-identification-with-body-parts chart on the right hand side and a long, white leather massage table in the middle of the room.

For the next half an hour she took me on a long, drawn out tour of the space and its contents, explaining each item's history and significance. 'And now for de resistance piece,' she said in a strong

Aussie accent. I think she meant *la pièce de résistance.*

Zelda lifted a purple curtain that covered the lower shelves of the bookcase and pulled out a small white case, with a gold key protruding out of a tiny lock. I thought it was a child's jewellery box which would open to reveal a plastic, twirling ballet dancer in front of a mirror with the tinny strumming of *Swan Lake.* Instead there were five rows of tiny, multi-coloured stones. 'Aren't they beautiful?' she sighed.

They looked more like plastic beads from a Christmas cracker than precious gems. 'I like this one,' I said, handling a dark, red specimen.

'Don't touch that!' she screeched and snatched the box back, away from me. Her face flushed with a similar crimson colour, and she apologised. 'It's just that these have been charged with my energy and have to be handled specially.'

'Sorry,' I said. I wanted to get out of this claustrophobic pen and back into the garden as soon as possible.

She brushed her hair with her hands and breathed deeply. 'What's your date of birth?' she asked.

'Sorry?'

'Date of birth,' she repeated, firmly.

I felt like I had been arrested and was facing charges down at the local police station. 'Twelfth of January, sixty-four,' I replied.

She sighed again and held her palms up, towards the roof of the hut. 'Of course, Capricorn. Garnet. That's why you were drawn to that stone.' She closed the lid on the box and tucked it away, back under the purple curtain. Zelda, walked over to the picture of the body and chakras. There was a long, silver chain hung over a corner of the frame. She carefully lifted it off and I noticed another gem, clear this time, swinging at the end.

'This is my pendulum,' she told me. 'I need you to lie down for me.' She walked over to the table and pumped up the pillow.

I checked my watch and walked towards the door. 'I think I'd better get on,' I said.

'Nonsense.' She rubbed the leather surface clean with her hand. 'Up you get.'

I had my hand on the door knob. 'No, really.'

'It's my gift you to you,' she said, gently. 'Now lie down.' Her voice was very insistent.

I walked over to the flimsy table and pushed myself up. It felt like it was going to snap, but I managed to turn myself round and lie down. It was cold on there, like butter from a fridge, and I pulled my shirt and jacket tightly around me.

'Now just relax,' she said. 'I'm going to begin here, at the root chakra.' Zelda held the chain in one had with the gem suspended over my groin area. She supported this hand with the other, to ensure the clarity of the reading. 'Please keep still.' Sure enough after a while the pendulum started swinging in a clockwise direction over my body. 'This is good. There is a good flow of energy here.' Her voice had changed, it sounded flatter and more monotone; almost automatic. 'Now let's check the sacral chakra.' It swung again and Zelda concluded this was also fine. The third measure was just below my ribcage and the movement was a lot smaller and more confined. 'There is some blockage in the solar plexus,' she announced. She relaxed the grip of the supporting hand in case it was affecting the movement. 'This definitely needs some work.' She closed her eyes, contemplating the results. 'You are experiencing a lack of identity at the moment. You've lost your usual confidence.' She opened her eyes again. 'Is that right?'

It certainly felt true at that moment. 'Maybe it's been the move over to Spain?' I suggested.

'Could be.' She moved the stone above the centre of my heart. It started swinging with much more energy in large, open circles. 'Steady, Zelda,' she told herself. She gripped the elevated arm harder and the swinging gem continued to spin around in large, swirling circles. 'Too much energy here,' she cried. 'There's too much.'

Perhaps I was going to have a heart attack?

She pulled away from the side of the table. 'It looks like you are putting too much love into your relationships.'

This didn't feel true and I was about to disagree.

'You dear, sweet man. You are full of love; so full of love. You must take care of yourself. This is causing the blockage in your solar plexus.'

I sat up on the table. 'Thanks, Zelda. That has helped.'

She put her arm on my shoulder. 'But we haven't finished yet. We still need to examine the throat, third eye and crown.'

I swung my legs around, so they were hanging over the edge. 'Perhaps next time,' I said.

Her head dropped forwards and she stifled a yawn. 'Yes. I think it's a good idea. That has really taken it out of me. I 'm bushed.' She led me through the door, back into the bright sunshine. She showed me around to the rear of the house. There was a large square of overgrown grass that ran along the length of the house. 'I'm sorry it's got away from me.' She put her hands on her hips. 'There are the roses over there.' She pointed to a huge pile of shrubs edged in red petals, under an olive tree on the far side. There must have been about two hundred of them.

'No problem. I'll soon get this down with my strimmer,' I said, walking past her back towards the car. 'Once I get the growth down, I'll be able to rotavate and clear the soil.'

'Stop,' she yelled. 'We don't do that here.'

I turned back to face her. Zelda's relaxed smile had turned into an angry frown. 'What do you mean?' I asked.

Again, she looked embarrassed from her uncontrolled outburst. 'It's just that, this is a place for peace, for tranquillity. We don't use machines here in this natural haven.' She walked over to an old deck chair, in the corner of this meadow and picked up an empty wine glass and a pair of nail scissors.

I scratched my head. 'How can I do it then, Zelda?'

She held up the scissors and pointed to a long handled scythe and a pair of shovels.

You've got to be kidding, I thought. The blank look on her face said otherwise. At least it wasn't by her nail scissors, I considered.

'I'm going to meditate,' she said. 'If you need anything, just call or knock on the window.' She walked back to the front of the house and slammed the door closed.

I had never used a scythe before. But I remembered *Monty Don* demonstrating one on *Gardener's World*. It was important to get into a routine; to swing the blade in neat semi-circles, trying to avoid slicing your feet off. At first I was cursing Zelda and her strange ways but, after a while, the motion became almost hypnotic and easy to repeat. There was a sense of soft harmony in the November sunshine, as I quietly sliced the weeds down and the birds sang in the trees. The only man-made noise was the groan of a distant radio or television programme talking away, banally, to itself.

After two hours of labour, I needed to ask her where she wanted me to leave the cuttings for composting or burning. After I began rapping on the living room window, I noticed that she was asleep on a black leather sofa, with another empty wine glass at her side, dwarfed in the shadow of a huge plasma television. It was the biggest screen I had ever seen. It must have been about seventy inches across and the room was tiny. If she had stretched her arm out, she could have touched it.

On the screen was a presenter on some chat show interviewing a tearful mum, who only looked about sixteen. She was arguing with her husband or partner about more money for her three kids.

I decided to rake up the debris and stack it into a pile in one corner. Then I went back over the area with a pair of shears, to cut it shorter. My face and legs were covered with sweat, dried blood from tiny cuts, and shreds of green and brown splinters. The whole site needed to be dug over but I was getting tired. I went back to the car and guzzled down two cans of lemonade and demolished a six pack of *KitKats*.

At the far side of the building, I could hear the credit music from the t.v. on my way back, but there was still no sign of the mistress of the house.

The first cut of the dirt was easier than I thought. It was much softer than the rocky soil we had at our mountain house. It looked fertile and was probably part of the dry river bed area, which had loads of minerals washed down from the hills, and is commonly used for growing the many fruits and vegetables this region is well known for. The roots and grasses surrendered to my efforts and in three hours I had dug over the whole area. Blisters were swelling up on my right hand, but the results were pleasing.

I guzzled down some water, rinsed my hands and devoured the ham and coleslaw sandwiches I had packed in my cool box. I counted out the rose bushes and, despite my usual rubbish maths, I found that there were two hundred bushes, more or less, and decided to dig ten, long troughs along the length of the plot and plant twenty in each line. They were all good specimens, full of heavy blooms. This could be a problem. The wind was getting stronger and would put a lot of strain on the long stems and rock the newly planted roots. Also, with new plants, you need to encourage root growth and should cut off the flowers. I decided to ask Zelda what she preferred, but she was still asleep on the sofa. I had remembered from Janet and John's hedge that you could always cut more off, but couldn't put it back on once it had been chopped. I planted the shrubs intact and decided I could take the flowers off later, if needed.

The flower blooms were heavy with a deep perfumed scent and my head became light and unclear as I continued to plant. The first two rows were neat and tidy but each subsequent one became more bent and curved, like they had been carved into the dirt by a drunken artist. As I was putting in the last five bushes, Zelda appeared. The sun had set behind the mountains and her white silhouette looked ghost-like, apart from the head that was still bludgeoned in purple.

'Strewth mate! You've really got through that quickly,' she yelled.

'It looks amazing.'

I was glad that she was pleased and explained about possible wind damage.

She ruffled her hands through her violet hair and screeched, 'Off with their heads.' With renewed energy she skipped down through the lines of shrubs with a pair of shears, slicing the flowers off in glee. At first she was careful and took them off, one at a time, but as the frenzy increased, she cut lower down the stems severing clumps of petals and buds in one clean cut. She was The Queen of Hearts in *Alice in Wonderland,* ordering the execution of every offending bloom with her own happy guillotine. I was instructed to pick up the heads and put them in the wicker baskets at the side of the house. Sometimes her cutting was so feverish that I managed to catch the heads before they hit the floor.

'That was fun,' she announced, as she decapitated the last bush.

I looked back at the trail of destruction behind her and doubted that any wind could have caused such devastation. 'I should water them in before I go,' I said.

'No, don't bother. It's going to rain tonight. Come in and have a drink.'

I looked up at the cloudless sky, shrugged and followed her into the lounge. The television was still playing away to itself and had just erupted into the droning theme tune to *EastEnders.*

'Is it that time already?' I asked, thinking of the hour time difference with the UK. The room was as purple as her hair and was making me feel queasy.

She walked behind the sofa and into an adjoining room. 'No silly. It's on catch up.'

We walked into a narrow hallway, which was painted indigo. There was a small shower room off to the right, painted in blue, and we walked into the kitchen that was decorated in green. There was something oddly familiar about this sequence of colours. The yellow dining room beyond, followed by what looked like an orange guest room and a red master (or should I say *mistress*) bedroom, confirmed my beliefs; we were walking through the chakras.

She motioned me to sit at a green lacquered table.

'The heart of the home.' I said, quietly.

'Clever boy!' she said, pulling two boxes of tea and a couple of cups down from a shelf. 'Camomile or Rose Hip?'

Strewth I thought. *More bloody roses. I'd rather have a beer now.* 'You choose,' I said.

The kettle boiled quickly, as if it had been used a few moments ago. 'Camomile, methinks. I always find it helps with a good night's sleep.' She put some dried green leaves into a stained teapot and poured in the boiling water. 'Care for a cookie?' she asked, retrieving a dented cake tin. 'Ginger and Almond. Made them on Monday.' I tried to refuse but she had put six on a cracked green plate and insisted. 'Go on. There's nothing of you. You need feeding up.'

'Thank, you,' I tried to say, but the biscuit was so dry that I ended up coughing and swallowing the words.

'There, that should be brewed now.' Zelda picked up the teapot. 'I'll be mother.' Her arm started shaking as she poured and half of it went into the saucer. 'I'm such a clumsy ox,' she cried. She looked tearful.

I dabbed the spill with a dishcloth that had been left on the table. 'It doesn't matter.'

She spilled more as she poured her own. 'Silly, silly Zeldy. You ruin everything.' Streams of tears ran down her face and her chest heaved as she started to sob.

I got up and grabbed some kitchen towel for her to dry her face and tried to soothe her.

Whilst the soap family argued and yelled at each other from the massive television in the living room, Zelda told me how her mother had abandoned when she was six. She was left with her Nan and her mum ran off with the milkman. They were two of the last *ten pound poms* and bought the subsidised sea tickets to find a new life, without kids, *Down Under.*

Years later, when she was in her thirties, Zelda decided to try and find her mum and she tracked her down to the small, suburban town of Narara, just north of Sydney. She wrote to her ten times but received no reply. Her intuition told her just to fly out and everything would be fine. Her intuition was wrong. She was sobbing even harder now. 'I knocked on her door and she near slammed it in my face.'

I poured her some more tea.

'Thank you, Rob.' She blew her nose into the kitchen towel. 'She asked me how I found her. She told me that Darren, the *spunky milkman* who became her lover, had seen the letters and decided to leave her. She said it was all my fault. "Silly, Zeldy. You still mess up everything for me." She told me to leave and said she never wanted to see me again.' The weeping started again and Zelda's chest was heaving so heavily I thought she might collapse.

'What did you do?' I asked, passing her more tissue.

She dabbed her eyes. The blue eyeshadow had smeared onto her cheeks. 'I decided to stay. Just for a few months. I got time off from the bank. I hoped she would calm down, change her mind. I was drinking too much at that time and ended up spending too many nights in the bars. That's where I met Jerry, but he left me. I'm a good woman, a strong woman but everybody leaves me.' She blew her nose into the soaked tissue.

Finally, Zelda pulled herself together, paid me and I walked over to the car in the dwindling light as the night was drawing in.

Before I left, I gathered up a huge bunch of her red roses from one of the baskets and gave them to her.

It started to rain.

'Oh Robert. How lovely. Red roses. My favourite.' She held them close to her nose and buried her face in the petals. 'So thoughtful of you.'

It's amazing how roses can be so cathartic. It reminded me of another emotional .time, back in Westminster.

***

Normally September was a quiet period for us. Both the Lords and the Commons were still in recess and the staff slowly returned, from long summer breaks, to the political headquarters, like reluctant children returning to school for the start of term. This particular day should have been very quiet and non-descript, looking after a few private members' parties. Most of the political activity takes place outside the building during this period, at the party conferences which seem to alternate between Brighton, Bournemouth and Manchester.

I had been promoted to head waiter and was responsible for managing the newly formed dining rooms: the Atlee Room, the Hulme Room and the Reid Room.

On that day in 2001, towards the end of the long summer recess, only half a dozen of the Lords, the usual suspects, were rattling around. For them it was like a second home; a grandiose garden shed to hide away from the misses and think about world affairs and pragmatic stuff. Some of the members always seemed to be there, such as Lord Ampthill who lived just across the road. Others were mainly the Lords who resided in London and used it as a private gentleman's club; somewhere to have an inexpensive lunch and connect with some like-minded company.

In my department, we had a lunch booked in for twelve people in the Atlee Room, hosted by Lord Cavendish, for some of his co-directors of Nirex Ltd. He had been the company's director since 1993. He was made a life peer as The Baron Cavendish of Furness by Margaret Thatcher in 1990. He always wore colourful bow ties, was kind and cheerful and not too demanding, so it should have been an easy day. Only a few of us who had volunteered for overt-time were drafted in. Most of the Lords were still abroad on holiday or relaxing in their country retreats. I had followed some of these Lords' examples and moved down to the coast, to Brighton, two years previously. This meant that I had the joys of living by the sea but, consequently, a long daily commute.

There was only one chef and a handful of waiters on that day; it was very much a skeleton staff operation in a ghost town.

Before the luncheon, like silent spectres we floated around this abandoned mausoleum, serving occasional food and drinks to the living, who were cheerily enjoying their splendid isolation. Between service, we laughed with the security men who were watching three mice scampering up the empty staircases on their monitors. The corridors were deathly still. The two main chambers above us were swallowed in a vacuum of voiceless silence. The time was moving slower than the proverbial tortoise in its race with hare and I was doubtful that any of us would ever get to the finishing line.

I don't think I had ever heard the building so quiet before. I stepped out into the corridor and was relieved to hear the faint hum of conversation from a small luncheon being served in the Peers' Dining Room, upstairs. I heard the muffled voice of Lord Longford who had probably jogged in, as usual, in his lace-less trainers, looking for some sustenance.

Lord Ampthill was in the Hulme Room moaning about the menu which had been reduced for the nominal number of diners. There were only two or three hot dishes that day, instead of the usual half dozen.

Every manager had favourites in their team and I was lucky to have the company of mine. These in included the audacious Sandra, charismatic Alfredo and Mumsie Lena. In fact most of my team were in and there was very little for us to do. Even Victoria who was in the gift shop was equally bored, twiddling her thumbs and flirting with one of the security men. It was a genuine busman's holiday. Between intermittent bursts of laughter from one of Sandra's jokes, the long, slow ticks of the innumerable clocks were counting down towards Lord Cavendish's lunch.

Finally, his guests arrived and came in through Black Rod's Entrance. Sandra and I raced each other to welcome them in and show them where the cloakrooms were located. Also we pointed out the gift shop, en-route to the dining room, and startled Victoria who had nearly fallen asleep. Alfredo served them drinks from a makeshift bar we had created in the Atlee Room and announced their arrivals to

Lord Cavendish.

The lunch service was pretty routine and uneventful. The diners didn't mind the reduced choice from the menu and were happily engaged in muted conversations, about visits to their holiday homes in the Dordogne, new wines they had discovered on their travels and the imminent departure of their offspring to Oxbridge and other esteemed educational establishments.

Just as the end was in sight, and the party started their desserts, a muffled scream came from Victoria, who was running around from the gift shop with her hand held over her mouth. 'Oh my God. Have you seen what's happening on the news?' she cried.

Normally we ignored the monitors, which were strategically placed in the corners of the dining rooms. They were used to update the members with tele-typed information, broadcasted from their respective chambers. It was interesting at first, but you don't usually get time to read the text on the green or red screens during service. Occasionally, the BBC or CNN news is turned on, but often it's just text.

'Sandra can you switch it on, quietly, in the Hulme Room?' I asked, as I carried a tray of empty glasses into the kitchen.

'I would if I could find the remote,' she said.

Alfredo scratched his grey moustache. 'I'm thinking it's-a, by the cash register,' he told her and set off to find it.

Sandra was impatient. She was shorter than the rest of us but more resourceful. She pulled her shoes off, dragged one of the tables over to the wall, jumped up and switched it on.

'What's going on?' Lord Ampthill said, through a mouthful of his lunch.

I ran back into the room, where Victoria was ordering Sandra to press the channel-up button.

What appeared before us were scenes of what looked like a terrible accident. In fact the concerned voice of a young American newscaster confirmed this, announcing that a plane had crashed into the north face of the North Tower of the World Trade Centre. The news banner across the bottom of the screen read: WORLD TRADE CENTER DISASTER.

'How terrible,' said Sandra, as reports came in that the plane had entered between floors 93 and 99. 'Those poor people.'

We heard how people on the floors underneath were evacuating but that others were trapped or killed above. Since it was declared to be an accident, the staff working in the South Tower were ordered to go back to their desks and continue working.

It was only after the second explosion, at 14.03 (GMT), when there was a genuine concern of terrorism, that we realized we needed to inform all the guests. The Palace of Westminster is the number one U.K. landmark and if these attacks were global it was very likely we could be next.

One of my responsibilities during that period was being the fire marshal for this section. A few months before, I had been involved in a real evacuation situation and had to deploy the skills I had learned in my training.

All the Marshals were obliged to carry a fluorescent arm band with the words *fire marshal* printed in bright red ink. We had been trained to inform the Lords and their guests when this was not a regular test or drill, but a genuine fire. We had to urge them to remain calm, to leave their belongings and to make their way quickly out through the Cholmondeley Room and onto the assembly point, which was behind Black Rod's Garden Entrance. We were also warned that the Lords would be unlikely to follow any instructions from us staff and would probably ignore any fire bells; they were accustomed to hearing many bells within the building. There were bells to signal voting, bells for the start and finish of sessions; for them, it was like being back in a public boys' school where chimes summoned you to assembly, class, lunch, and signalled the end of the day. If they ignored us, we should tell them once again that this was a real fire and then make our own escape.

During that real fire event, back in July, black fumes were found to be seeping out of the recently installed kitchen. Within this newly formed space were three small corridors which housed a thin galley with all the cooking equipment, a washing-up area with views over the Thames, and the Servery which consisted of a counter-top with heat lamps for dishing out the plates.

The source of the fire turned out to be the cooker; black breaths of thick smoke were pouring out of the angry mouth of the oven door. I immediately smashed the glass on the alarm, the fire bell erupted through the building and I waved the staff and members out of the rooms. Soon after, an army of fire engines descended on us, within minutes, from three different London Boroughs. It was true that a lot of the members were reluctant to leave but the patrolling firemen gradually got them all out.

Later investigations revealed that the fire had been smouldering for about three weeks before then. The cooker had been incorrectly fitted directly onto the wooden floors, with no space for ventilation and had consequently caught alight.

As the events of *9-11* unfolded, I was confident that with this surging state of emergency in New York, we would soon receive orders to clear the building.

I went back into the Atlee Room to inform Lord Cavendish, found a remote and pointed it at the screen. 'Excuse me for interrupting, M'Lord, but America is under attack. Some planes have gone into the twin towers in New York.'

He put down his glass of wine. 'Thank you, Robert. Yes, please do switch it on.'

There was a scene of both the towers choking in thick smoke, like two giant, combusting chimneys. Tiny dark pixels of life, like ants tumbling out of a burning nest, fell, screaming from the towers.

'Turn up the sound,' he ordered.

Scenes from the first and second impacts were replayed on the news. The seated party put down their pudding spoons and watched the fall of the first tower in absolute silence; reports came in that people were jumping out the windows of the South Tower and choosing to fall to their deaths rather than be consumed by fire. I rejoined my staff in the Hulme Room. They were very agitated and anxious to get away. Their fears were compounded by the newsreader speculating where would be next, Paris or London? We felt like sitting ducks silently waiting in the marshes to be shot at by poachers and kept listening out for any orders to evacuate.

Lord Cavendish called me back in. 'Be a good chap and switch that off now.' He picked up his glass, drank a mouthful of wine and then continued to eat his dessert. The rest of the party looked numb but calm and seemed to be waiting for some cue from their host.

This came when he turned to the guest on his right and said, 'How are your roses coming along for Chelsea?' He must have been an exhibitor for the Royal flower show.

I thought this was unbelievably calm and unaffected. It reminded me of that scene in *Carry On Up the Khyber* where Sir Sidney Ruff Diamond and company continue to enjoy their meal as bombs and shells explode around them. Then I realized that Chelsea was in May. Most of the roses would be over by now. Perhaps this was some kind of flowery Morse code or a secret language they had picked up at Eton College?

Eventually the lunch finished and they slowly departed. We were all keen to follow them and leave, but our duties demanded that we stay until the end of service for a single dinner party, later that evening. An evacuation order never came and we were recommended to stay inside until service had finished. At the final dinner, less than half the invited guests turned up. The others had been, wisely, too scared to enter the building.

It was one of the longest days of my life.

7   DIFFERENT ON THE INSIDE

In December, the sun continues to shine. It is lower in the sky and weaker but still bright and cheery. Whilst UK shoppers maintain their Christmas spending frenzy, following Black Friday, here the residents harvest their own home-grown treasures.

This region is highly productive in citrus fruits. Fields of orange, lemon and lime trees sway in gentle breezes, heavy with colourful orbs of delicious fruits.

I asked José if the Spanish are keen on *Black Friday*. His answer was that he didn't believe there was much need for it here, as racism isn't really an issue. Things are changing though and the commercial aspects of the season are slowly increasing within Spain.

There are some large shopping centres in this area. We have *Plaza Mayor,* near Málaga airport, *La Miramar* in Fuengirola and *La Cañada* near Marbella. They do engage in the holiday season and decorate their interiors with fairy lights and tinsel, and often have at least one huge, artificial cone to represent something tree-like.

Christmas here is still a decidedly religious affair. It starts on December 8th, with *Dia de la Immaculada Concepcion* (Day of the Immaculate Conception). It's on this day that the Christmas lights are switched on. The most impressive display is usually found in *Calle Larios,* Málaga. This varies from lights arranged to represent the city's high, vaulted cathedral ceiling, to a twinkling night sky with the Star of Bethlehem. Local shops and street vendors display elaborate nativity scenes *(belen)* and encourage you to buy figurines, to create your own three dimensional depiction of the Birth of Jesus Christ.

Amongst the decorated streets, rows of orange trees, laden with sun-ripened fruit, lure you to quench your thirst with their sweet temptations. However, not all is as it seems. The city trees only have enough soil to produce blossom and immature fruit; they are incredibly bitter and can make you very sick. Many a seduced tourist has spent an unwelcome afternoon in the A & E department of the local hospital with agonizing stomach pains.

The bakeries and sweet shops are full of *Polvorones* (almond cookies), *Turron* (nougat) and marzipan figures. These are normally consumed on Christmas Eve, following late-night family meals of lamb or suckling pig. These meats have usually been hand reared in sheds by locals who live in the countryside. Guide books will tell you that the Spanish only exchange very small gifts at this time; their main presents are given on *La Dia de Los Reyes Magos* (Three Kings' Day), which is Epiphany, on January 6th. This seems more logical since it was when Balthazar, Melchior and Casper actually offered their gifts to the holy infant.

However, this is deceptive. In reality, a lot of Spanish kids have been swept up in the aggressive t.v. marketing campaigns and now want presents on Christmas Day *and* Three Kings' Day.

Christmas was still on my mind, as I followed Simon's directions to meet my next clients, Ben and Abigail Snipe. I wanted to pick up a fir tree from the local garden centre but the car was too crammed with tools.

That day was a public holiday. You weren't supposed to work, so I just hoped I wouldn't get pulled over by the civil guard.

The Snipes' house was near La Cala, a growing sprawl of coastal development below Mijas. As I drove past the empty brick shells of another half-finished development, I left the dusty, rocky terrain behind me and continued up between two lush, verdant golf courses. Small clusters of white golf carts rolled along the undulating surface, like snooker balls across a crumpled felt table.

Despite the intense sunshine here, it is possible to create your own green Eden with a good water supply. We rarely have drought restrictions and, ironically, water is about a fifth of the price than in rain-soaked Britain.

I found *Casa de Imogen,* at the top of the next hill. Behind a short line of metal railings and an ornamental gate was a small patio of white marble. This led to a thin, wooden door, attached to a small white bungalow with a few squares of grass at the front. My first thought was, *this will only take me ten minutes to cut and trim.*

There was only one plant, a tall vine of jasmine climbing over the entrance and, although the white flowers were a mistake against the walls, the scent was aromatic and sweet.

I pressed the door buzzer but heard no sound. Sometimes the chimes are located at the back of the house and you don't hear them. This place was so small that it meant it probably wasn't working. I tried it again and heard the motorized whir of a small oblong device above my head. It was a security camera. I was being watched.

Five minutes later, I was about to leave when the speaker erupted into a low-pitched groan and started crackling.

'Yes. What do you want?' It was a deep, mechanical voice.

I wiped my head and straightened my *Garden Butler* polo shirt for the camera. 'Hello. Is that Ben? This is Robert.'

'What do you want?' It was sounding more like a recording.

'Robert the gardener.' It still felt great saying those words and I was pleased I had omitted the word *Butler* in the introduction.

'Very well. My wife will see you in.'

As soon as his voice died inside the hissing speaker, the front door flew open. A short, thin woman with long, black hair and a spiked up fringe darted out across the patio and, with a huge bunch of silver keys, began unlocking the security gate.

'I can never find the right one,' she said, thrusting one after the other into the small hole. It was like watching an angry woodpecker jabbing at a tree for an elusive grub. Her tiny head rocked backwards and forwards as she tried to free the locks. Finally, the fastening clunked and she pulled the door open. 'Quick! Quickly. In you come.' She directed me to the closed front door whilst she re-fastened the gate.

I looked behind me. *Were we being followed by some armed gang?*

After a further fumbling of keys, and a screech to take my boots off, I was led into a dazzling entrance hall, with high glass walls and an atrium roof. There was a mature magnolia tree stretching up from a hexagon of white picket fencing to the crystal roof above. It was even brighter in here than outside.

'Welcome. This is Casa De Imogen,' the lady of the house proclaimed, stretching her short wiry arms up to the tree and vaulted ceiling, in case I had somehow missed them.

I dutifully looked up again and tried to shield my eyes from the blinding whiteness.

'Very impressive, isn't it?' she said clasping her hands together in ritual praise. 'My daughter designed it. Our own Spanish hideaway. So naughty, really. We only use the house a few weeks a year.' She took a deep breath and slowly exhaled her immense pride. Her eyes were hidden behind large, oversized Philippe Chevallier sunglasses. The big pools of lenses looked like those worn by a young Iris Adfel, but her clothing was more modern and shipshape. She was wearing a blue and white striped dress and white deck shoes. This nautical theme gave her the appearance of a Captain's Mate.

Having secured three heavy deadlocks on the main door, she waved me across the white marbled floor and down a short flight of stairs. The house was divided in two halves, lengthwise, separated by a dark stairwell in the centre. We walked along the right-hand side and into the kitchen. It was a long galley, about sixty feet in length, with a line of six portholes mounted over the work-surface. Beyond the kitchen was a dining area with a long white table and eight designer chairs, with a bunch of white roses in a white porcelain vase. Further back was a living room area, which seemed to continue around the corner, in an l-shape, along the entire width of the rear, glass wall.

'Would you like a drink?' she asked.

I glanced over at the racks full of expensive wines and champagnes. 'Yes, please.'

She took down a tumbler from one of the cabinets and poured me some water. 'There. That should be nice and cold,' she said, handing it to me. 'Ben, do you want a drink?' she yelled through the house.

'What?' he growled from a room on the other side of the partition.

She raised her eyes to the cream coloured ceiling. 'Drink darling?'

He grunted something from his den.

'What darling?' she cooed, refusing to move from where she was standing.

'Are you deaf woman? Sancerre! In the fridge.'

More raised eyes. 'Coming darling.' She poured a large glass of wine into a crystal goblet. 'Come and meet Ben,' she said to me.

I'd rather not, I thought. 'That would be good,' I said.

I followed her back into the hall and down the other side, to the far end. There was a small, blue room, off to the left; the only concession to this endless canvas of whiteness.

A big, wrinkled man in a colourful Hawaiian shirt and pink shorts was slumped over a desk in a navy-blue armchair, in the far corner of the room.

Abigail shot through with the wine glass to where he was sat. 'Ben, darling. This is Robert. The new gardener.'

He shook my hand, without looking at me and then said to her, 'Well, let him get on with it then, woman.' We had been dismissed. I noticed that there was a small black cat on his lap, purring loudly from the attention it was receiving from his other hand.

She put the glass down, hurried out of the room and led me

back though the kitchen and into the living room. 'Let me show you around,' she said. She slid one of the three sets of sliding doors open and led me out onto a high terrace. From here there was a great view of the golf greens. The strong blanket of outdoor colour soothed my eyes from the stark, clinical interior. I couldn't bear to look at the shiny white carts, for some reason.

Abigail ignored the outlook and pointed down to the garden which was three floors below us. There was a small infinity pool in one corner and half an acre of grass with six fig trees planted along the bottom. She pointed to some raised beds and told me that these needed to be weeded, regularly, and about her plans for half a dozen lemon and lime trees, for their gin and tonics, on the other side. She giggled with the thought of picking her own fruits next summer.

She walked back into the kitchen and up to a half-glazed side-door. 'Would you like some more to drink?'

I looked down at my half-full water tumbler. 'I'm fine,' I said.

She unlocked the door and pushed it open. There was a high rock face on the right and a small patio framed by some empty borders. 'It needs to be *Imogened,*' she said, pointing to the empty beds. She must have seen the blank expression on my face. 'That's what we call it when our darling girl goes all creative on us and uses her *imogenation.* She just has heaps.' Her polished English accent kept slipping when she became excited, revealing a foreign twang.

Abigail walked outside. 'I want to *imogen* a kitchen garden. I want herbs, cut flowers and salads. 'She pointed to a three metre square piece of dry, baked soil. 'Immy would do it for us, but she's overseas.'

'Australia?' I asked.

She put her hand over her mouth and then pulled it away. 'No. Hong Kong,' she snapped.

I looked away from her, embarrassed and was dismayed by the scene in front of me. Beyond the kitchen garden, there was a steep slope of grass, two metres wide, dropping down by about one hundred and fifty feet to the bottom. It ran parallel to the side of the building and the garden wall. As I walked up to the perimeter, in my socks, I could see that the house was a series of overlapping blocks, which descended the hill like steps made for a giant. I thought of Oscar Wilde's, *The Selfish Giant,* and decided that no happy children would want to play here unless they wanted to break their necks. It would have been good for sledging in a British winter, but that was extremely unlikely to happen here, on the Costa del Sol.

The grass was long and hadn't been cut for months. What it needed was a few resident goats rather than this middle-aged man with a Flymo.

'I want it cut in stripes,' Abigail told me. 'That's what Stanley does for us back in Surrey.' She tilted her head up to look at a passing plane. 'He trained at Wisley.' She looked back at me and I saw my worried reflection in her sunglasses. 'Perhaps you know him?' she added.

The only *Stanley* I knew was our best friend's border terrier, who was more in favour of digging up plants than putting them in. 'Perhaps,' I said, following her back inside. 'Have you always lived in Surrey?'

She shut the door behind us and locked it. 'Good heavens, no. I'm a Kiwi and proud of it. I'm surprised you couldn't tell from the accent.'

I shrugged.

'Let me quickly show you the other side and the pool.' She scurried back into the hallway and stopped by the staircase. 'We are so proud of this.' She switched the lights on and a highly-polished, glass staircase was illuminated below us. It dropped all the way down, through the successive floors and finished at a glass door leading onto the pool.

'Wow!' I said, stepping forward. The effect was dazzling, though not good for vertigo sufferers.

'We love it, but some of our friends won't use it. Also, it can be quite tricky for Maria to keep clean so we only use it when it's too cold outside.'

Since we were in December, I felt sure that she would lead me down it today.

She put her arm across. 'No. Not today. It was only cleaned a few days ago.'

We walked away from the crystal avalanche and over to a further external door. This led onto another patio area with a white and blue striped table and matching chairs. Six columns of jasmine had been trained up the walls and over a pergola on the far side.

'Isn't it heaven?' she sighed.

As I looked at the sheer drop of stone stairs down to the bottom, it certainly felt like we were up in the clouds. There were several flat plateaus of grass, bordered with flowers, punctuating the steep descent.

'You can access from there,' she nodded her head up to the top of the hill above us. I could see the edge of the gate I had entered and excused myself to quickly retrieve my boots.

As we walked down the steps, she was issuing lists of detailed instructions of the work that she wanted me to do; I was thinking about how difficult it was going to be to carry the equipment down the hill and to access the different areas in the garden. Finally we arrived at the bottom, next to the pool. It was a relief to be back on flat ground. She showed me the pump house for the infinity pool and I saw the sheer rise of the other slope that led up to the kitchen garden. At least this side was only grass, I thought. Then the realization hit me: there was no external access to this side of the garden. I would have to carry the lawn mower down one side, hike to the top of the other, and then carefully climb back down, cutting the grass. I would be lucky to survive, let alone create lines of stripes.

'Well, I'll let you get on,' Abigail said. 'I'll leave you some more water on the top terrace.' She unlocked the glass door, opened it and relocked it. I saw her take off her shoes and begin to clamber up *Crystal Mountain*, inside.

I began my own ascent on the stone ledges outside. By the time I had got to the top and reached the approach to my car, I was out of breath. Fortunately, Abigail had already opened the gate, so I could retrieve my tools.

So much for this being a small bungalow with a tiny yard. There was a lot of strenuous work ahead.

The only other house I remembered being so surprising was Number 10, Downing Street.

***

Dear Sandra, in my team in the Lords, spent many of her breaks walking around the palace trying to spot famous personalities and introduce herself.

She had two main hobbies: trying to win the jackpot prize in her local bingo club and meeting as many of the members as possible; she had a particular fascination with the Prime Ministers. She would always ask me, in the nineteen-nineties if she could leave early on a Tuesday or Thursday, so she could see John Major arrive in his car from Downing Street for *Prime Minister's Question Time.* I thought that she just had a passion for Major but this was proceeded by Tony Blair. She would often rush out on her break and chat to the policemen on the gate, the private secretaries and personal assistants. Eventually she got to know Blair's P.A. in the Commons, through numerous visits to the small ante-chamber and private office behind *Speaker's Chair,* which the Prime Minister in power would use. This acquaintance-ship led to us having a small private tour of Number 10. Our party consisted of other members of my team and Sandra's daughter, Christina, on our day off. Even though we weren't working, we all dressed up: me and my team wore our service attire, apart from Alfredo who was sporting his old Italian jacket and Christina had on her best party dress.

We approached the iconic black door through stolid, wrought iron security gates which were installed during Margaret Thatcher's time. Before this, members of the public could wander freely through the street and it was frequently used as a short-cut between Whitehall and St. James's Park. Our names were on a list held by a heavily-armed policeman, who let us in through the gates and past the newer Foreign and Commonwealth Building on the left, which is sometimes used to hold cabinet meetings.

He led us up a short flight of steps and to the front door of Number 10. The first thing I noticed was there didn't seem to be any lock on this famous, black, shiny door. Our escort just knocked and a porter from somewhere inside casually opened it.

I later learned that within this *open house*, not even the Prime Minister has keys. There is always someone on duty to let him, or her, in. Another interesting point is that the house was originally Number 5, when it was first built in 1684, and was not renumbered until 1779.

The building is deceptive. As soon as you step inside there is a feeling of going into *Doctor Who's Tardis*. It's far bigger on the inside than it appears from outside. Behind the polished door there is a labyrinth of rooms and offices. The first thing you notice is that it isn't just one house. From the black and white chequered floor you can see a corridor extending down the left into numbers 11 and 12 of this classic Georgian terrace. Also it is far deeper than it first seems. From the early 18th Century it was annexed to a very large and elegant manor house, which was adjacent. These are all part of the same building now which is simply referred to as *Number Ten*. It has been an important building for British Prime Ministers since 1735 and some of the most significant political decisions have been made from here in the past 275 years. Also, it is the official residence of the serving Prime Minister, their office and the place where the PM entertains guests, such as The Queen and other world leaders.

We were instructed to hang our coats on temporary racks which had been installed in the entrance hall, next to one of the custard coloured walls. Our mobiles and any electrical items had to be left on a small occasional table, next to the unlit fireplace, with yellow *Post-It* notes, which had our names scribbled on them. We were invited to join a small party of Lord Mayors who were being escorted around the building.

From here, we were led along a thin corridor, past a lift, through a large ante room and to the bottom of *The Grand Staircase*.

Our tour guide was a retired colonel-looking chap, complete with a grey handlebar moustache and a red, weather-beaten face. 'Right men. Get in a neat line and follow me,' he commanded, as he walked up the stairs.

'What about me?' Sandra asked, in her most feminine voice. 'And Christina?' She pointed to her daughter.

He waved his arm, dismissively. 'Yes, you two, too.'

Sandra nudged me in the ribs. 'He's a right character,' she said, loud enough for him to hear and continued to salute him as we climbed the stairs.

We were led up the famous yellow painted staircase, with its polished iron railings and white marble floor, with a narrow strip of plush carpet fixed in the middle. It was commissioned by Sir Robert Walpole in 1735. Above the panelling there were portraits of all the Prime Ministers hung in ascending tiers, in chronological order, with the latest incumbents at the top, including John Major and Margaret Thatcher. I don't recall seeing Blair's there.

When we reached the top we could see a small reception room which is for the Prime Minister's private use. Ted Heath, allegedly, used to tinkle the ivories and ebonies of his grand piano in there. Nowadays, according to our guide, it had been reinforced and requisitioned as a safe room, or *Panic Room,* where the PM could safely lock themselves in during an attack. We weren't permitted to enter.

Sandra pulled herself up onto the landing using the balustrade. 'What's this piece of old crap?' she asked, pointing to a small lump of grey coal, which had been placed in a bowl, on a thin shelf.

'Madam, please!' The Colonel shouted, more red-faced and heated, than before. 'Don't touch anything.'

She remained as cool as the burnt out embers. 'Call me Sandra. What is it then?'

'That, my dear lady, is a priceless piece of moon rock.' He twiddled with his moustache. 'Four pieces were given to Harold

Wilson by President Nixon in January 1970. They were brought back from the lunar landing by Buzz Aldrin and Neil Armstrong. They were sent to our London museums for public exhibition.' He sighed with enormous pride.

Sandra pushed forward to get his full attention. 'What's it doing here then?'

He combed the thin layer of hair over his head with his hand. 'It was later put into storage, madam, due to falling interest.'

Sandra laughed. 'I'm not surprised. Not very interesting is it?'

He brushed his black blazer down with his hand. 'I'm afraid the Prime Minister of the day, Ted Heath, wouldn't agree with you there madam. He brought the pieces back to Downing Street for display, until he left in 1974. Let's move on shall we?'

She was a sucker for attention and nudged me again, to indicate she wanted to continue this banter. 'Then what happened?'

He was getting irritated now. 'Well if you must know madam, they were hidden away in a broom cupboard.'

We all started laughing.

He cleared his throat. 'That was until Lady Thatcher found them and put them back on show.'

'Because no one else wanted them,' Sandra teased.

'They were offered back to the Science Museum but it seems they had received some better samples.' He looked somewhat defeated.

'Now that it is interesting. We like Lady Thatcher, don't we Robert?' she grinned.

I winked back at her. 'Yes, Sandra, we do.'

As we walked back down the stairs to the ground floor, she leaned over the step above me and tried to whisper, 'I don't think they ever did land on the moon. It's one of those *constipation* theory things, isn't it Robert?'

I just nodded.

'It probably came out of an old bonfire or the fireplace downstairs.'

'Shush,' one of the mayors said, angrily.

She ignored him and laughed.

From there we were led into a room called *The Terracotta Room*. In fact the room is frequently changed and renamed according to the individual taste of the resident Prime Minister. When Margaret Thatcher came into power she changed Callaghan's cool, cold-looking *Blue Room*, to the *Green Room*, ostensibly to reflect her favourite colour and her roots from the greengrocery business. There were many famous works of art on loan here from the Government Art Collection. Like the colour, the PM is given the choice of which artworks they want to exhibit.

Nearby was the Cabinet Room, with the long oval table where the Prime Minister and the cabinet meet at least once a week. This used to be on Thursday mornings but Gordon Brown changed this to Tuesdays. The room was enlarged in 1796 by removing walls and inserting columns. It has been totally soundproofed and reinforced since an IRA terrorist bomb exploded in the garden in 1991, whilst John Major and his Cabinet were in session.

Our escort ordered us to gather around the table and told Sandra off for trying to sit down. He was conducting his own cabinet meeting and we were all summoned to attention. 'Number 10 has seen many PMs come and go,' he barked. 'Although you may think of it as a home, I think it's more important to think of it as an office.' He strummed his fingers on the highly polished table until Sandra tutted at this indiscretion. He cleared his throat, noisily, to demand attention; like he was some kind of de facto PM appointed to take over when Blair was absent. 'I want to tell you about the greatest Prime Minister who ever lived.' He paused, trying to build tension. 'Winston Churchill.'

He told us that Winston Churchill loved Number 10. During the Second World War, keeping Downing Street safe became the priority of the Prime Minister and the War Cabinet. Steel reinforcements were added to the *Garden Rooms*, and heavy metal shutters were fixed over windows as protection from bombing raids. In reality, though, these would not have saved them from a direct hit. The Garden Rooms included a small dining room, bedroom and a meeting area which were used by Churchill throughout the war.

By October 1939, the Cabinet had moved out of Number 10 and into secret underground war rooms in the basement of the Office of Works opposite the Foreign Office. Nowadays these are known as: *Churchill's War Rooms*.

Following near misses by bombs in 1940, Churchill and his wife, Clementine, moved out of Downing Street and into the Number 10 Annex above the war rooms. Furniture and valuables were removed from Number 10 and only the Garden Rooms, Cabinet Room and Private Secretaries' Office remained in use.

Churchill disliked living in the Annex and, despite the danger and lack of furniture, he continued to use Number 10 for working and eating; it was a place which helped him centre his thoughts and resolve to win the war.

The fear of attack was so imminent that a reinforced shelter was constructed under the house for up to six people. Even George VI sought shelter there when he dined with Churchill in the Garden Rooms. Although bombs caused further damage to Number 10, there were no direct hits to the house, allowing Churchill to continue to live and work there right up until the end of the war.

As soon as war was over, Churchill and his wife moved back to Number 10, where he made his Victory in Europe (VE) Day broadcast, which was delivered from the Cabinet Room at 3pm on 8th May 1945.

The Colonel clearly knew his facts on Churchill and, although it sounded like he had swallowed a generic history book, I did find it interesting. The rest of the party had started yawning and Sandra and her daughter were drifting around the room.

146

He tried to reassert his command. 'Downing Street has seen many Prime Ministers come and go. Some loved it as their home but some never actually lived here.' He twiddled his thick lip hair, deep in thought. 'At the start of the nineteenth century, up until the eighteen twenties, this was not the favoured home for our PMs. It was first and foremost a place of work. Many of our esteemed leaders kept private residence outside.'

'Is that right, Robert?' Sandra asked me.

I nodded. His information agreed with the facts rattling inside my head.

The Colonel held his hand up to silence her and muttered *madam* under his facial hair. 'That was until Sir John Sloane was commissioned re-design the dining rooms.'

He had missed out some essential information. 'By Prime Minister Viscount Goderich, I believe,' I said.

'Yes. Yes, indeed. However, Lord Wellington decided it was too small and only used it whilst his own grander residence was being refurbished. As everyone knows, the current Prime Minister, Tony Blair and his family have thwarted convention and don't live here.' There was a disapproving tone in his delivery. 'He considers it too small so has swapped residence with Gordon Brown, the current Chancellor of the Exchequer.' His voice trailed away in disappointment and he added, in a subdued voice,' Whatever next?'

Sandra tugged my sleeve. 'I didn't know that, Robert. Is he right?' she whispered.

I nodded.

'In 1826, number 11 became the official Chancellor of Exchequer's residence,' he added and pointed to the adjoining rooms, next door.

That wasn't quite right. It was two years later, but I was too nervous to challenge his command. His voice and confidence were trailing off. He had had enough of this contrary company and wanted to leave.

'Towards the mid nineteenth century, the area fell into disrepair and wasn't considered safe anymore.' He looked down at his reflection in the table.

'Brothels,' I said.

'What!' His face again detonated in anger.

'Brothels,' I repeated. 'Houses full of ladies of the night. I believe it became an area of guilty pleasures.'

Sandra twirled the plastic beads on her long necklace. 'Right me lovelies,' she cooed, leaning across an armchair. 'What can I do for you today?'

I thought The Colonel was going to have a heart attack, but he looked away.

We all laughed loudly, apart from her daughter who said, from under her breath, 'Mum. Really!'

One of the mayors, who had been silent during the whole tour, was rummaging his hands though his pockets – maybe he was trying to find some loose change?

The Colonel took a deep breath and turned back towards us. 'Murder!' he yelled.

We all fell silent and looked over the floor and scanned the room.

Sandra couldn't resist. 'I think it was Colonel Red-face, in The Terracotta Room with the moon rock.' She pointed at him.

We all laughed, and even the accused managed a wry smile. 'You got me there, madam,' he surrendered and held up his hands in front of him, together, ready to be handcuffed. As she moved forward, he withdrew them and dropped them by his side 'They tried to murder Prime Minister Robert Peel, in 1842, but, fortunately, they failed.'

The year was right. 'Not so fortunate for Edward Drummond though,' I told the group.

'Who was Edward Drummond?' Sandra asked our tour leader.

He didn't reply and looked at me for assistance.

'He was the Prime Minister's secretary. He was murdered carrying dispatches in Whitehall by a killer who thought he was the PM.'

The Colonel walked away from us and over to a tall, white, Regency bookcase with double doors, fitted with grills, so you could see the outline of the books inside. 'Ramsay Macdonald brought the building back to its splendour in the 1920's with the creation of the *Prime Minister's Library*. All Prime Ministers now donate books to this private collection, some which they have written themselves.'

We walked over to join him.

'Not very big, is it?' Sandra said, with her hands on her hips, leaning forward. 'Even the crappy library we've got in Willesden's bigger than this.'

He tried to ignore her. 'Of course this is only a small selection. The prize pieces.' His face was beginning to re-flush with pride. He pointed to a thick book spine which read *Ten Years at Number Ten*. 'We are very privileged. This has even been signed by Lady Thatcher.'

Sandra pushed through the assembled group to the front. 'Robert's got this one.' She looked back at me and I gave her a thumbs-up. She added, 'And about six more. And loads of other books from Prime Ministers. All signed.'

I looked back at our host who, like a tired balloon at a late-ending children's party, was looking increasingly deflated. 'Yours is in better condition though,' I admitted to him.

'What's next then?' Sandra asked, her energy still surging.

The tour guide frowned and bent slowly down towards her. 'That's it for today madam. It's time to leave.'

'Can we see the kitchens?' she asked, unabated.

He was having no more and leaned into her face. 'I said, it's time to go now.'

He walked past us, marched through the corridor and we all followed him back to the entrance hall and retrieved our belongings. Our happy troop had been summarily dismissed.

'How rude,' Sandra said, as we walked back down the steps and out into the cold wind.

I smiled. 'Just think. You're like Lady Thatcher now. You've been chucked out of Downing Street.'

'I like that,' she chuckled. 'But just remember, Robert, this lady's not for turning.' She turned to the group of people following her and asked, 'Anyone up for a game of bingo now?'

We all shook our heads apart from the quiet mayor, who had been fiddling with his pockets again, who said, 'I'm up for a game.'

Alfredo winked at me. 'I-a bet he's after a full house.'

8   IT'S A MYSTERY

Winters are mild here in Southern Spain and relatively frost free. Snow does fall on the high peaks of the local mountains but, in most parts, the patches of intermittent cloud swirl fast overhead, occasionally releasing much needed precipitation.

It's amazing but even with low rainfall, the fields and mountainsides turn green and yellow. This is rendered by the abundant growth of yellow flowers; the clover-leafed Bermuda Buttercups. Also, dark green hedges erupt into cascades of bright orange trumpets. These flame vines are a popular type of hedging. The colourful palette is further complemented by the red stars of high flowering poinsettia trees.

In January, the trees gradually begin to look snow-covered but this is an illusion. They are covered in white but these are not snowflakes, but prolific pentagons of almond blossom flower, with a honey scent.

Graham and I went into town for fish and chips. These were served up by another expat, from Leeds, called Rosie. After her third divorce and failed attempts to distance herself, from a selfish son who constantly wanted money, she had met a kind older guy, Dave, whilst serving him across the bar at *The Black Horse*. They had both given up on ever finding romance again. However, after a passionate week of constant love making in her caravan in the pub car park, they were married; as soon as his slipped disc had settled down sufficiently for him to drive down to the registry office. It's true that sometimes love is found where opposites attract; where he was tall and thin, with grey hair and a pallid, almost ghostlike complexion, she was orange and ruddy, short and dumpy, with long tails of auburn hair which curved over her shoulders; he looked like he was allergic to daylight, she looked like she had fallen asleep under a sunbed. Her bank balance was heavily in the red, his was healthily in the black. This was a fact that the wayward son, Karl, had somehow found out about and turned up, uninvited, to the wedding. Unusually, his appearance turned out to be fortunate. They only had Rosie's aged father as a witness and Karl was happy to fulfil the role of the second, though the receptionist had offered to step in. She would have done it for free, whereas Karl managed to extort £250 from his new father-in-law, for his services.

Rosie wasn't interested in Dave's money. She just wanted a simple life. They had a private reception of cod and chips, wrapped in creamy-white paper, (the same colour as her dress), back in the caravan.

'So what's next me love?' He asked her, crunching on a pickled onion.

After making love so vigorously that the wheel suspension broke on her side of the van, she told him she had always dreamed of running a fish and chip shop and then, perhaps, retiring somewhere warmer. There was still the matter of her aged father who needed to be taken care of.

Dave scratched his head and a small clump of hair fell out. 'Life is short. Don't know how long we've got. What say we get a fish and chip shop in the sun? Besides, I fancy taking it easy and playing a few rounds of golf.'

Three weeks later they had sold his cottage in Horsforth, given Karl the caravan and a few hundred to keep him going, and moved to Spain, complete with two dogs, three cats and her dying dad.

We were the only customers but as usual Rosie was busy on the other side of the counter, cleaning out the fryers, wiping down the work-surfaces and unloading palettes of drinks.

'Hello boys.' she yelled from under the counter. 'Two of the usual?'

I stood up to try and see her. 'With mushy peas and a pickled egg please.'

She got off her hands and knees and ran her fingers through the hair, that was piled up like a damp mop on the top of her head.

'No egg for me,' Graham said and put his hand in front of his mouth. 'I hope she washes her hands first,' he added, quietly.

We heard the clash of metal as she grabbed her weapons. It was always like watching Joan of Arc going into battle, as she kicked implements out of the way and started coating things in hot oil.

We heard the gurgling of chip fat as the fryers started to heat up.

It was sad to see that the restaurant was still so quiet. It was a great location, near the library dedicated by Gerard Brenan, with the mountains in the background. However, the old whiteboard with its faded list of food items was not enough to entice people in to eat.

Graham had offered to take some photographs and help her make a more colourful and attractive display, but she was always too busy. Dave had discovered that he loved golf and often disappeared onto the greens and left her alone to run the business.

'What can I get you to drink?' she yelled.

We checked our watches. It was only twelve. 'A couple of Cokes, please.'

She wiped her hot face with her apron. 'Does Dickie want some water?'

I couldn't hear what she said.

'That would be great,' Graham replied.

She brought around two cans of Coke, some glasses with ice and a big bowl of water for the dog. 'How's the gardening?'

I poured my drink into the glass. 'Not too bad. It seems to be picking up slowly.' I looked at Graham.

'He's doing really well. It takes time,' he said. 'I think you've got to give it a year to know if it's working or not.'

Rosie wiped her forehead with her stained apron. 'That's for sure.' She put her swollen hands on top of her hips and looked at the empty chairs. 'I've still got your flyer up there.' She pointed to one we had posted up in July that was partly torn and tatty. 'I could do with a new one.'

Normally we carried extra cards and flyers, but I didn't have one today. 'Thanks, Rosie. I'll bring one down. How's things with Karl?'

She threw her head and her hands up in the air. 'Didn't you hear?'

We both shook our heads.

'Little bastard did a shift for me last week.' She rested her hands on top of one of the vacant chairs. 'On Wednesday night. Curry Night. It was probably our busiest evening.'

'That's good then,' Graham said. 'Good it's getting busy.'

She opened her mouth wide and swallowed a big gulp of air. Her face was turning redder even with the fresh breeze outside. 'He went off with all the takings after telling me he hates me, wishes I was dead and says he wants to go back with 'is dad in Manchester.'

Graham was dumbstruck.

'Where is he now?' I asked. Dickie was getting agitated so I pulled him in towards me.

'Damned if I know, damned if I care.' Rosie raised herself up and tried to straighten her back. 'Good riddance I say.' Having made the main announcement, she forced her legs forward and shuffled back into the kitchen. 'If he knows what's good for him, he'll stay away from here.' Her voice was getting lower as she disappeared inside, but then peaked again in renewed anger. 'If he comes anywhere near hear again, I'll frigging kill him.'

We'd heard these threats before but somehow she always forgave him, let him back into her life and let him take her for another ride.

'It's like Nick and Dot Cotton in *EastEnders*,' Graham said to me, over the table.

A thin man with a long beard and five dogs walked in front of us and claimed the next table. 'Hi Rosie. Pint of Carlsberg,' he shouted.

'Sure, Clive. Coming right up.'

He let his dogs off and they all started jumping over Dickie who was tying himself up on his lead.

'Let him off, Rob,' Graham told me. 'He won't go anywhere.'

Rosie came back out with two pints, gave one to Clive and put the other down on our table. She rubbed her hair and continued. 'Where was I?'

'Karl?' Graham prompted.

She pulled a chair out and sat down with us and took a big swig of beer. 'That's better,' she said. 'Yes, not my problem anymore. We're moving soon and I've no plans to let him know where we're going.'

'That sounds like a good idea,' I said, keeping an eye on Dickie who was on the other side of the terrace, sniffing the largest of the dogs, a solid, black Rottweiler.

I'm not sure if it was the strength of this new resolution, or perhaps the effect of the beer, but Rosie seemed visibly relaxed and a bit happier with her decision.

'Any chance you can help us move?' she asked. 'I could really do with some help with the dogs and the new garden needs a bit of sorting out. '

'Yes, of course.' I said. 'I can put the back down in the car.'

She finished her pint. 'Don't you have a van, Rob?'

Graham looked at me. We had been talking about this for a while. It was becoming impossible to squeeze all the tools into the Kia and I had to guess which ones I would need. On more than a few times, I had made the wrong choice.

'No he doesn't, Rosie. I keep telling him he needs a van.' Graham said, finishing his Coke. 'There's no getting away from it, Rob.'

Rosie dismissed herself, saying the food was ready and we talked about making this next step.

'It's not just the gardens, I need the car for my teaching,' he said.

Normally his teaching was in the evenings but he had already turned down some private hours that he could have done in the mornings.

I had no idea how much money we had left and how much a van would cost. 'Can we afford one?'

'You've got about three thousand euros left from your pension. It won't be a new one but you should get something decent for that. It's Spain, after all.'

Rosie plonked two huge piles of fish and chips down on the table, toddled back inside and brought out ketchup, vinegar, salt and pepper and my pickled egg and peas in a bowl.

I squeezed the wedge of lemon over the dish and cut off a large chunk of fish and crunched through the crispy, beer-flavoured batter. 'Ah. That's good.' A large spoonful of mushy peas gave it a smooth after-taste.

'Alright, boys?' Rosie asked.

Graham still had a mouthful and muttered, 'Bloody luverly.'

She smiled, satisfied.

'I did see one opposite Mercadona,' I said, biting into my egg.

Graham looked puzzled. 'One what?'

'Van for sale.'

'Oh. How much was it?'

I scratched my head, trying to remember the hand-written *se vende* sign. 'Two thousand eight hundred, I think.'

Graham started coughing. 'Too much. I put too much vinegar on.' He coughed again and swallowed a mouthful of my Coke. 'We should take a look at it.'

Rosie popped back onto the terrace. 'No. Don't do that!' She was louder than she had intended and lowered her volume. 'You never buy a car off the road over here.'

'Why?' we asked together, with mouths full of chips.

Rosie had her head bowed down, as she picked a piece of fried potato off her apron. 'Cos, you'll end up with a load of unpaid fines. That's why.'

'That's right,' added Clive. 'Happened to a neighbour of mine. Sixteen hundred and fifty euros in parking and speeding fines.'

I looked at Graham. *Was this just another expat horror story?*

He put down his cutlery and dipped a chip in the ketchup. 'How come?'

Rosie walked over to pick up Clive's empty glass. 'Same again?'

He nodded.

She turned back to face us. 'Because over here everything goes by the car, not the owner. What you need is a garage. Go and see Jesus down by the Tabac on Carretera de Mijas.'

Graham laughed. 'What Rob needs is a van not a donkey in a stable.'

She ignored him. 'We get all our motors down there.'

I poked Graham in the ribs. 'Is he near the ferreteria?' I had seen a large warehouse building that looked like a garage.

'That's it.'

'With cars for sale, parked out on the road?' Graham said, ironically.

'Yes. That's the one,' she said and pinched a chip off his plate. She often did this, saying she could never resist a freshly fried chip.

He pretended to look shocked. 'Does he speak English?'

She looked at Graham, mischievously, grabbed a handful of chips and ran back inside. 'Better than what I does.'

We laughed. It was like being back at school.

'I think it's the guy Suzie Partridge told me about,' I said. 'And, yes, his English is supposed to be good.'

'That's just as well,' he sniggered. 'Your Spanish is about as good as your car skills.'

'I drive very well, thank you.' I gave Dickie a chip and the Rottweiler started growling. It was time to leave.

Graham drove us past the garage on the way home. We saw five vehicles for sale with an *ocasion* (special offer) sign on each of their roofs, but no price signs.

'You shouldn't buy a car off the road,' Graham said, as we got out the car.

I hit him with the jumper that was tied round my waist. 'Behave.'

There was one van; a small, white Opel Combo with clean, shiny paint that looked in perfect condition. The garage was closed so we decided to go back the next day to investigate.

Jesus (pronounced *Hay soos,* he told us) was a short dark skinned, middle-aged man with a clean-shaven head, like mine, with a thin, uneven line of moustache, which looked like it had been drawn on his face by a child. He had bright, hazel eyes which seemed to sparkle when he started speaking.

His English was good. He told us that the van was three thousand euros. It had been his, from new, twelve years ago. It had been well-looked after and maintained and he happily agreed, on Graham's insistence, to extend the warranty, from six months to one year. 'More than this, my friends. I will be giving him a new *ee-tay-vay* and will be making a new belt of timing for you.'

I looked at the clean, rust-free body work on the van. 'What's an *ee-tay-vay?*'

'It's their version of an M.O.T,' Graham answered.

Jesus opened one of the front doors to show us the clean interior. 'That's right, my friend.'

I sat in the low seat and, like Maggie in *The Simpsons,* turned the steering wheel pretending to drive.

'You take it out for a driving,' he said, handing me the keys and pointing up the road.

'No that's alright,' I said.

'You should try it,' Graham advised.

After realizing they were on the other side of the driver's seat, I checked the gears were in neutral, turned the key in the ignition and it started first time. The engine sounded much deeper and rattled more than the KIA.

'It's diesel,' Jesus told me.

I looked at Graham who nodded in silent agreement.

I looked up through the clear windscreen at the road that was full of double-parked cars and people trying to reverse into non-existent spaces. I turned the engine off. 'It's fine,' I said.

'Are you sure?' Graham asked, leaning into the cab.

'It's got a year's warranty,' I reminded him.

We followed Jesus into the garage. It must have gotten cold as he was rubbing his hands together. He led us into his immaculate, polished office, where all the paperwork had been filed in strict alphabetical order. He took out a receipt book and said, 'This is special price. Price for cash. You pay deposit today. Twenty per cent.'

We delved through our wallets to find as much as we could for a holding deposit. He accepted the three hundred and eighty-five euros we had, checked each of the notes under a desk light, locked them in his safe and wrote us out a *recibido* ticket.

'You pay the rest on Tuesday next. Cash only. The government is thieves. He is asking too much from us small people.'

We agreed. We could both take out two hundred and fifty euros per day and would have the balance ready by then.

He rubbed his hands together again and went over to a small crystal decanter on top of the filing cupboard. He poured three small glasses of Spanish rum and handed us one each. 'Salud!' He yelled, we clinked the glasses together.

We were both about to drink when he shouted, 'Wait!' He slammed the bottom of the glass down on the desk top and held it up again. 'That is most important before you drink.' We followed his lead and slammed our glasses down.

He held his up to his mouth and said, '*Quien no apuya, no folla.*'

'Cheers,' I said. We downed the thick brown spirit in two long gulps. 'What does it mean?' I looked at Graham but he just shrugged.

Jesus took the glasses off us and wiped them clean with some kitchen towel. 'It means, he who doesn't slam doesn't fuck.'

We all laughed.

We shook his hand, agreed that he was a very nice man and virtually skipped out of the building, happy with our new acquisition.

The following Tuesday came and he mechanically implemented the same ritual as before: the notes were checked; the money was deposited in the safe; the receipt was written and we clunked glasses and cheered again with that funny Spanish expression.

I was sure that Jesus would now give me the keys.

'My friends,' he said. 'Please you sit down.'

We did as we were told, confused.

As he was wiping the glasses, he turned and said, 'My friends, there has been a small, *como se dice* hiccupping.' He stroked the thin line of hair over his top lip. 'We were making the belt of timing for you, like I said. But, Manuel. Manuel!' He shouted the mechanic's name and his small eyes grew wide and menacing. 'Manuel was not making the fitting well.'

For the next half hour he paced up and down his office, explaining in long, drawn out, convoluted and often confused English that, effectively, a screw had become loose and had somehow worked its way inside the engine and damaged one of the pistons. The whole engine needed to be rebuilt and readjusted. He assured us it would only take a few days and added, 'Manuel, he is no here now. Antonio is coming. He is much more good.'

As we left his office, we noticed that there were about six other vehicles in the workshop up on ramps, with raised bonnets and discarded body parts at the side. There was no sign of any mechanics and the site looked like the forensic department of *CSI* for dead cars.

Graham stopped and surveyed the ghostlike scene. 'Where is our van?'

Jesus ushered us towards the half-closed doors. 'My friends. No problem. He is in my other garage. I see you next week.' He gently pushed us out of the doors and double-locked himself inside.

'Oh shit,' I said, as we walked back to the car.

Graham jumped into the driver's seat. 'At least it's covered by the warranty,' he said, doubtfully.

I may be no expert at cars but I knew that having major repairs on a van we had just paid for, and which there was now no sign of, couldn't be good.

Rosie rang me the day after and asked me to help her move. I told her about our experience and she told me not to worry. 'He has done a good job mending both our cars recently, the Peugeot needed shit loads doing to it and it didn't cost too much.' Remembering that she had bought them both from him, this wasn't reassuring.

I emptied the car out and put the back seats down. Rosie had five dogs: a couple of old Corgis, Thelma and Louise, a Podenco, Dusty, a Jack Russell, Jack and a very old Alsatian called Rocky. The latter was now aptly named as he was very wobbly on his aged legs and I had to lift him into the back of the car.

It took two trips and the hounds all seemed pleased with their new space. The house was a large white block of building on one floor which looked like it had been dropped on a huge square of tiled terrace, with a small pool on the south side. The ground was unusually flat and that was the reason for the move so, that Rosie's father, Ed, who was *on his last legs,* could move around more easily. The edges had been planted out in with hundreds of oleanders and several large, overgrown shrubs.

January is the perfect time for pruning as you can easily see which parts of the plant are dead. I cut back the dead shoots apart from two large forsythia bushes near the house, as they produce flowers on the previous year's growth.

It's also the best time for breaking the soil up for new plants, before the earth gets too dry and baked. Rosie apparently knew this as she gave me clear instructions to dig a very deep hole, beyond the pool area.

'How big do you want it?' I asked.

She looked back at the house. Ed was sorting through some of the moving boxes which were piled outside. 'About this high,' she said with her hand a foot over her head, still looking at him. 'And about this wide,' she showed me with her hands a few inches inside her own portly frame.

'What's it for?' I asked.

'Do you want a beer or a Coke?' she offered, walking back to the house. Either she hadn't heard me or had chosen not to answer.

'Coke please.'

There was a crash on the floor as Ed had dropped a plate which smashed into smithereens. Rosie started running and swaying, towards him. 'For Christ's sake leave that father,' she yelled, with her arms in the air. 'Bloody useless,' she added.

I spent five hours sweeping, pruning and digging. The bushes looked great, the hole was impressive but the terrace was disappointing. I kept scrubbing and blasting it with the hose but the stain would not come up.

'You need a Karcher,' Rosie said.

There was a cry from inside the house.

'What have you done now!' she yelled and told me she had to go. 'Bloody man. I'm sorry Rob, I've got to go. Can you come back next week and finish it?'

'Yes. Sure.'

She waddled back into the house, slammed the door and I could hear screaming and swearing at the poor man who was falling about inside.

I remembered seeing a Karcher in John's massive shed and found out, from Graham, that it is a high powered jet wash machine which you attach to a garden hose and an electricity supply. We found one on sale at *Bricomart* for sixty euros and purchased it as an investment for another service I could offer with the gardening.

With still no sign of the van, I continued to haul my gardening equipment around in the car.

My hours were starting to increase to a healthy level. I was doing four hours every week at Janet and John's and beginning to see a great improvement in the overall look of their garden. There were also two hours per week at Abigail Snipe's place, or as I called it *The Garden of Death*. The actual garden work was simple enough but scaling the slopes was still exasperating.

I went back to Rosie's a week later. She had left the back gate unlocked for me as she was taking Dave to the golf course as his car had broken down again. It was deathly silent there, in her absence. All the boxes had been cleared off the patio area, so there was an even greater tiled area to clean. There was a fresh film of dog hair on the top, so I brushed it down and then set to work on the jet washing. As the machine thundered into motion, Thelma, Louise, Jack and Dusty all raced over to check out the action. Dusty was trying to grab the thin black nozzle whilst Jack was barking at the yellow body of the machine. There was no sign of Rocky.

An hour later their mistress returned. 'Hey! You lot. Get back in here,' Rosie called, from the opened front door. Most of them dutifully followed her voice back inside, but Dusty continued to wrestle with the attachment. Under the blackness there were squares of cream, marbled tiles. As the dirt lifted off, they started to sparkle and shine in the bright sun. The only problem was that with the removal of the sticky layer they were very slippery.

Rosie shuffled onto the terrace in a Pink Panther onesie, with a jacket over the top and white bunny slippers. The path she made gave an even greater sheen on the newly exposed surface. I wondered if she had driven Dave wearing those. The answer was, probably, yes.

'That's looking great,' she said, as her back foot slid away from under her centre and she threw her arms to the side, to remain upright. Her face looked sad and tired. Thick lines of mascara had been smudged around her eyes and she looked like she hadn't slept for the past week.

I grabbed her arm to steady her. 'Yes, but please be careful. It's quite slippery now. I hope Ed will be alright with it.'

She grabbed Dusty by the scruff of her neck and pulled her back towards the house. 'That won't be a problem anymore,' she uttered, with no emotion.

'How's he doing? I called out, but she was nearly back inside.

'There won't be any more problems with father,' she yelled, without turning round. 'That's all been sorted.'

As I reached the far side of the terrace with the jet washer, I noticed that the large hole had been filled in. The earth had been flattened and was decorated in a mosaic of broken tiles. A small metal cross, made from two old fish slices tied together, had been placed at one end.

Rosie closed up the fish and chip shop soon after this event, and I never went back to that garden again. The object buried in the hole remains a mystery. It was like something penned in a puzzling crime novel.

***

I first met Ruth Rendell in the late 1990's, when she became one of several female life peers for the labour party, who were affectionately known as *Blair's Babes.* Tony Blair brought many new faces into the Palace of Westminster and it was my duty to show them some of the dining rooms they could access. After being shown the main Lords' Dining Room, they were sent down to me, normally in twos or threes, to show them the rooms I was responsible for: the Reid Room which now had a bar that led into the Attlee Room, and the Hulme Room. Sandra would call for me and I showed them around. The Hulme Room is for peers only and we had four hot dishes plus a small *a la carte* menu. Effectively it was a club, within a club.

Baroness Rendell was like a character out of one of her crime novels. She had a sharp, curious face, with a short-cropped mound of blonde hair which bobbed as she pecked her way around, uncovering all the facts and characters of the building. She was accompanied by her partner in crime, Baroness Pitkeathley. These two were often seen together.

Ruth Rendell was very easy to talk to and was very much in favour of fighting for the needs of women. She introduced the bill into the Lords that would later become The Female Genital Mutilation Act 2003.

There was much evidence within this gentlemen's club of women who had gone the extra mile to fight for their sex.

An interesting example of this resides in the recesses of St. Mary's Undercroft Chapel. This is a wonderful medieval chapel under Westminster hall; the only original section to survive the terrible fire. The chapel is a great example of a place of worship before Henry VIII's reformation of the Catholic Church. It is a highly decorated building, with its original green mosaics. It is still used for weddings, christenings and civil partnerships by M.P.s or favoured individuals sponsored by an MP. At the back of the chapel behind the ornate organ is a broom cupboard. Behind the door there is a small brass plaque to commemorate the life of Emily Davison. The money for this was raised by Tony Benn, labour MP. On the night of April 2nd 1911, the night of the census, Emily had concealed herself in that cupboard in order to claim the House of Commons as her place of residence. She was found hiding in there and was arrested for previous acts of protest. In June 1912, when Emily was near the end of a six months' sentence for arson in Holloway prison, where she and dozens of other suffragettes were being subjected to force-feeding, she threw herself down a 10 metre iron staircase in protest, to try and end the suffering for all others. Although she suffered severe head and spinal injuries, this act did not kill her. It was a year later, on June 4th 1913, when she drew further attention by throwing herself under King George V's horse, Anmer, and died of fatal head injuries four days later. The mystery still remains as to whether she tried to kill herself in an act of martyrdom, or if she was simply trying to attach a scarf with the suffragettes' emblem for publicity of their cause.

Whatever the motive, her death had the outcome of inciting male political support for suffrage and her legend lives on.

In addition to the changes being brought in by Tony Blair, there were several changes coming into my department. Rupert Ellwood was brought in as assistant Banqueting Manager, fresh out of Eton College. There was talk that the strict, uncompromising, Miss McWilliams would be retiring and was grooming up her younger counterpart to take over our catering business, which was becoming busier every year and more difficult to manage. In fact this new relationship hit the headlines in the tabloids, when this new couple were accused by one of the casualties of the department, an over-worked secretary. She cited them as being racist, when she heard them refer to the dining hall as looking more like a *curry house* than a Members' club.

After Miss McWilliams retired, with her MBE, Mr. Ellwood took charge. Mr. Bibbiani continued as superintendent of the Refreshments Department and I became one of the longest-serving, remaining faces. Due to my experience, I was given a lot more freedom to manage my team and the service in our rooms.

Another change that was introduced was that staff of my grade or higher were allowed to bring up to four guests on a Friday into the Peer's Dining Room, but not many did.

When Sandra found out that I was turning forty at the start of the following year, she encouraged me to ask if I could use the Attlee, Hulme and Reid Rooms to host a party for my birthday and also for my mother who was turning sixty. To my amazement they said *yes*.

I carefully wrote out a guest list consisting of most of my family and some of my favourite Lords and ladies from within the House. I had invitations printed and embossed and sent out, with the official stamp, from the banqueting office.

A lot of the peers were busy with other engagements, but wrote very nice letters of apology for absence and best wishes. Maybe this was just as well as. In the case of my family, anyone who was remotely related to me or my mother, who were old friends of hers whom she hadn't seen in years, all accepted. They all wanted to experience the magic of Westminster. Second cousins, more than a bit removed, and people who hadn't seen me since I was a baby turned up. They all arrived on a chartered coach from Hampshire.

I was very fortunate to have all the members of my team who volunteered to come in and serve the party. We had a running buffet in the Reid Room and set up tables in the Attlee and the Hulme Rooms. Two of the doorkeepers: Tim Healey and Jumper Collins, offered to take visitors around the building on small guided tours, up to Big Ben and into the main chambers.

As well as hosting the party, it was my responsibility to introduce my family to some of the members and share some of my knowledge of who they were and what they had achieved.

In all there were about fifty guests. From the peerage, these included: Lord Ampthill, and Lord Williams of Elvel, who gave me a book he had written about Charles de Gaulle. He was married to Baroness Jane Portal who served as Churchill's private secretary. Her son, Justin Welby is the current (105th) Archbishop of Canterbury.

It was an honour to be joined by Lord John Richard Attlee, whose grandfather was Clement Attlee, the labour Prime Minister (1945-1951), whom the dining room we were using was named after. Although he looked like his grandfather he had no memories of him. He had the same, distinguishing moustache and had made his mark in the newly appointed Attlee Room by replacing a cartoon sketch of Clement, by Cummings (which he had hated), with a portrait from the family's private collection. The caricature was sent back to the National Gallery. I found out, after the party, that Earl Attlee was actually looking for a wife at that time. Had I known beforehand, perhaps one of my cousins could have been introduced as a potential suitor and improved my own family tree.

Lady Julia Cumberlege also came. She had recently campaigned for improved procedures for accommodating pregnant refugees seeking asylum, and was one of my favourite Conservative peers. She had quite a long journey as she lived in Lewes and was well-known in the building for always being nice to the staff.

The Baronesses Ruth Rendell and Jill Pitkeathley also came and my naughty brother, Paul, who was fascinated by the former's books, made it his mission to try and get them both tipsy on the steady flow of wine and champagne I supplied.

After the lunch, I gave a small speech and the lovely Luciano, who used to work with us, acted as Master of Ceremonies for the event. In his usual flamboyant style, he had decorated all of the pastries, including the beautiful birthday cake made by June, with lit sparklers. He presented *official* cards of merit from Buckingham Palace, where he now worked. In truth, these were large, garish cards he had bought from the Pound Shop, covered in photos of the

Royals, cut out from magazine clippings. With his great mound of coiffured hair and exaggerated hands, looking like Liberace, he beckoned us into the centre of the red carpet for a few special presentations. He even made my mother an M.B.E. medal (Mothers of the British Empire) out of a Persil powder box, with a length of cut washing line, and placed it over her head.

As my team were all working on the event it made it feel very special. It did feel a bit extravagant but it livened up a normally quiet Friday.

Near the end of the lunch, a lot of the Lords and ladies politely gave their thanks and slowly filtered away, out of the building or back to their offices or chamber.

As she was going, Ruth Rendell suddenly announced, in her recognisably high pitched voice, 'I seem to have lost my purse.' She stood looking up at the ceiling. 'Please can you help me find it.'

The whole family sprang into action. Nephews and Nieces crawled under the tablecloths to look for it under chairs and tables. Aunts and female cousins seemed to be checking their handbags to make sure it hadn't somehow fallen into them. I was embarrassed in case one of the visitors, who I didn't know well, had taken it. We searched for an hour but we couldn't find it.

Suddenly, whilst observing the crime scene, like a reporter gathering notes for a news story, she directed us to stop and dismissed herself, saying that she was feeling a bit dizzy.

The party continued for another couple of hours and then the family and remaining guests departed. My team and I needed to clear the dining rooms and set up for a private dinner which we would be serving afterwards. Just before I started service, a phone call was put through to me. It was Ruth.

'Robert, Robert. You must forgive me. I must tell you when I got home I found my purse on the little table in the hall. I feel so silly.'

I didn't mind. It was a relief.

When I later read a similar event described in one of her mystery novels, I often wondered if perhaps the act had been staged as research for her book.

9   POLISH IT UNDER THE TABLE

With spring around the corner, it's a great time to have a spring-clean in the garden. You need to clear, weed, plant and mulch in that order, before any new growth appears. General leaf debris and cuttings can be put into a composter, but dig out any diseased rhizomes and roots. These need to be burned, never mulched, so it's a good excuse to have a bonfire whilst the permit season is still effective.

As I drove over for a meeting at Simon and Steve's I chuckled to myself at the realization that I was going to become a White Van Man. The roads are pretty empty over here and with generous loans from the EU a lot of the area had benefitted from brand new roads and motorways. There is very little road rage. In fact, whereas the White Van Man in Britain pushes past you to get to his next job on time, and to meet unrealistic deadlines, their counterparts here drive slower than everyone else as if to say: *I don't rush when it's work.*

Unfortunately, this was never the preferred work ethic at the Pink Palace.

When I arrived there, Simon was pacing up and down, looking flustered. 'We're going to trim back the dead wood and focus on our big clients,' he told me, puffing on a cigar in his conservatory. 'The small ones just aren't worth the bother.'

Steve, who was cleaning the table, didn't agree with this. 'We can't put all our eggs in one basket, Simon.'

Simon started coughing from the smoke and bellowed, 'You don't even like eggs.' He turned to me and added, 'We had chickens back in the UK. Steve would feed and water them but a boiled or scrambled egg makes him sick.'

'Oh come one. That's not fair. I eat yer cakes, don't I?' He fanned some smoke away with his duster.

Simon nodded. 'Talking of cake. Bob can we offer you a cuppa and a slice of coffee and walnut?'

I looked at my watch. It was eight thirty in the morning. 'Sure,' I said. 'Thanks.'

The reason for the early morning meeting was that they wanted to give me first option on the *dead wood* they were trimming off their client books.

Despite Steve's protestations, it was Simon who wore the trousers and made the final decisions. He told his skinny counterpart that there were ten bags of washing which needed to be put into the machines and Steve duly ran downstairs to the laundry.

'You can have the Pratts, for starters,' he told me, cutting a big wedge of cake. He must have seen me smirking. 'Yes, that is their name and their nature, I'm afraid.'

'Thanks,' I said, both for the cake and the new clients. I didn't care what they were called as long as they gave me some paid work.

'Ah, that is a good bake.' He had filled his mouth with the light brown sponge and was catching some crumbs as they fell out. 'It's only a couple of hours but we also need to use you for their cleaning.'

A lump of cake caught on the back of my throat and I started choking.

'Have a swig of your tea,' he said, pushing my mug forwards.

The tea was scalding hot and made it worse. I coughed out the cake onto my hand and put it back on the plate. 'Sometimes I bite off more than I can chew,' I said, without explaining my double meaning. The idea of cleaning was not palatable. I wanted to be a gardener, not a cleaner. However, he made it clear that if I wanted their garden, I had to do the cleaning as well.

'You can do the Murrells', too.'

172

Steve had overheard him and came running into the room, face flushed. 'No way,' he said. 'Gerry and Pauline are like family to me.'

I picked up a smaller piece of the cake and continued eating. 'I don't want to cause any problems.'

Steve folded his arms and stared at us.

'Steve, you won't have time. Not with the new Sun Ray Villa contract.'

He put his hands behind his head and then thumped them on the table. 'I'll make time.'

'We'll see,' his older partner humoured him.

'Simon.' He was seething and started frothing through the large gaps in his teeth. 'I need to talk to you. In private.'

I quickly finished my cake. It was time to leave.

Simon stood up. 'Bob, stay. You don't need to go.'

'It's fine. I need to meet Graham. We're supposed to be finally picking up the van.'

As I left, I could hear Steve shouting and screaming at his partner. It felt good to be getting more work but not at the expense of someone's relationship. Also, I vowed, that I didn't want to take on too many clients. The idea was to have a good life in the sun, not a stressful one.

When we got down to Jesus's, the garage was closed.

'It must be *siesta*,' I said to Graham.

He checked his watch. 'It's only nine thirty. Have you got his phone number?'

The receipt was in my back pocket and I dialled the number printed on the top. No answer.

We went back down at eleven and were met with the same

closed doors.

'This is ridiculous,' I snapped, feeling stressed.

Graham looked over at the *venta* at the end of the road. 'Let's go and have a beer.'

It seemed like a better solution than pacing up and down.

As soon as we sat down, my phone rang. 'Roberto? It's Jesus. Are you wanting your van or not?'

'*Si*, señor,' I replied.

'Please you be coming now. I have to be coming out again soon.'

'*Si, si*. I'm on way.' I hung up.

Graham had finished his small caña. 'What's happening?'

I pushed my chair in. 'Jesus is there but he is *coming out soon*.'

'What did I tell you? I knew he was gay.'

I swiped him with the receipt papers. 'You coming then?'

He shook his head. 'No. You're the gardener, not me. Down to you now.'

'But the steering wheel's on the other side.' My face and the back of my neck felt hot.

He took another swig and grabbed my full beer glass. 'That's cos we live in Spain. *Salud!*' He raised the glass, as I slowly left.

I found the van, parked just inside the open metal gates. It looked even better than before, almost newer.

Inevitably, picking it up took a lot longer than it should have done. I was coaxed back into the office, given innumerable explanations for the delay to the repairs, offered another glass of rum, told that Antonio had now been replaced by Alejandro and then finally received the keys. I had spotted a very handsome black-haired man with a thick, clipped beard. He looked more like he had wandered off the front cover of *Men's Health* magazine than had started working in a backstreet garage.

'You must be remembering that the ITV is being every six months and you must be going to the hall of the town to pay the tax.'

By the time I left, my head was swirling with all his information. He and Alejandro had a good laugh as I opened the front door on the right-hand-side and discovered the passenger seat. I put the paperwork in the glove compartment and coolly walked around to the drivers' side.

Once I found the ignition, the engine started first time. It rattled a bit more than before, but I guessed that was due to the new pieces installed. '*Adiós*,' I shouted and pulled the gear stick into reverse. It wouldn't move. I revved harder; exhaust fumes began filling the workshop.

Jesus waved his hand and walked back towards his office. 'Alex, *le ayudas!*'

The model walked through the carbon monoxide mist to help me. I felt so stupid. He effortlessly leaned across, pulled the gear knob up and pushed it into position. Fortunately, my foot was still on the clutch.

Very red-faced, I gingerly reversed the van onto the pavement, missed the oncoming traffic and slowly pulled away. I drove it down towards Graham.

'Finally,' he yelled, standing up. 'Now, take it for a spin. Get used to it.'

Secretly I was cursing him for not helping me, but he is the eternal teacher. He knew that the only way I learn things is to be thrown in at the deep end.

I took the van up to our house and was enjoying it so much that I continued on to the roundabout and took the empty road down towards Fuengirola. The engine was far more powerful than the Kia and, as I swerved along the mountain hillside, I felt like I was playing a driving game on a computer. It flew down the hills.

It didn't have much fuel, so I pulled into the petrol station, wrestled with the fuel cap and reminded myself to fill her with diesel. She took forty-five euros worth.

When I got back to the house, Graham had parked the car at the edge of the driveway so that I could manoeuvre the van up by the house and put all my tools inside.

It was great to have so much space. I got all my tools inside, even the stepladder and there was still an empty roof rack I could use.

Graham had bought a cheap bottle of Cava, tied a piece of string around the neck and gently swung the bottle so that it clipped the top of bonnet. 'Ladies and Gentlemen. I give you the official launch of The Garden Butler.'

I gave a short acceptance speech to him and the dog.

It seemed like this dream of a new business in the sun was gradually turning into a happy reality.

The next day I drove down to the Pratts' to meet Duncan and Elena.

They lived in Fuengirola in a small, mustard-coloured house behind The Miramar Shopping Centre. As I pulled up the steep driveway, I could see that an old mannequin had been playfully placed in the porchway next to the front door. It had clearly been rescued from the depths of a closed department store, which had gone out of fashion, or discovered at the local car boot sale. The figure was of a tall woman, probably from the nineteen fifties, although the overall look was somewhat confused. It was modelling an old fashioned floral print dress, in greens and purples, but the hair was too sharp and severe: more Annie Lennox than Doris Day.

Thin, white, alabaster arms were folded over each other, below a flat bosom, with the head tilted slightly back to depict an air of sophistication. It could also have been a reaction to the thick smell of sewerage I discovered as I closed the van door.

I decided to play along with the scene. 'Good morning to you,

176

my lady.' I bowed my head.

'And a good afternoon to you,' a voice shrieked above me.

I jumped up and saw the figure had become animated and was pointing at her watch. 'You're three minutes late!'

She sounded so fierce and her gaze and expression were so hard that I felt nervous, like a naughty schoolboy in the headmistress's office. 'You must be Elaine,' I said and held my hand out to shake.

She ignored it. 'I am Elena. Are you very train-ed in zee world of gardens?' she demanded, as I climbed up the steps to their house.

I was impressed that she had worked out that I was the new gardener. 'Yees,' I replied, unintentionally echoing her East European-sounding accent.

She looked down and kicked a fallen rose head off the path and into a flower bed.

The flowers all looked extremely dry and parched. Some were beyond the realms of Tutankhamen's journey into the Underworld but others, I believed, could be resuscitated and brought back to life. 'I see you have a problem with the irrigation,' I said, looking up at her.

'Don't give me problems. Give me solutions.' With that she turned around, stepped inside the house and slammed the front door.

Nice to meet you too, I wanted to say.

Without any instructions, I looked around to see what needed to be done. José had taught me that the most important parts of the garden are the areas the owners see most often. He told me to always make sure the plants and borders next to the front door were neat and tidy and that the edges of the paths were well presented.

The Pratts' garden was a simple layout of four borders at the front arranged either side of a path which led up to a gate and onto a pool and patio on the same level as the house.

Irrigation can be a constant source of trouble in Spain. There are so many systems ranging from a single hose with a clockwork timer to a complex system of pipes and valves which would look more at home on a life support system in a hospital than a garden watering operation.

The sprinklers here had been placed too far away from the plants. I decided to pull the whole thing up, relay it and insert some new, additional heads. A few months before I could never have entertained doing this, but José had taught me how, and this had given me newfound confidence. 'It's just water and *plástico,*' he had told me.

There was an old wisteria hanging over a pergola by the pool that had been left for years and became my next project. These need to be trimmed back twice a year in Spain. Look for thin stems that were produced last year and cut these back to short spurs 2-3 buds from the base to encourage flowering. Tie in any shoots that have appeared at the bottom or remove if you are creating a standard.

I was only contracted to do two hours a week, but I often got so involved in the gardening, that I ran over time.

'You still here?' A kinder, man's voice, with a public school accent asked, from inside the back door. 'I'm Duncan,' he announced. 'You must be Rob.'

I looked up from the dustbin sacks I had been filling with cuttings. 'Good to meet you. I needed to take a lot off that wisteria,' I told him.

He walked out to inspect the result and put his hands on his rounded hips. 'Good job, my man.' He walked around to the other side of the huge bush and spoke through the twisted stems. 'You've done a good job there.'

'Cheers,' I said, still clearing up.

Duncan came back around to the other side and stood over me. 'It was a pretty little thing when I first bought it. But then it took hold, planted its feet in and took over.' He sighed and looked back towards the house. 'A bit like the misses,' he added and grunted, snorting through his flattened nose.

I didn't respond to this.

'I would give you a hand, old chap, but bad back, I'm afraid.' He stretched his tubby body into an arch and put his hands on the base of his spine. His hair and moustache were a light ginger colour and his blue eyes looked a bit watery, beneath a pair of thick rimmed glasses which were covered in greasy smudges. 'Right, better get on. Got another charity do to organise at the golf club.'

From inside the house, Frau Pratt yelled from the recess of the hallway. 'Phone for you Duncan. Tell the garden man to go now. We're not paying extra!'

'Any chance you could trim her back to a manageable size,' he chortled. 'Thanks a lot, Rob. See you next week and we'll pay up front for the rest of the month.'

I tied up the last of the sacks. 'Actually, I'm back on Friday afternoon, with Steve to do the cleaning for you.'

He rubbed his face. 'Oh yes. Of course. Good luck with that,' he said and disappeared inside.

On my way home, I needed to call in at the Snipes', to cut the grass, check the irrigation and pool level and water some of the pots. It didn't surprise me that they were still away. They had gone back to their country estate in Surrey for New Year and wouldn't be out again until Easter.

As I parked up outside Casa de Imogen, and sorted through the sets of keys I had started amassing from the different clients, in the glove compartment, my mobile bleeped. It was a text from Abigail.

When you next visit, please take away the old sunbeds stored in the pump house. Imogen and some girlfriends are coming over for a few days next week and I'm having some new furniture delivered. Abi.

It seemed an amazing coincidence that she had sent it just as I was arriving.

I decided to tackle Mount Verde and cut the grass first. I thought it would get easier, as I got used to it. It didn't.

There was no short cut to carrying the lawnmower down the steps on the left side, pushing it across the terrace and then lifting it to the top of the grassy slope. At least, once I was back at the top, on the other side, the cutting was all downhill.

The garden was looking really good. Two of the borders were a mass of colour. These osteospermums had balls of dark-green foliage and daisy-like flowers in deep-purple and white.

Whilst the sun shone brightly but quite softly on my face, I noticed that there was snow on the mountain beyond the golf course, where a few electric carts buzzed, slowly, over the green, like early pollen-drunk bees searching for nectar.

Not bad for February, I thought.

After watering the new hibiscus hedge I had planted at the bottom a few weeks ago, I went into the pump house. Stacked in the far corner, there were four white plastic sunbeds, a patio table and four chairs. The moulding had dried out a bit, but they were still in great condition. I was worried that she had made a mistake but there was no other furniture in here.

I dragged the collection outside and, even in the sunshine, they looked good. Carrying them up in as few trips as possible, I lugged the pieces up the tower of steps and stacked them inside the van. There was no way these were heading for the skip; they would look very nice around our own pool.

Just as I was about to get back into the van, my phone bleeped again.

Don't forget the parasol base, a new text read. *It's on the terrace near the pool shower.*

I looked up at the windows. Was she hiding indoors? All the metal shutters were down but perhaps she was peeping through the gaps. I ambled over to the car port but it was empty.

As I climbed back down the steps, I heard a further mechanical whirring which was much closer than the golf-course. One of the elevated security cameras had swung round to face me. I was being watched. At first I felt quite shocked, even embarrassed. But as I walked down and retrieved the stand, I felt annoyed and mistrusted. It was bizarre to think that the little Kiwi woman was perched somewhere in her English nest, in the lush confines of a mansion in leafy Surrey, spying on me.

It was very tempting to show her a finger or drop my trousers and give her an eyeful, but I needed the money and was enjoying the work. My face blushed with the sudden realization that she had probably seen it already. A couple of weeks ago I had been caught short by drinking too much water and had had to relieve myself, in a hidden corner, next to one of the flower beds. The spot was in clear view of camera number two.

I told the story to my favourite clients, Janet and John. They just laughed and John added, 'If she wants to see a real show, she should stick a camera in here.'

They told me how they had been to a great naturist resort near Estepona, last July.

'It was great fun just to hang out and relax.' John told me, whilst repairing the cable to the hot-tub that the dogs had chewed.

'What about Eleanor?' I asked.

He tightened the join between the wires. 'No. She'd have melted.'

'Stop it John,' Janet said. She sounded annoyed.

Shorty made me jump, as he came up behind me and started licking the back of my legs.

John stood up and winked at her. 'You enjoyed the volleyball. Didn't you, love?'

'Not as much as you did,' Janet laughed, looking down at the swollen bosom beneath her low-cut t-shirt. 'It's alroit for you,' she told him. 'These bad-boy-puppies nearly knocked me out.'

John walked over and kissed her. 'I'm a lucky man Rob.'

She pretended to be embarrassed. 'Ah get away with you. You're all hot and sweaty.'

He ran over to the swimming pool with his dirty shirt and shorts still on. He did an impressive dive bomb into the water and spun himself from side-to-side. After a couple of minutes he pulled himself out using the steps, shook himself and said, 'There we go. That's the washing done for this week.' The water must have been freezing.

She pretended to be angry. 'Unbelievable,' she said.

'Oh, come on you love it. How's about another kiss?' He started running towards her.

She turned and hurried back towards the house. 'Get away,' she cried.

'You love it!' he replied and the two of them disappeared inside, laughing loudly.

After planting a new pittosporum hedge, along the far edge of the pool, to block the neighbour's house out, I drove back home. On my way I spotted a cane sofa and chair which had been dumped by the communal bins and loaded them into the van. It was great to have all this extra space.

That afternoon, I drove over to meet Steve for the Pratts' monthly clean.

He was waiting outside their gates and called me over, before we went in. 'Just to warn you, it's always a pig sty in there,' he said, loudly enough for them to hear him.

I locked up my van. 'Really?' I said, more quietly.

He pulled a Henry hoover out of his transit. 'She's a dirty bitch. Never picks up anything.'

I was cringing, afraid that they might have heard him.

'And he just sits in his office, like the Lord Mayor, organising people for his next charity events. He won't get up. The office is full of shit and you just have to clean around him.'

He passed me some buckets and bottles of cleaning liquids and put on his old Quicksilver baseball cap. I followed him to the front door.

'Right, let's go and muck out the pigs,' he snarled, putting on a new pair of blue rubber gloves.

Elena let us in, wearing another pristine floral dress, this time in orange and white. It looked like it had just come back from the dry-cleaners. Her immaculate appearance of an efficient housewife belied the dire state of her dwelling.

t was gloomy inside. All the windows, shutters and curtains were closed. The rooms were lit by dimmed ceiling lights and lots of small table lamps and the strip of a white, fluorescent bulb that buzzed from the kitchen. There was black dog hair all over the carpets. Piles of shoes and jackets had been discarded in the hallway, as if someone had thrown them on the floor as soon as they had come in and left them there.

'You can start by hanging those up, Bob,' Steve told me. 'What a mess,' he said, with Elena only a few feet away.

She walked past us and over to the front door. 'I'm just heading out to the hairdressers, but I'll be back soon.' She flicked her hand in the air, in dismissal and left the door open.

Steve marched over and slammed it closed. 'Lazy bitch.' He grabbed some kitchen cleanser and headed off to the left. 'You dust and hoover the bedrooms, Bob,' he yelled. 'I'll meet you in the bathrooms.'

'Sure,' I said, still placing the shoes back on the racks. The bedrooms were at the far end of the hall. There was a small guest room on the left, the main bathroom, and the main bedroom on the far right, at the end of another corridor. Between these was another small room, with the door open. Beneath columns of paperwork and old magazines, Duncan was sat in front of a big monitor, with a full headset and microphone. He was barking commands to a grey man on the other side of the screen, like he was an air traffic controller directing a wayward plane.

'Tom, I need you to you sort out more chairs. Bloody Charlie's gone sailing again and left it down to us chaps. Cheeky blighter.' His voice was loud but friendly sounding. He noticed my reflection in his screen. 'Just a minute, Tom.' He placed his headset down. 'Hello, Rob. Very busy morning. Don't mind me. Just give it a quick flick over in here. Don't bother much. There's a good chap.'

Before I could respond, he had re-engaged in his video call, so I took care to creep around him, lifting and dusting, the piles of paperwork, trying to not to mess up any of their chaotic order. He pushed himself back, so I could wipe the screen, and continued talking. I felt very awkward. After about ten minutes, he shook his hand and told me, 'that'll do.'

'Do you want me to close the door?'

He didn't look back at me. 'What? No, no. Leave it open. What was I saying, Tom? Oh yes, about that auction next month.'

I grabbed my cleaning tools and headed down to the main bedroom. The whole room was littered with dirty underwear which had been thrown on the floor. Heaps of dried out contact lenses, which crunched under my feet, had been dropped from the bed. There was far too much furniture, crammed into every space of the room, covered in more dirt and rubbish. What this place needed was a bomb squad, or preferably, a large bonfire. I shot through the detritus with the hoover, polish and duster like Taz the Tasmanian Devil, having a meltdown in a Looney Tunes cartoon.

Half an hour later, Steve called me into the en-suite. 'You need to slow down a bit. We're supposed to be here for three hours,' he told me.

I looked over at the pile of soiled towels dumped by the bath tub. There was a framed drawing of a caricature of Her Majesty The

Queen, sat on a throne, in full coronation robes sat on a throne, with a bent sceptre, hung over the toilet. Underneath were the words, *If it's brown, flush it down, if it's yellow then it's mellow.* Although I appreciated the effort to conserve water, the picture was in very poor taste.

For the first time, since leaving the U.K., I wished I was back there. I had moved over here to be a gardener and had not worked as a cleaner since filling in for the contractors in the House of Lords when they failed to show up.

***

When I first started in the House of Lords, there was a team of dedicated cleaners, including a pair of twin sisters. The team took great pride in their work and the palace was always spotless. Inevitably, after a change in management who wanted to cut costs, they were all made redundant and replaced by contract cleaners who rarely turned up when they were supposed to. Often they would arrive late, so me and my team would have to quickly grab a hoover and duster and give our rooms a quick flick over before the parties started.

In the 1970's an inventory was made of all the furniture inside the House of Lords. There were found to be over a thousand original pieces of about three hundred different functional types. Most of these were designed by Augustus Welby Pugin. After Barry won the competition in 1835 to redesign the palace of Westminster, he realized that he needed a gifted assistant to realize his extravagant plans. He chose Pugin who was only 23 years old but had devoted his career to Gothic architecture and was paid £400 by Barry to help him with drawing up his plans. Barry became very reliant on his younger counterpart and in fact Pugin took responsibility for the detailed design of the superb interiors including the wood carvings, panelling, gilt work, stained glass, upholstery and also the furniture. In every room and in multiple materials and aspects, the legacy of Pugin lives on.

One of his most notable achievements within the palace was the Royal Throne and elaborate canopy in the House of Lords' Chamber, carved from mahogany and completely covered in a sunburst of gold leaf. He also revived the distinct portcullis emblem of Westminster which was emblazoned on every chair, thousands of floor tiles and ceiling decorations, and incorporated into the rich design of the Clerk's Table in the Prince's Chamber. The sumptuous Lord's library carved from oak and much of the metal work throughout the buildings, including the door hinges, were all designed by Pugin.

I was very fortunate to see and serve The Queen and members of the Royal Family on many occasions. In addition to the twenty-one State Openings of Parliament that I provided service, one of the most memorable was the anniversary of the Privy Council. My team and I had to re-organise the furniture and transform the Robing Room and the Royal Gallery into dining rooms. On one side of the Royal Gallery, Her Majesty The Queen was seated and on the other H.R.H. The Duke of Edinburgh.

Prince Charles and his party were served on a series of round tables placed inside his mother's Robing Room. I always found him quite entertaining and fascinating. When I presented him with a basket of bread rolls, he smiled and said to me, 'How very exciting.' The Prince of Wales was sat with the Welsh Labour politician, Cledwyn Hughes. It has been well documented that Hughes was a close friend and a reliable counsellor to Charles. Since the main role of the Privy Council is to give advice to the Sovereign of the United Kingdom, their happy company seemed auspicious to this occasion. One of its main duties is to confer the Royal Seal of Approval to companies and institutions which are considered worthy.

I heard Charles say to Cledwyn, 'I'm not sure they (the people) are going to want me to ever be king. Do you think it will end with mummy?'

He just put his hand on Charles's shoulder and smiled, and they continued to admire Martha, one of the very pretty, black kitchen porters from the Caribbean who was attending to them.

One member of the Royal family who had received the Royal Charter was Princess Margaret's son, David Armstrong-Jones, The Viscount Linley. This was affirmed during another occasion when I served Her Majesty at a dinner party in the Attlee room, hosted by Lord and Lady Westbury who were close friends of the Royals. He was very distinguished-looking and charismatic; reminiscent of the actor Howard Keel with his classic platinum-white moustache. During his years of celebrated military service, Lord Westbury, then Lieutenant David Bethell, was famous for receiving punishing shrapnel wounds in his chest and hand, dismissing himself from hospital and returning to the front line, to take back command of his platoon, and then leading them to an enemy machinegun post and successfully capturing it.

In his post-military career, he was popular for his charming personality and engaging sense of humour; joking that he kept escaping death, even from the Pharaoh's curse which had claimed his father and grandfather. The Honourable Richard Bethell, his father, was a keen Egyptologist and was with Howard Carter at the opening of Tutankhamen's Tomb in 1922.

Lord Westbury had a great talent for public relations and was appointed as PR Officer for Moet Chandon in Britain and latterly for some of the top London hotels, including the Ritz and Dukes. As an ebullient entertainer he attracted the company of many famous personalities and was deeply respected for his fundraising efforts for charities, such as St. John's Ambulance, whereby he raised more than £10 million pounds. As a good friend of the Royals, they would arrange to meet up somewhere new, whenever their diaries allowed. On this occasion it was the brand new Attlee Room and Committee Room G. These had previously been used to accommodate the dowdy-looking HQ for Parliamentary Security, with its bank of telephones and dull, municipal furniture. The decision was made to relocate these to Canon Row police station. The two rooms were transformed into Pugin-styled rooms with detailed replicas of his wallpapers and textiles; new furniture was commissioned by Princess Margaret's son, The Viscount Linley, who had a gift for replicating Pugin's style. Once the refurbishment had been completed, these two new entertaining areas looked like they had been there for years.

About a week before the dinner party, a palace official came and said that queen loved lamb, so the menu was constructed to include lamb cutlets. The Southeast Return, which housed the restaurant, was given special security lock down. We set up Committee Room G as a bar area with some soft, antique chairs brought down from the Lords' Library.

187

Princess Margaret came in with The Queen who was wearing a beautiful peach coloured dress, with semi-precious stones inlaid in the fabric. It was going to be one of her outfits for the Australian tour the following week and she seemed to be test-driving it on home territory before wearing it abroad. Princess Margaret led her, excitedly, into the Attlee Room but the dress seemed heavy and she was only able to follow her slowly.

Princess Margaret walked over to one of the new Lindley tables and lifted the table cloth. 'Do look at the table legs. He's used two different in-laid woods,' she told her sister.

'I'm not getting down there Margaret,' she replied. 'I'm sure it's all very splendid but I may never get back up again.'

They both laughed, took seats back in the Committee Room and The Queen had a dry Martini cocktail.

I remember that it was a laid back dinner with about fifteen diners. The Queen was enjoying herself, looked relaxed and was laughing and joking a lot.

It was funny for me too as it was *butler service* which takes much longer. You have to try and gauge the correct pace as you present the platters with tongs and forks, so the guests can choose the items and place them on the plates themselves, whilst continuing conversation with other members of the party. Sometimes the serving instruments are used more like a conductor's baton, waved in animated expression to emphasise a point being made, and you have to duck out of the way.

Dessert was a marmite of different sorbets for The Queen to select. After presenting these to Her Majesty for approval, I took them over to the dumb waiter and had to crack the nougat casings, put all the bits to the side, and then ask her which colours she preferred. She picked out two with a small piece of the cracked lid.

After the dinner they had drinks. The Queen was enjoying a glass of dry, white wine and Princess Margaret was finishing her whisky. When Lord Westbury ordered me to get another drink for Margaret, I brought one over and tried to remove the empty glass.

She grabbed it back and yelled, 'No, no, it's not finished yet.' She waved me away with her hand, put the old glass back down next to the full one and sighed.

Before the party left, Lord Westbury got us to open the gift shop to get The Queen an enormous box of chocolates to take home with her. The only sad thing was that, when the Royal sisters requested to go up onto the principal floor and take a peek into the House of Lords' Chamber and Library, whilst there was no one else around, Black Rod refused, due to a lack of security clearance. It was at moments like this this that you realize the lack of freedom privilege sometimes affords.

***

My own sense of freedom of living in Southern Spain was being compromised by Elena Pratt. Steve had quit the cleaning and I was left to do it. Unfortunately, each time I did it, she stayed in the house drinking coffee and reading her *Ideal Homes* magazines, and I had to keep asking her to move whilst I cleared up, around her. She never thanked me and would always check if I had forgotten anything. She was obsessed with the bathrooms and insistent that I got every speck of lime scale off the tiles and taps. She went on and on about it. In the end I decided to go down to my local ferreteria to get something powerful for removing the lime scale and was very proud to show her my chemical warfare. In addition to the lime scale it also removed the silver plating on their cheap taps and it was decided that my cleaning days for them were over. Like a naughty dog, I was banished outside, to the garden.

In a way it was a relief and I felt that my freedom had been restored. That was until I got home and discovered three speeding fines for 300 euros from the Spanish *Trafico* Police.

10   OUT WITH THE OLD

At the beginning of March, interest in my advertisement suddenly peaked. I was becoming more experienced to finding out what people needed and always offered to go over and give a free estimate first. Sometimes the enquiries were from Spanish people and the call soon ended once we realized we couldn't understand each other. Other times they came from too far away. I was happy to travel as far west as Málaga and east as Marbella, but needed to keep my fuel costs down by servicing a realistic area.

One good lead I got was from a very posh sounding lady, with a young voice, who was called Claudia Dunn. She lived down on the coast in Mijas Costa which was only twenty minutes from our house. Her voice on the phone had been very warm and polite and she told me to pull up onto the driveway when I arrived. It wasn't far from the Snipes', so I organised to come and see her after working in the Garden of Death.

With the help of my trusted satnav, I eventually found her house, *Villa des Pinos* on a side street, off the main A7, overlooking a busy gym. Before I pressed the buzzer, I noticed the main gates had already been opened and I drove through the wide entrance and onto a crumbling bricked driveway.

There was no sign of the lady of the house, but the front door was wide open, with a locked metal railing gate providing security. Dance music, which sounded like Kylie Minogue, with a very upbeat tempo, was emanating from nearby.

'Hello. Anyone there?' I called through the railings.

All the windows were open but fortified by strong iron bars across the edge of their frames.

I tried walking around the side, calling through the windows, but, again, no answer. There was a stairwell leading up to the main body of the house, with a covered terrace, but that seemed too private to intrude. Perhaps she was doing her daily workout?

As I walked around to the back of the house, I was distracted by the music becoming louder and the vision of a dozen fit, muscled bodies pulsing and grinding behind a large picture window, beyond the canopies of about two dozen pine trees which edged the garden.

'Aren't they fine specimens?' The voice I had heard on the phone said, from behind me.

I was embarrassed but made a quick recovery. 'Yes, they're the native Spanish pines, aren't they?' I turned around and found that the owner of the voice was entirely different from what I had imagined. Instead of a young, athletic woman, was a frail-looking elderly lady, with waves of white-grey hair and bluish grey eyes beneath a pair of spectacles. She was sat near the pool, at one of three wrought iron patio tables, on one of the many chairs and was laughing.

'No, not the pesky trees, those beautiful creatures up there.' She pointed up to the gym window.

I nodded in agreement and smiled.

As I walked over to the table and took the seat she had offered, a tall, bronzed Scandinavian guy with shiny blonde hair, stopped exercising and leaned out of the window to cool off. I gasped, involuntarily.

'I'll take one of those to go,' the lady chuckled. 'But don't bother to wrap it.' Her eyes twinkled, gleefully.

I took an instant liking to her. She reminded me of my grandmother and it felt I had known her for years. 'Too right,' I said. 'Maybe they do home delivery?'

She laughed again, introduced herself as Claudia and began pouring tea into two fine bone china tea cups, with a delicate red rose pattern and matching saucers. Her hand was sure and steady. 'Let's get two. One for me and one for you.'

'I can see why you moved here.' I helped myself to milk and sugar and stirred it in.

After she took a small sip from her cup, she sat back and her face became more serious. 'To be honest, Robert, everything's changed. Is *Robert* alright or do you prefer Rob?'

'Robert's fine.'

'Please help yourself to a custard cream. What was I saying?' She looked up at the sky to regather her thoughts. 'Oh yes. The gym wasn't here when Gordon and I moved in. In fact none of that line of shops was here. There was only us and one other villa.' She paused, filtering the memories that were flowing through her mind. 'So many changes. Too many changes.' She took a big gulp of her tea, wiped her nose with a handkerchief, which had been tucked inside the sleeve of her cardigan and found her smile again. 'What can you do? It's life.'

After the tea, she walked me around the garden. She explained that her husband had died six months ago and that she wanted to get the garden back to looking neat and tidy. It seemed that she had somehow managed to pull on some deep inner strength, her voice sounded calm and cool and there were no further sniffles. They had always enjoyed doing the garden together, but nowadays she kept falling over and couldn't manage it on her own.

The garden was laid out in a square that wrapped around the base of the elevated house. All the borders were overgrown, the pool was cloudy and a lot of the old terracotta tiles were stained with green-black mildew and damp. 'I can soon clean these up with my jet washer,' I reassured her.

'I tried scrubbing them with some soda and bleach but can't seem to shift it.'

It became clear that she felt everything was slipping away from her and that if I could help her reclaim the garden, she might feel like she was regaining some control in her life.

The main difficulty in this garden was the pine trees. What she and her husband hadn't realized was that they are very strictly protected by the Spanish authorities and that the needles drop throughout the year and cause no end of problems. Large sections of turf were receding due to a lack of sunlight from the canopies and layers of their invasive debris. She still wanted to do some of the gardening, so I agreed to help her to rake them up, bag them up and take them off site. Also I would cut back the hedges and dig over the borders to get the whole garden back to how it used to be.

'I know it's only a garden,' she sighed. 'But it meant a lot to me and Gordon and I just don't want to lose anything else.'

I gave her a hug and said, 'It's not just a garden. It's your garden and you can have it any way you want.'

We agreed that I would do three hours a week on Wednesdays and as I drove out through the gates, which shut behind me automatically, sealing the lonely widower inside, the realization hit me: *It was so much more than just a garden.*

I knew that this was a job I would look forward to doing every week.

As I continued around the corner, I saw that my mobile was flashing from a message that had been left. I pulled over and dialled the mail box.

'Yes. Hello. You there?' There was a pause in the recording. 'Right, name is Richard. I need a new gardener. Can you come today? I'm in Marbella, in El Rosario near the international tennis centre. Flying back to the UK tomorrow.' The line had gone dead. He hadn't left his number but I managed to retrieve it from the *missed calls* folder and called him back.

His house was only fifteen minutes from Claudia's, so I agreed to meet him half an hour later, to give me sufficient time to find it.

It never fails to surprise me how much the neighbourhoods and their inhabitants vary within a short distance, on the Costa Del Sol. As I came off the busy dual carriageway, that links Málaga, Fuengirola and Marbella together, there was a steep, narrow, lane which led through an avenue of trees with a series of sharp bends. Dispersed along this route were impressive, bespoke, individual dwellings which ranged from Mock Tudor styled mansions to Art Deco inspired town houses and newly created white blocked villas, with the statutory excess of glass balconies, glass curtains and huge picture windows and, of course, that much needed infinity pool.

The house I was looking for was number 127 and was at the bottom of the hill on the left hand side. It was hidden behind a high white wall with several deep purple bougainvillea which had been neatly trained along a spider's web of wire.

Set into the wall were a huge pair of solid wooden gates, with a smaller inset door in one of the panels. I pressed the buzzer and before anyone answered, the small door flew open and a tall, confident man, with a shiny face and thinning blonde hair, stepped through and grabbed my hand and shook it very firmly. 'Richard. Richard Harrington-Smythe. Perhaps you've heard of us? Chartered accountants.'

Before I could answer he had delved inside his suit jacket pocket and thrust a business card into my throbbing hand. The only casual aspect of his appearance was the pair of blue denim jeans he was wearing.

'Don't just stand there,' he added, and stepped back through the door. 'We don't bite. Come and have a look around.'

Dutifully I followed him in and onto a newly laid flagstone driveway, where there were several expensive looking cars. I don't know much about cars but reading the emblems of Porsche, Audi and Land Rover Discovery it was clear that there was several thousands of pounds worth of vehicles here.

'Follow me,' he said. 'What I need is it all cutting right back.' He pointed to a border of well-trimmed lantana bushes. As we proceeded to the back of the house, which had recently been repainted in a pale blue colour, there was a magical avenue of shade, created by long throngs of established palms which gently bowed down on either side. 'All this needs clearing, right back.' He smacked one of the offending branches out of his path as if he was cutting his way through rainforest. 'Last chap was bloody useless. Only stayed three months and bugger knows what he actually did.'

We emerged from the tree tunnel and back into brilliant sunshine on the far side of the property. This was mainly laid with lawn, which was very patchy, with clusters of decaying pine trees. 'I told him, I wanted all this dug up and new turf laid. He just kept cutting it every week, without raking up the needles. Bloody useless.' His face was becoming redder. 'I need someone who just uses his own initiative.'

'Can you get rid of those?' he pointed up to the pine trees. They were over two hundred feet high.

'No. Aren't they protected?' I felt small and inadequate in this man's presence.

'Don't worry about that. Got a good friend in the town hall. Can you do it?'

'No,' I repeated, feeling smaller. 'You'll need a tree surgeon. I just do maintenance.'

He had started walking along the grass, kicking some of the needles off the receding areas. 'That's a bugger. No matter.' He had marched over to the far wall which was covered in mature, twisted vines of wisteria and Argentinian trumpet vine. Patches of dark green and brilliant orange from the flowering flame vines broke up the woody branches and half a dozen bushes of jasmine were budding up getting ready to flower. There was a faint smell from large clusters of denoche plants. They look a lot like privet bushes, but have thin feathers of white blooms which give a heavenly scent in the evenings.

Richard walked over and kicked one of them. 'I want all this old cut down. Just use your initiative. I'm sure you can see what needs doing.'

I couldn't believe what I was hearing. 'All of it?'

'Yes. All the hedging. Too messy and it just takes over.' He strode across to the other side of the lawn, which was about 30 feet wide and over to a raised border of roses and hibiscus. 'I want all these out and just put in some succulents or even better, cacti. At least those will keep Nicole's bloody cats from digging and shitting everywhere.'

He walked back toward the front and stopped beside an old kidney-shaped swimming pool with pale green tiles. 'You do pools?'

'Yes, no problem. Where's the pump house?'

He pointed over to some steps descending down the side of the house. 'It's over there. Gwyn can you show you when you start.'

My face revealed my surprise. I thought we were still negotiating. 'So you're happy for me to do your garden?'

'Yes. I need six hours per week. Three on Mondays and three on Thursdays. The same day as the housekeeper. Advert said ten euros per hour?'

'Yes,' I nodded.

'Right, then. I'm away for a while. You won't see much of me and Nicole. Let's keep it tidy, you can start the first Monday of next month. Be here at nine and Gwyn will let you in and give you a key. Gotta get on. See yourself out. Good to get is sorted.' He grabbed my hand to seal the deal and walked back inside.

As I got back inside the car, I realized that I had only said about a dozen or so words during the whole meeting. Fortunately, I wasn't usually working on Monday and Thursday mornings and would make sure I was there on time to start clearance duties. If he was hardly ever there, it should be easy; provided that the housekeeper wasn't a monster.

It did seem a shame to rip out all those beautiful, old specimens without anything substantial to replace them.

***

Before Tony Blair came into power, one of our regulars, Lord Longford, during one of his weekly complaints about the rising price of his omelette, asked me what I thought about things. 'So, Robert. What do you think of our Mister Blair?'

I had already given this much thought. 'I think, Lord Longford that he has been packaged and sold to us like a new brand of baked beans.'

'How so? Lot of hot air that'll give us wind?'

I laughed. 'Like a tinned product that is new and good for Britain. Really it's just the same stuff that has been repackaged from the Conservative government, sold as Labour, but with only a few new ingredients.'

Lord Longford took me by the hand and said, 'Give the boy a chance. Give the boy a chance. He's a good Christian.'

Boy was a good description. At age 43, he was our youngest PM in history, apart from William Pitt, The Younger who became PM in 1783 at the age of 24. The main problem was that Blair wasn't really a politician. He was a radical barrister who had become PM by default following the early demise of John Smith who had had a tragic heart attack. I was concerned that he was obsessed in making his mark and changing things rather than reflecting the needs of the British people and this was evident in his plans for the reformation of the House of Lords. However, the voting public were hungry for new beans.

As soon as Tony Blair became Prime Minister in 1997, he was determined to implement his promises to reform Britain and take away privilege and power handed down through inheritance and to distribute it more fairly to the people of our country. It is no secret that he, and especially his wife Cherie, were anti-monarchists and vehemently against parts of the parliamentary system which they felt were outdated and unnecessary.

Fortunately for The Queen, Mr. Blair became more convinced of the role of the monarchy after the death of Princess Diana. Furthermore, even at their lowest point, polls taken around this time showed that three quarters of the population were still in favour of the monarchy and it would have been politically suicidal to challenge The Queen's Sovereignty.

However with a landslide victory and promises to reform and modernise the old establishments, he turned his attention to the Houses of Parliament, particularly the House of Lords.

The two main types of Peers of the Realm are Life Peers and Hereditary Peers. The former are appointed by the Prime Minister in power and can be anyone ranging from businessmen, academics, politicians and labourers. They are given the title of Baron and can enjoy the privileges of being a Lord, but unlike the hereditaries, cannot pass down their title and power to subsequent generations. The main consequence of this peerage is that typically the Prime Minister will appoint candidates from their own party who will support their bills and manifesto.

Tony Blair quickly took advantage of his new position and flooded the chamber with the rapid appointment of an unprecedented number of new life peers. My team and I were kept very busy showing all these new faces around our dining areas and explaining how and when they could access the facilities; they were like new groups of first years attending Fresher's Week or Induction Day. In some ways it was interesting as they weren't all young, brash, businessmen; many were old and retired and had led very interesting lives.

For most governments, redressing the balance of the leading party within both Houses was enough. After all, the House of Lords does not make new bills, it is a revising body, designed to ensure that an eager government cannot pass any new law that it wants without thorough consideration and consultation, exercised by experts and experienced members.

The Prime Minister still felt that the House of Lords was undemocratic as the majority of its members had not been elected. He was frustrated that with 750 members in the Lords, the majority of which were Conservatives, and only 650 members in the Commons, he was still accountable to the competition. This was not a realistic viewpoint. It's true that the Lords can delay bills by up to a year through scrutiny of the Law and investigations by Committees, but the purpose is to revise and improve the government's proposed legislation and not to abolish it. They can't. At the end of the day, the government can still decide to reject their amendments and pass it anyway.

Unlike America, we do not have a rigid, written down constitution. This means that we are able to adapt to changing lives and conditions with more flexibility, but this needs to be done with the two Houses of Parliament working collaboratively and not competitively.

Tony Blair, propelled by huge support from the public that voted for him, continued his campaign for change and power inside the House. He claimed that although there was a Labour government in the Commons, the hereditary peerage meant that there was an overwhelming Conservative majority within the house, of 3 to 1, which was undemocratic. Although the government could reject amendments and revisions from the Lords, this could often take a year and was seen as inconvenient and annoying, especially for a PM who wanted to make a lot of changes as soon as possible.

However, the complete abolition of the hereditary peers was unrealistic as everyone was too concerned about what would replace them. New laws still needed to be examined and reviewed and many of the life peers openly expressed that they lacked the education or experience to do this. Besides, such a massive reformation would have caused huge anger and protests within the building. Some concession would have to be made.

Reluctantly, Tony Blair agreed with Lord Cranborne, the Leader for the Lords, that during this transitioning period, a core nucleus of 92 hereditaries, from the existing 750 should be permitted to stay and the expelled majority would then leave, peacefully.

With this agreement, Cranborne's deputy, Lord Strathclyde, introduced the government's Reform Bill to the Lords and, inevitably, a lot of anxiety and anger developed. Who was going to be able to stay and what would replace the main body of the House?

Meanwhile, Tony Blair, knowing that there was going to be a massive vacuum from the 668 who were forced to leave, continued to appoint more and more life peers, in unprecedented numbers. Interestingly, the media showed no attention to what was going on and I sincerely feel that *Joe Public* was kept completely in the dark about how their parliament and constitution was changing. At that time, only the internal members and staff were affected.

'Who are all these new people, Robert?' Sandra asked me, blowing the top of her hot coffee, at our weekly Monday morning meetings. 'They don't seem to know anything about the building and keep asking me to give them a tour.'

Alfredo thumped his cup on the table. 'It's-a not our job to give tours,' he said, over folded arms.

Sandra wasn't finished. 'Some of them are damn right rude. One lady told me I needed to clean the toilets better.'

Alfredo gripped her hand, affectionately. 'You should-a said, "show me which one." Or given her a toilet brush.'

Sandra squeezed his arm and laughed.

It was important that we all tried to keep a sense of humour with these fast changing times. We had been so lucky to work in such a historical bubble, away from the ever-changing, modern world. It seemed like an unwanted intruder had finally broken into our rooms and was stealthily taking over.

Sandra took a big swig of her coffee and a mouthful of a digestive biscuit. 'This will make you laugh,' she said, checking we were all listening, again. 'One young man asked me if we had a McDonald's and whereabouts was is it.'

We all gasped and waited for the punch line.

She leaned towards the centre of the table. 'So guess what I told him Robert? I told him, "Yes, sir. It's right at the end, past the Commons. Just keep following the green carpet to the end." ' She took another bite of her biscuit. 'Then guess what I said? I told him they do a wonderful McLord Burger and to ask for a Blair Shake. It's quite bitter and bits can get stuck in your teeth, but you get used to it.'

Hysterics erupted and many exclamations of: *Oh, Sandra, you didn't!*

'I bloody did,' she howled. 'And the silly sod set off to find it.'

Privately, I was thinking, *I'm not sure I will ever get used to that blend of newly mixed up ingredients.*

A lot of people were very angry with all the new individuals coming in, refused to help them and even ignored them.

Black Rod sensed the indignation and several meetings were called and instructions were given for everyone to remember where they were and to uphold the traditions of etiquette and gentlemanly behaviour. It was not, after all, their fault that the Prime Minister was acting so aggressively.

Even some of the Lords, who knew they were going to be forced out, agreed with him. Earl Romney said that it was a difficult time but that we should all be nice to Blair's new favourites.

During the year that followed, whilst the mechanics of how the expulsion should proceed were developed, the House was becoming increasingly unhappy and unsettled. In the end, the PM decided that the most democratic process for the selection of the 92 hereditary peers to remain would be by an election. They must put themselves forward as candidates, like he had done for the Commons. As the public had no idea who they were or what they did, he declared, that they should vote for themselves.

This was not a well-received decision.

As one of my favourites, Lord Westbury put it, 'There is nothing democratic about voting for ourselves.' He added, later on, 'I'm sure he [Blair] wants to be President.'

It's important to state here, that a lot of the Hereditary Lords are not politicians. There are a lot of negative general misconceptions about the Lords. Due to bad media coverage in the past, people believed that a lot of them were very old fuddy-duddies who occasionally rocked up, drank too much fine wine, ate too much rich food, had too much power and fell asleep in the Chamber. Hence the expressions: *Drunk as a Lord* and *To Lord it over People.*

Of course, within any groups, if you look hard enough you can find the stereotypes; there were certainly some characters that befitted this description, but they were normally backbenchers, had little to say and were only there to make up numbers or engender party support. It could be said, that some of the Royals, such as Prince Edward, also play a seemingly insignificant role. Look inside your own place of work or family and probably you will find that there are some strong, motivated *Go-Getters* and some quiet, content, *Couch-Potatoes*. Sometimes it's better to look at the role of the group as a whole than to single out offending individuals.

In terms of attendance there were some hereditary peers who came in everyday and some who only attended, intermittently, when a bill that had been introduced, needed their area of experience or expertise to enable the revision process. Of course, frequency of attendance was also down to how far away the Lord lived. What many people don't understand is that the hereditary peers do not become involved because they want to make a career out of politics or secure a salary. A lot of them already have their own careers, businesses and other interests. They simply want to give their advice and suggestions based on decades, sometimes centuries, of inherited knowledge and experience. Most of these peers do not spend much time in the actual Chamber; they use the House for running and organising much needed committees or raising millions of pounds for charities.

However, the impending internal 'election' started drawing members in from all the remotest reaches of the British Isles, and beyond. There were normally around 400 of the 750 in attendance on any given day, who needed to be looked after, fed and watered. During those last remaining months there were about 800, which included some of the retired life peers who had turned up to give support to the House and its existing members.

'How are we going to feed them all?' Sandra asked, distressed.

As we looked through the rooms we could see that all the tables were full and some diners were even sat on radiators. However, they were so busy engaged in conversations that food seemed a secondary concern.

I knew what we had to do. 'Don't worry, I've told the chefs to keep cooking up sausages and potatoes, and order in more liver and bacon. Lots of comfort food. It's what they all love.'

'It's true,' she agreed. 'They do love their bangers and mash.'

Actually they were much easier than the New Labour life peers. If anyone started complaining during this time, it was likely to be one of them.

For the election, each party had to select about 10 per cent of its members for election and these members could write an optional 75 word c.v. to strengthen their candidacy. For some this was an easy task to complete; for others it felt like a complete character assassination and undermined all their efforts and hard work over the past decades. Some decided that it was all too terrible and quietly left the building, forever.

During this period, normal parliamentary business continued. Bills were still introduced, debated in the Commons and sent to the Lords for revision before being inaugurated by Royal Assent.

The most significant of these was the Welfare Act. The Labour Party wanted the act to be reformed, to make it a legal requirement that all people receiving Incapacity Benefit were thoroughly means tested to check their entitlement. This was opposed in the Commons by the opposition, insisting it was unfair and cruel to get people who were already struggling to fight for help. Unfortunately, the government seemed unstoppable. They started using the Welfare Act as a test case for their increasing power. Arguments in the Commons moved away from the act, itself, into base criticisms of the Lords and overt speeches about how their power had been broken and they were no longer in a position to tell the government what to do.

Jack Ashley, a life peer for the Labour Party was so incensed by the government's loss of ability to let common sense prevail that, for the first time, he voted against his own party. This is a clear demonstration that the two separate Houses are not just simply Conservative or Labour but have been designed to determine fair and just laws for all. However, in this landmark case, there were several threats to invoke the Parliamentary Act and to reject <u>any</u> revisions provided. The government ignored the revisions and the tidal wave of means testing for all forms of welfare was established within The Welfare Act, 1999.

At the same time the Lords had to vote on the final draft of the Reform Bill. This is done with an eight minute walk from the House of Lords to the division lobbies, which is essentially a corridor that splits in two. One side is for the *contents* [YES] and the other for the *not contents* [NO]. The result was 221 for the *contents* and 81 for the *not contents*.

The government finally got its own way. The bill was expediently sent for Royal Assent and on November 11th The House of Lords Reform Act 1999 was passed.

Inevitably, there was a lot of distress in the House at this time.

The registration process for the hereditary peer election was promptly closed; there were, in the end, around 220 candidates. Three Committee Rooms were designated for the different parties to use as polling stations.

The procedure for voting was, in itself, punitive. Like naughty schoolboys lining up to take the cane, the Lords were channelled into tiny, cattle-like, pens of chipboard. On the voting slip, they had to select <u>42</u> candidates in order of preference to remain. Many of them found it highly confusing and a few couldn't even fit inside the booths.

During all this time, there was no sign of the media. It was like a closed shop, in the dead of night, that was being plundered of all its goods and riches.

When the votes had been finalised and counted, and the results were announced, the press suddenly arrived, like flocks of vultures, tearing through the building to find every Lord that had been voted out and to get a few sentences from each one, as if compiling a centre page of obituaries. All the staff were asked to point out who each Lord was or where they could be found.

In the weeks that followed, there were numerous leaving parties for the departing Lords, which we were asked to host and even attend. There were many sad farewell speeches and fond recollections of days gone by.

As they drifted out of the building, Sandra asked me, 'What will we do now, Robert?'

My heart was breaking but I told her, 'Same as before, Sandra.'

We walked back down to clear one of the tables. 'It will never be the same, will it?' she added.

'It won't be the same, but we will be fine,' I told her, not believing it. 'At least we haven't been expelled.'

She looked up at me with watery eyes. 'No, not yet, eh Robert.'

The fact was there had been a revolution inside the British Parliamentary System; an almost silent, bloodless coup that the public neither knew nor cared about. Also, we worked in The House of Lords and without the Lords what would it become? Tony Blair's House of Friends?

11   MODERNISING FOR PROFIT

As I turned my diary over, into April, it was becoming clear that the pages were beginning to fill up with clients. Some of the people I had met had already come and gone, like Suzie Partridge and her family of cats, Mystical Madame Zelda and Fish 'n' Chips Rosie, but others were now firm regulars.

On Monday and Thursday mornings I now had Richard's for three hours, the Pratts' was two hours on Tuesdays, the Snipes' was two hours on Tuesdays or Wednesdays and Claudia's was another three on Wednesdays, and there was still 4-5 hours every week at Janet and John's on Fridays. They were still my favourites, so it was good to have this at the end of the week.

In addition to this, I still helped José at home, around Isabella's, for a few hours here and there. I didn't do much work for Simon and Steve any more but there was a promise of some villa cleaning (*yuck*) for the Easter holiday season.

'I think I'm going to have to start turning work down, soon,' I told Graham, as I thumbed through my diary.

He was busy marking some practice written papers for the Cambridge English exams. 'Don't you dare. If you keep going at this rate, I can retire from teaching and laze by the pool all day.'

I started counting up the public holidays that were coming up soon. 'You might have to wait for a while. There's Easter this month and the Spanish take a whole week off for that.'

He put his pen down. 'We'll have to go down to the English shop and stock up on Cadbury's Cream Eggs and Mini Eggs.'

'You do know that's not the true meaning of Easter, don't you?'

I teased.

'Of course! There's hot cross buns as well.' He licked his lips. 'Why is Easter on a different date every year? Christmas is always December 25th, so why not make Easter on the same day?'

'Are you joking, Graham?'

He wasn't. It still surprises me that for someone with such a quick, academic mind he has literally no idea about history and events.

With chocolate still on his mind, he went into the kitchen and grabbed a multi-pack of Jaffa Cakes and ripped them open. 'I suppose you can't really have Good Friday on a Tuesday or Easter Sunday on a Monday, but at least they could do it on the same week.'

I grabbed the Jaffa Cakes off him. 'That's enough for you, or you'll start looking like one.'

He still had a small pile of them beside him and held one up. He recited the words from the advert: 'Full-moon,' he held one up in his fingers and then bit half of it out. 'Half-moon.' Then Graham swallowed the rest in one mouthful and shouted, 'lunar eclipse!'

'Actually you've just said the answer,' I told him. He looked back at me, quizzically. 'The start of Easter begins on the first Sunday after the first full moon of spring. That's why it changes.'

He ate another one. 'Trust you to know that, Beany.'

I was on a roll now. 'And the reason why they carry the statues out of the churches in processions was that in the early days they used to transport the remains of the Christian martyrs.'

Graham grimaced. 'That's gross.'

'It was. Sometimes there were just a few bones, with some dried skin or a skull.'

'Robert, please!' he added and put down the biscuits.

'Of course there's always a representation of Christ as well.'

We are not particularly religious but do believe that some amazing guy called Jesus did exist and people thought of him as a prophet. A few months ago, a replica of the Turin Shroud was displayed in Málaga Cathedral. The exhibition was so technological, with laser beam projections, that it was like *CSI* for Jesus; very impressive.

'You're a bit like Jesus,' Graham told me. He observed my blank face. 'Your working life was practically dead and with all this gardening work you've been resurrected from the scrap heap and brought back to life.' He laughed.

'It does seem to be working, doesn't it?' I don't know why I needed reassurance.

'Of course. Anyone's lucky to have you working for them. Now make me a coffee servant.'

Typically in Spain, the holidays are longer. Instead of an Easter weekend there is a whole seven days of celebrations during holy week, or as they call it, *Semana Santa*.

'Right I'm off to meet the housekeeper at Richard's,' I said, pulling my boots on.

'Housekeeper? That sounds a bit grandiose. Where are you going? *Downton Abbey*?'

'It does sound a bit over the top for a little villa, doesn't it? Hey ho. Let's hope she's nice.'

It took about forty-five minutes to drive there and I was very cautious to observe the speed limits and to look out for cameras and unmarked cars, which they use as speed traps over here. I didn't mind if anyone got frustrated behind me; I was going to go slow and avoid any more fines.

When I arrived at Richard's house, there was an old, beat-up four by four parked next to the gate, on the road. There was a key with a green fob in the gate, so I let myself in, put the key in my pocket and walked up to the house. At this time of year, the winds get stronger, heralding warmer weather to come. There was a calming sound of the breeze whistling through the trees above.

As I got closer, I could hear someone shouting inside the house. It was a woman's voice, down in the basement area, near the pump house, with a strong-sounding Welsh dialect. Normally I find this accent soft and almost musical but not in this case. She was on the phone, shouting at some poor repair man that the washing machine still wasn't working.

I decided to leave introductions until later and headed back into the garden to start my clearance work. The line of hedging seemed to be the most offending area for Richard, so I walked across the lawn, took out my secateurs and started pulling the long limbs down to be cut. As I did, a beautiful hoopy bird, with its soft brown neck, long pointed crown and zebra striped wings and body, shot out and flew to the end of the garden. They are very elusive, so I was lucky to see it.

Suddenly a high pitched bleating sound rose up from behind where I was standing. I could see a woman with bright orange hair, which was cut harshly as if it was a small bale of straw on her head, scurrying across the lawn. She looked like a human sized version of G.P. the Guinea Pig from the children's television programme: *Tales of the Riverbank*.

Her voice was getting louder. 'Wot are you doing mun?'

I turned around and saw a short woman, with an old wrinkled face, in a grey faded sweat shirt and jeans. 'You must be Gwen,' I said and put down the secateurs, to shake her hand.

She kept her hands firmly inside her pockets. 'It's Gwyn, not Gwen. But you must call me Miss Gwyndoline.' She took a deep breath and continued, 'Wot you do-ing, anyways?' The second syllable kept rising up, higher than the first. 'And how did you get in?'

'There was a key in the gate.' I pulled it out my pocket to show her. I looked back towards the hedge and told her, 'I'm cutting it back, like Richard wanted.'

'Give me that,' she demanded, pointing at the key. She walked over to inspect my handy work. 'Well, I wouldn't do it like that. It needs to be cut down to the root ball. She grabbed my cutters off the lawn and hacked the bush down as far as her creaking hips would allow. 'It needs to be shorter than this. Right down there,' she pointed to the dirt.

I wanted to tell her I had only just started but she wasn't listening.

'I've been with Dicky and Nicky for ten year now. They have a certain way they like things done.'

I managed to stifle a giggle when I heard the words *Dicky* and *Nicky*, and walked back over to continue the work.

She followed me and stood over me with her hand on her hips. 'Yes, that's better. Dicky wants the garden cut right down. Of course that's not how I would do it, but we work for them, so we do as we are told. That's just the way it works.' I noticed, a twang of regret in her voice, as if she was here against her will.

'I had fifty acres, back in Wales. Everyone said it was the best garden for miles. I love gard-ning, I do. I would do it here but I'm seventy next year and it's too physical.'

I turned around to give her more attention. 'You don't look seventy,' I lied. She looked a lot older.

She ignored my compliment, as if she knew it wasn't true. 'I should be retired now. But me damn husband went off with a bar maid in Fuengirola. He was seventy five and she was about forty.' She looked up at the trees, recalling the time of her abandonment.

Instantly, my feelings of irritation turned to pity. 'That's sad,' I said.

She looked down and wiped her face with her hands. 'Well, I never complain. There's many folks worse off. My sister back in Aberystwyth has a man who's always drunk. She barely has enough money to feed the little ones. She used to call me *The Lady of the Manor*, back home. It's true it was the biggest house in the area. Even had a sit on mower. Much bigger than this place. I send her a bit of money when I can.'

I looked back at her tired, torture-filled face, at a loss of what to say with all this new information of someone I'd only just met. 'That's good of you,' I managed to say.

'Well enough said. You're keeping me from my work. I've still got the bed to change and all the windows to clean. Make sure you cut it all back hard. Come and see me when you're done and I'll make a note of your hours and give you the keys.'

Before I could reply, she had turned back to the house and was scampering away muttering, 'Much to do. So much to do.'

I continued without taking a break, for three hours, and had created a huge pile of clippings which I had added to the compost heap in the far corner of the garden. I looked back at the hedge which was now a bare wall; all the colourful blooms and green shoots had been torn out as demanded. It looked so sad.

As I approached the house, I could hear Gwyn's raised voice chastising another poor sod on the other end of the phone. It wouldn't be a good idea to interrupt her, so I sat on a stone bench, near the pool, close to the basement area which she seemed to inhabit. Ten minutes later, the voice stopped but she didn't come out. I walked over to the open door, under a stairwell and called in, 'Gwyn. I've finished now.' There was a shriek indoors and something heavy dropped on the floor.

'Good heavens mun. You gave me the shock of my life,' she yelled, out of sight. 'Come in.'

I walked through the small PVC door, into a thin, white chamber. Along the entire length of the back wall there were a series of shelves with freshly washed and pressed clothes, towels and bedding. Gwyn was stood over an industrial sized ironing board, wrestling with a large white sheet. It was quite cold in here as there was no sunlight; just a couple of strips of flickering, fluorescent lights.

She put the iron down on the sheet. 'Isn't it marvellous?' she said, pointing around the utility room. 'They had it specially made for me.'

Marvellous was not the word I would have used. It was more like a newly constructed prison cell, or oversized hamster cage, to harbour this rodent inmate in solitary confinement. In place of an exercise wheel were a washing machine and tumble dryer to keep the interned occupied; the water dispenser on the side of the cage had been substituted with hundreds of bottles of cleaning fluids.

Gwyn was still grinning with pride. 'The important thing to remember is that Dicky and Nicky like everything to be kept here like a five star hotel. They work hard and are very particular about how things are done. If I leave a tea towel in the wrong place, then Nicky will leave me a note to remind me.'

There was a faint smell of acrid smoke and it seemed that the sheet was starting to singe under the iron. 'Gwyn, the iron!'

She quickly clasped it up in her hand and put it on a metal stand. Fortunately the sheet seemed alright.

'The most important thing to remember,' she added, folding the sheet over, 'is to never let the cats out. Always keep the gate shut.' Gwyn put the ironed sheet on a shelf behind her and looked at me intently. 'She is very demanding and it can seem that she has far too much. They also have a finca in the mountains and ski chalet in St. Moritz. It's cos they couldn't have kids.'

'Who, Nicky?' I asked.

'Of course, it was never a problem for me. I always fell pregnant easily.' She appeared to snarl under her thick lips and continued, 'The cats, Dolce and Gabbana, are like her kids. There was a another one, Versace, but he got crushed under the rubbish lorry last year. She cried for weeks.' A thin smile of satisfaction broke between the circles of her puffed out cheeks. 'Dicky is a great man. Very respected. A true gentleman.' Her eye lashes had started fluttering as if she was a teenager with a crush on her teacher.

It was starting to feel very uncomfortable and claustrophobic down here. 'Poor Nicky,' I added, checking my watch.

She saw me. 'Sorry! Are we keeping you?' She kicked a linen basket out of her way and walked over to the washing machine. 'Right let me note down your hours. She retrieved an old ledger from behind a large box of Aerial. 'The last gardener was always claiming hours he never worked. Make sure you find me when you arrive and before you leave and I will clock you in and out.'

I nodded, diffidently.

She rummaged in her back pocket and handed me something. 'And this is your key.'

It was the exact same key I had retrieved from the gate three hours ago.

'Oh, and Robert. You'd do best to remember that you must address me as *Miss Gwyndoline* and it should always be *Richard* and *Nicole* to you. See you Thursday.'

Before I could apologise, she had turned her back on me. It was time for me to go.

During the days that followed I realized that some of the work was much more enjoyable and easy than others. Elena Pratt was still quite stiff and cold but after I had trimmed all the bushes that Tuesday, she came out and said, 'You know. Zee garden is starting to look a lot better. Thank you Robert.' I was speechless. I had noticed that she had become less frosty after Steve left, but this was more than I could ever have hoped for. It was a pretty little garden and a real sun trap; even on a spring day I ended up just wearing a polo-shirt and work-trousers.

The Snipes were due over the Easter break, so I put in a few extra hours trimming back some of the climbers. Abigail had transferred fifty euros into my account for planting out the kitchen garden a few weeks ago, together with strict instructions that plants should always be planted in blocks of threes or fives. I had delayed buying the plants, so they would still look great for her visit and went to *Casa De Flores* and bought loads of herbs, three white rose bushes, some different lettuces and a couple of bags of compost to dig into the hard soil. I did four hours over my time, but it didn't matter as the result was so satisfying.

Dear Claudia greeted me with a cup of tea and biscuits on Wednesday, which we had on the top, covered terrace overlooking the pool. Although maintaining the garden is important for people, sometimes the need for company is also significant. She started telling me more about her husband who had been a successful television and film producer, mainly for the crime and mystery genres. They had travelled all over the world with his work.

One of the things she really wanted to get working again was a water fountain which they received as a gift for their fiftieth wedding anniversary. She led me indoors though her sitting room, where there were many framed photos of Gordon, looking very dapper, in suit and tie, with some of the famous people he had worked with, these included: Oliver Reed, John Thaw, Helen Mirren and even Shirley MacLaine. Most had been signed with best wishes.

It was clear they had had a very interesting life and now she was home alone, with her memories which she was struggling to keep alive.

Beyond the lounge was an inner courtyard, with a small atrium roof, filled with potted ferns and small palms. The floor was tiled in a mock Roman mosaic pattern, with a cast iron, pedestal fountain with a cherub emptying a water pitcher, which had now run dry.

'It stopped working the day after he died,' Claudia said, woefully. She began sniffling and dabbing her nose with her handkerchief but there was no sign of tears.

My dad was pretty good with electrics and I had learned quite a lot from him. 'Don't worry. We'll get it working again. It's probably the pump.' I went out to my van and got some tools and stripped the pump down and after about an hour, found nothing wrong with it. Claudia had gotten a couple of buckets of water in the hope it would soon be working again. I decided to check the plug, even though the Spanish ones don't have individual fuses. It was tucked behind a large Swiss cheese plant in a corner. I discovered that it was a standard

British three pin plug, inserted into a European adaptor. Having replaced the fuse and emptied the water buckets into the base, I asked Claudia, 'Would you like to do the honours?'

She walked behind the ornament and flicked the switch on and started jumping up and down, and shaking as if she was being electrocuted, shouting, 'zzzz, zzzz!'

The pump started whirring and soon after the water began trickling out from the top.

'That got you worried,' she laughed, re-joining me at the front.

My heart was still beating in my head. 'Yes, slightly,' I chuckled. 'Perhaps your husband should have put you in films?'

As the lifeline of water trickled down into the small pond reservoir, onto the small plants inside the base, she grabbed my hand and said, 'Thank you so much.'

I left her, feeling that gardening was probably the best job in the world.

The next day, I was due back at Dicky and Nicky's at 9 a.m. sharp. I arrived on time, let myself in with my key and luckily managed to stop one of the cats shooting out between my legs, onto the road. It was very keen to escape.

As I started walking up to the house to report to *Madame Gwynny* for duty, (I had to entertain myself somehow with all this silly protocol), I noticed there was a large delivery of garden materials on the corner of the driveway. There were some sacks of white gravel, a box of galvanised steel pins, some reels of black plastic weed suppressant and a selection of cacti and succulents, in pots, ready for planting. Beyond this was a high, pyramidal stack of rolls of turf, which was shiny green and looked like the Emerald Tower in *The Wizard of Oz*. As I walked closer, the explanation for this strange colour became apparent: it was made of artificial grass. I counted about thirty rolls of the stuff.

'What time did you get here?' a voice squealed at me. Gwyn was stood behind me with a pen and her ledger in her hands.

'Oh, it was er..nine o' clock,' I stammered.

She checked her watch. 'Well it's eleven after now, so that's what I'll have to put down. You should have come straight to the house.'

Words failed me. As the bright Mediterranean sunshine radiated in the sky and the soft whistle of the wind flowed through the trees, her angry presence just seemed too incongruous to comprehend.

Like a factory floor inspector, in a large industrial warehouse, she marched over to the sacks of gravel. 'You're to lay these today. Take the roses and shrubs out from those borders, put down the black plastic, plant all these and cover with the gravel.' As she spoke, I noticed there were some partially eaten nuts churning in her mouth; they were being tossed around the opening, like clothes seen through the door of a washing machine on rinse cycle.

This seemed straight forward enough. 'What do you want me to do with all the old plants?'

She was already scuttling back to her burrow and threw her empty hand in the air. 'I don't care. Just get rid of them.'

I set to work, dragging the equipment over to the borders which needed to be reworked. It would have been good to have had a wheelbarrow and I made a mental note to add this to my wish list for the business. The old plants came out easily enough and I decided exactly where these were going to go. I would take them over to Claudia's next week and give them to her for one of the borders she was trying to reclaim.

After digging the empty borders over, I laid the black plastic and trimmed the edges to fit. I placed the new plants over the surface to give the best coverage and effect and then cut out holes to plant them. It would have been useful to have had some compost for the new plants, but I reassured myself that these native spiky specimens were probably fine in poor, dry soil. Having watered them all in, with a nearby hose, I spent the remaining hour neatly spreading the white, sparkly chips of gravel over the surface and raked them over.

When the job was finished, I stood back to inspect my handy

work. It did look good and was certainly neat and tidy, but was reminiscent of the stones you see in a cemetery, decorating a grave and what lies beneath, complete with a few, dotted, plastic, floral tributes. I much preferred what was there before but, concluded, this would be maintenance free.

After Gwyn recorded my clocking out time, I asked her, 'Do you want me to do the grass next time?'

She spat out a piece of peanut shell from the side of her mouth onto the ground. 'Well, yes. I would have thought that was obvious. Have you laid grass before?

'Yes!' I replied a bit too sharply, annoyed. But I had never put down artificial grass.

'Richard will be here on Monday and he'll tell you exactly how he wants it. I've got you down this week for five and a half hours. You can make up the half hour you've lost next week. Now, I've got to get on.'

Cheeky bitch, I thought. 'Have a lovely weekend, Miss Gwyndoline,' I said.

She had already scampered away and didn't respond.

Thank God for the weekend. I was looking forward to some time off in our own garden and I would try and find out some hints and tips for laying AstroTurf from José.

I found him working in the poly tunnel on Saturday afternoon. There was a new pile of horse hoof clippings in one of the composters, presumably for a new Isabella Vincent potion. I wasn't quite sure how to explain artificial grass to him in Spanish, so Graham looked it up for me on Google Translate. 'Do you know how to use *césped* artificial?' I asked him.

He looked up from his watering and seemed very tired. 'Kes-ped? What is kes-ped?'

There was a small patch of grass outside, so I pointed to it.

'Oh you mean *Thes-ped*. Artificial, I understand. Why you want grass of plastic?'

I laughed. *Plastic grass* did seem a ridiculous idea. 'It's not me, it's for one of my clients in Marbella.'

He walked over to blue, chunky cool box which he brought into the garden when he was working, pulled out two cans of *St. Miguel* and gave one to me. We sat on the floor, near one of the compost heaps.

'*Salud!*', we cheered.

'Thoses people in Marbella, they are a bit loco, no?' he said, with a wide beaming smile. 'They have houses too big, so they need to have many peoples to have them clean, no?'

'Yes,' I nodded. 'They do.'

He stood up and stretched his arms. 'And they have gardens too big and need men to come and do them, no?'

'That's true. But then that's good. Good for us gardeners.'

'And they have big, big boats, as big as this, no?' He walked down to the other end of the tunnel, emphasizing the length with long, deep strides.

I swigged the beer and yelled, 'Bigger!'

He walked out of the entrance and ten feet further. 'Like these?'

'That's it!'

He was walking back towards me with his hands on his hips, swaying as if he was an overweight model on a catwalk. 'And they all buy pretty shoes and clothings, to look big and pretty, like this, no?'

I couldn't stop laughing. I had never seen him like this before. Perhaps he was a few beers ahead of me? 'Exactly!' I said.

He fell down beside me and took out another beer. 'It's just loco, no?'

'Yes, my friend, it's loco. But it's also funny. Very funny.' I hadn't realized until then that I had really grown to like him. He had become my first local friend.

Back at the house, I did some quick research online and soon discovered that to create the perfect pseudo lawn you needed to do the following:

1. Clear old turf and excavate soil by 75mm and rake over.

2. Add crushed rock or sand and use a compactor to flatten.

3. Lay out turf and cut to size.

4. Secure corners and perimeter with galvanized turf pins.

5. Join sections by laying joining tape and secure with pins.

6. Apply turf adhesive and stick edges closely together.

7. Stretch out and pull lawn to remove any creases.

8. Sprinkle dry silica sand over turf and use stiff bristle brush

   to move sand inside to the base.

I was ready to commence operations.

When I arrived on Monday morning and entered the site, Richard was in the driveway inspecting the grass.

'Good morning. How was your trip?'

'Trip? Oh yes, it was business. All good. Now, are you alright with getting this lot down?' he asked me, looking very serious.

'Yes, but it'll take a few days.' I hoped he realized there was a lot of work ahead.

'What?' he snapped and then changed his tone, 'Oh yes, of course. Quite right. Quite right.'

I needed to ask him about some of the materials which seemed to be missing. 'Do we have some rock salt, joining material and adhesive?'

'What!'

'To lay out the foundations and join the sections neatly together.'

His face was turning red again. 'No need for that. The ground is flat enough. Just lay the stuff straight on top and fix it on with the pins.'

That really wasn't a good idea. 'The problem is the weeds and old grass will push up through, eventually,' I suggested.

'Nonsense. What grass? It's practically bare and the turf will suppress anything underneath. Anyway, need to get on.'

'Please will you let Gwyn know, I got here at nine.'

He didn't respond and was already making a call on his mobile.

For the next few weeks, I laid out the artificial lawn as instructed. I did remove some offending clumps of the old grass and used an excess of the galvanized pins to secure the pieces in place. By the time I had finished, it did look amazingly good; at least for now. With Gwyn's avid eye inspecting my work at regular intervals, I continued to trim all the other bushes and then re-trimmed them to her ever-changing expectations. She had, after all, as she reminded me every time I went there, *had fifty acres of land* back in Wales.

At the end of the month I dutifully went down to report to Gwyn, pick up my wages and find out what needed doing for next month. She was already outside, sat on the bench with a plate of grated carrot, her ledger and a big bag of coins on the table.

She made we wait whilst she finished her lunch. As she opened her mouth, there were two orange strips wedged between her ground-down teeth. 'So, then Robert. You've done a total of twenty-seven hours, times ten, that means we owe you two hundred and seventy euros. Nicky has been kind enough to count it all out.' She picked up and shook the heavy cloth bag of coins.

I had never met Nicky but had been told by Gwyn that she was also a busy chartered accountant and spent a lot of time in beauty parlours as she *wasn't born pretty* and had *very dried out skin*.

'How kind,' I said, as I went to retrieve the bag.

'No, not quite yet!' Gwyn snarled. 'I see you've left all the trimmings at the back of the garden. Thought I wouldn't know? Miss Gwyndoline knows everything!'

I didn't know whether to laugh or cry. 'I just put them on top of the compost heap.'

'That's not a compost heap! It's where Versace is buried! Thank God Nicky hasn't seen it. You need to take them off site, now, and then I'll pay you.'

Why hadn't she told me sooner? I'm sure she must have noticed as soon as I had started using that spot. I emptied all my tools out of the van and ferried the rotting cuttings across the plastic lawn and into the back. Fortunately, about half a mile from the house there was a derelict building site, where everyone put their cuttings. Three loads later, I pushed my tools to the back and stacked a final half load to drop off on my way back.

After Gwyn's inspection, she handed over the coins and asked for the key back.

'What about next week, Miss Gwyndoline?'

She smiled, knowingly. 'Well as you can see, there's nothing left to do. You've made it maintenance free.'

It was the first logical thing she had said. I shrugged, defeated, gave her the key back and walked back to the van. She locked the gate behind me. It didn't matter: I had other work.

As I was unloading the cuttings back at the dump, cheering myself up in the knowledge that I would never have to work there again, a Marbella Local Police Car, with flashing blue lights swung behind the van and I was given a fine of 200 euros for fly-tipping on an illegal site.

'It's turning out to be an expensive hobby this gardening malarkey of yours,' Graham teased, when I got home. 'I'm sure Monty Don doesn't have all this trouble.'

***

Having witnessed the massive changes that were happening in the House of Lords, I knew this was only the start of things to come and that things would become very different for me and my team.

I had been thinking of leaving London for some time and was drawn to the bohemian seaside town of Brighton, after many great weekends there. In 1999, it was incredibly affordable too. I could buy a two bedroom flat, with direct sea views for around forty thousand pounds in Kemptown Village. There were loads of hotels and restaurants, so I was confident that I would quickly find a job in hospitality. Meanwhile, my split-shift system in the Lords meant I could travel up to London Victoria by direct train, after peak times, and still be there before lunchtime service. The evenings might be late, but that didn't bother me.

So a month later, during our long Christmas recess, I sold my Shepherd's Bush studio flat, hired a man with a van and moved my stuff down to my new home in St. James's Street with my black rescue cat, Clementine. She had been found, abandoned, in Churchill gardens in Battersea, so it seemed only appropriate to name her after our greatest Prime Minister's wife.

My daily commute turned out to be what I had envisaged, but I had grossly underestimated the internal changes which were going to be imposed on the staff.

Within our own department, changes were afoot. Our dear Mister Bibbiani gratefully received an OBE for his services from Her Majesty The Queen and took early retirement soon after.

He was replaced by Tim Lamming, who had a strong background in corporate catering. One of his claims to fame was that he had been the man responsible for replacing live music on the Thames River Cruises with cheaper and more profitable canned tunes, which played in endless loops of Elgar's *Land of Hope and Glory*, as the boats went up and down the river.

His main agenda was to make the Food and Beverage Department much more modern and profitable. This was instrumented in a number of ways.

The first change we noticed was the rapid increase in the number of bookings. The pre-requisite that guests had to be invited in by an MP was scrapped. The restaurants were now forced to accept reservations from corporations such as *De La Rue* the money printers. They were welcome to use us whenever they liked to host breakfasts, lunches, tea parties and late night dinners.

Previously, we had always followed the pattern of the parliamentary business. We were only required when the Lords were in attendance. Sometimes this could mean late night dinners, if the debate and vote were extended, but usually business didn't start until lunchtime and was often concluded by nine p.m. Although my team and I had contracts for 40 hours service per week, the reality had always been that we worked only when we were needed, so had long extended breaks between split hours of service.

The House suddenly became known as *The Best Kept Secret in London;* an unusual place to host all your corporate functions in palatial settings and impress your staff and clients. For some large organisations, we became their hospitality venue. The most blatant example of this was British Airways. They literally took us over: there were BA breakfasts, brunches and lunches, afternoon teas, cocktail parties, presentations, and late evening dinners. Their patronage was so dominant that even the House of Lords merchandise in the gift shop was reprinted to incorporate their logo.

The hours were not the only things impacted by these changes. The reservation of certain rooms as private dining areas for esteemed members was disbanded. Everyone could eat where and when they wanted to. Consequently the different menu choices also became less varied and more standardised throughout the House.

All the staff within the building were enrolled in the *Investors in People Program:* we were forced to jump through bureaucratic hoops to prove on paper that we knew how to do our jobs. In reality it was all about lowering standards, reducing wages and increasing profits.

As a head waiter, I was forced to produce an annual appraisal on all my staff and give them a *box marking* from 1 to 3. The standard wage increment of two percent, in line with inflation, was scrapped. It was now up to only one percent but this depended on how good your *box marking* was. Like battery hens, we were being squeezed into smaller coops and made to fight each other for sufficient space and light.

It was incredibly divisive. Many of my team had happily worked with each other for years and provided excellent service. Now they were standing in corridors anxiously talking about their anticipated ratings and lower pay increases. Service and moral suffered; they became competitive not collaborative.

Thank heavens for Brighton. Not only had I found a city where I loved to live but for the first time ever I had fallen in love, with a teacher called Graham, and now had a dog and two cats; I had formed my own family outside of work.

The job that I had loved for so many years was now becoming more stressful and less remarkable. As the train arrived at the station around midnight, I could instantly smell the sea air and felt reinvigorated. Increasingly, I started looking forward to the next public holidays or periods of recess. I could use the time to get another job. If I was now a British Airways waiter, I may as well try and find a job at my local Weatherspoon or Harvester.

Unfortunately, the long periods of holidays were also slashed. Since we were no longer following the business of the House, our ten week summer holiday was reduced to three and Christmas and Easter, popular for corporate staff parties, were cut down to a few days. By the time the holidays came, I was simply too exhausted to apply for anything else.

The other benefits that we lost were the laundry allowance, for cleaning our uniforms, and the excellent free staff meals we used to enjoy in the House. We had always had food freshly prepared for us and would sit and eat together before we started service. In a further Tim Lamming cost-cutting exercise, it was decided that we would have the left-overs from the day before, which were turned into tasteless stews or bubble and squeak. Some of my staff started bringing in their own packed lunches, as it was so bad.

Unfortunately, some of the new customers were becoming more aggressive and demanding during this difficult time. Previously, if you were not an MP you had to leave the building by 11pm. When a Lord was hosting a dinner, he would normally graciously leave around 10.30 and then myself or one of the door men would bang the gavel and make the announcement: 'Ladies and Gentlemen, your host has now left the building, may I now kindly suggest we all do the same.' It was a well-respected etiquette which served the staff, members and facilities of the building well.

Again, this changed. After the parties dispersed, we were instructed to put all the remaining food from the day onto hot plates which there made available to anyone who wanted to pay for a late night snack.

Most people were more than ready to leave the House by this time, but a few decided to exploit this provision to maximum effect.

One memorable example was the night Lady Gould and Lady David came in, at 9.30 pm, escorting Lady Rendell, whom we loved and who seemed embarrassed to be with them. The last business of the House had been debating the welfare of Greyhounds which had finished at 7pm.

Clearly Lady Gould had been drinking and she stumbled up towards me and my exhausted staff, screaming, 'I want you to cook me a steak!'

Sandra had started snarling, so I told her to go and have a coffee and that I would deal with it.

'Good evening your ladyships. Welcome to the Hulme Room,' I said in the politest voice I could muster.

She turned and winked to her compatriots. 'Get me a steak,' she reiterated, nearly falling over.

'Let's go.' Ruth Rendell, nudged her.

'If I want a steak, I'll damn well have a steak,' she continued, unabated.

'Yes you will,' Lady David encouraged.

I pointed to the hot plates. 'I'm sorry your Ladyship, but the chefs have left and all we have left is on the hot plates.' I pointed to the overcooked remains of some sausages and chicken breast and the congealed remains of over-heated vegetables.

'I'm not eating that,' she scoffed.

In fairness, I would not have eaten it either. It really belonged in the bin, not reheated to be resold for more profit. But I had to obey orders and try and sell it. 'I'm sorry your ladyship, but it's after hours now and this is all we have.'

She threw her head back in temper. 'After hours! You'll stay here as long as I damn well want you to and give me my steak.'

Once again I apologised and suffered a barrage of insults until they finally departed.

The next day, she registered a formal complaint against me and I was summoned to a meeting. It was fine that I offered her the only food available but I was reminded that there were no longer any set hours of service and I was not to mention this again.

I was so incensed by the incident and what was happening to the place that I loved, that I decided to phone Simon Hoggart at *The Guardian* and expose the terrible situation that was unfolding behind our doors. This was published in his column, Simon Hoggart's Diary on Saturday July 14th 2001:

LORDING IT OVER THE WORKERS

A waiter phones from the House of Lords, giving his name but begging for my discretion. He says the place is going to hell in a handbasket with the departure of the hereditary peers and the consequent arrival of New Labour placemen and women. They are insisting, he says, that the restaurants, cafes, tea rooms and bars stay open much later than before.

"We are paid to work full time," he explains, "but it was always understood that the dining rooms would close half an hour after the House rises. That was in the days when peers were gentlemen, and the place was run like a gentlemen's club.

"The other day they rose at 7pm. They'd only been debating greyhounds and there wasn't even a vote. But two Labour peeresses marched in and loudly insisted that the restaurant stayed open till 9.30. They're just like the Bolsheviks; as soon as they got to power they started taking advantage of the workers."

As a result of the article, I was summoned in again and given my first official written warning.

For the next ten years, I kept my head down, motivated my team and looked forward to the next break and the few remaining gems of traditional service, including the State Openings, charitable events, dinners hosted by the hereditaries and The Children of Courage Awards. A lot of staff did leave, but with no new job offers in the pipeline, I was resigned to stay.

Meanwhile, Mr. Lamming continued on his barrage of modernisation and called a special departmental meeting to announce his biggest project. Placed on a small table in front of him, was a lumpy, three dimensional shape covered with a tablecloth. 'As many of you know, there have been discussions about the opening of a brand new restaurant, to meet the growing demands and to build upon the success of our Food and Beverage Department.' He paused, trying to light a positive spark of anticipation amongst the damp atmosphere of ambivalence that soaked the room. 'We have acquired the three vacant offices on this floor and they will provide much needed extra space. It is with great pleasure that I announce the construction of our latest jewel in the crown. The River Restaurant.' He lifted the cloth to reveal an architect's model of a new canteen looking room, which would have looked good in any school or college. He waited for a gasp or some sense of enthusiasm that never came. 'Yes, it made me speechless,' he sighed with enormous pride.

'It looks like Starbucks,' Sandra said, flatly.

Finally, a reaction. He strode up to her and her shook her hand. 'That's it, dear Sharon. That's exactly the look we are going for.'

As he walked back, she told him, 'It's Sandra.'

He ignored her. 'Are there any questions?' he asked the group.

'Who-a will be able to use it?' Alfredo asked.

Mr. Lamming was still admiring the expensive architects' representation. 'Anyone and everyone. Even you, dear man. Even you. Right, then. Let's all get back to our food stations. Mouths to feed.' He raised his arm and dismissed us.

'Do you like Starbucks, Robert?' Sandra asked me.

'No, I don't. They are taking over everywhere and pushing the small independents out.'

'I do like their Ginger beard Latte's at Christmas,' she said, licking her lips, as if there was some froth on them.

I laughed. 'I think you mean Ginger Bread not beard!'

'But I always end up looking like Father Christmas by then end of the cup.'

Thank heavens for my team. We all kept each other going and although other departments had had many people leaving, I still had all of mine.

We continued on and I did my best to try and make sure that everyone still had some sort of break in between the new ever increasing hours. We were permitted to use *Starbucks on the River,* but it was still only reheated leftovers for us staff.

The straw that broke this camel's back, came in the form of Lord Birt, a former director General of the BBC who was made a New Labour life peer and later became a personal advisor to Tony Blair.

For several years he had hosted a Thanksgiving Dinner in the Atlee Room, in honour of his American-born wife, Jane Lake. These parties were always difficult as he insisted in having the tables decorated in long, trailing ivy plants that tripped us up and candles on all the tables which were lit during service, with the insistence that all the lights were turned down. Not only could his guests not see what they were eating, me and my staff found it difficult to find the tables and serve them. Normally though, the event was a success, without any complaint.

However, on this particular evening, Lord Birt was really fraught and angry. Everything was wrong. I think, perhaps, it was the first time he had brought back the tradition since he divorced his American wife, after admitting adultery with Eithne Wallis and marrying her. Or, more likely the increasing powers of the life peers within the House had changed him.

In an effort to salvage the evening, Lord Birt was still demanding service at 12.30 a.m. I did politely remind him that my staff needed to go home and that security had now left the building. He continued on, unabated.

At 12.50, I turned up the lights, banged the gavel and made the old departure speech. He was furious.

I did manage to get all my staff home safely via taxis, but I had missed the last train and had to stay with friends in London for the evening.

The following morning I was summoned into the office, after they had received an official complaint from him that I had ruined his evening. I was forced to pen a letter of apology and ask for his forgiveness.

This humble servant did what he was told and also penned a letter of resignation.

It was time for me to leave.

12   A TIME TO CELEBRATE

Summer returns to Southern Spain like the flick of a heating switch, which turns the temperatures up instantly by ten degrees. There is about a week of heavy winds, normally around the end of May or early June, and when the air grows still you suddenly find yourself in beautiful hot sunshine with the need to jump in the pool to cool off.

At this time of year, I spend several hours going around the gardens, switching the swimming pools out of winter mode and back into life. You remove any remains from the wintering kits, check the chlorine and ph. levels, give the tiled walls and floors a deep clean and switch the pump back on. Like a dead-looking, hibernating aqueous beast, it precipitously starts moving and breathing again; inhaling and exhaling streams of water through its plastic gills.

There will be guaranteed sunshine now until at least November, so it's a great time to rejuvenate the garden borders with new bedding plants and start planning the many barbecues and parties for the season ahead.

Janet and John were busily preparing for Eleanor's birthday party on the next Saturday and asked if I could work the whole Friday before to help them get ready.

When I arrived at the house, Janet was wearing a pair of pink dungarees and was chasing after Toby and Oscar, who had run off with her trowel and gardening gloves. 'You's come back here, you terras!'

John was stood over a large white sheet of canvas, banging stakes into the ground and laughing at her. 'You'll have to run faster than that me girl,' he called after her.

I was stood behind the closed metal railing gate and should have shouted out but it was like watching live comedy or a *Carry On* film at the foot of the Spanish mountains.

Poor Janet tripped over one of the lines of rope John had laid out. He ran over to check she was alright.

'What you staring at you daft apeth?' she said, having rolled on her back, looking up at him.

He smiled. 'I'm looking at summit that's just gone arse over tit but still comes up smelling of roses.'

She smacked his leg playfully and he bent down to kiss her. Before they got too carried away and started getting amorous or naked, fortunately, Shorty announced my arrival at the gate.

'You'll just have to wait 'til laters,' she told him, as he pulled her back to her feet. She brushed her hair back with her hands and came over to let me in.

She offered me a drink and then started discussing plans for the party. All the guests were arriving around two tomorrow and she asked if I could get there an hour before. There were going to be around fifty people.

As we walked around the garden, which was looking really good now after all my efforts, she pointed out different areas which she had chosen for activities. 'The main area will be around the pool. I'd like to use the bar by the hot tub to give them all drinks and to set up the buffet. Do you think that's a good idea?'

I was grateful that she was asking for my advice. 'I think that's a great idea. There's lots of shade around there, which will be good for the children.'

'The pool is too deep for the little uns so we've bought a new inflatable paddling pool for them to cool off and I thought we could set that up over there.' She pointed behind the pool, next to a wall which was shaded by the tall trees.

'Good idea.'

I followed her back out onto the lawn. 'The bouncy castle is going up over there and John's putting up a marquee for the other activities.'

'It all sounds great.'

She stood back, imagining the scene. 'Yes, I think it should turn out alroit.'

'How old is Eleanor going to be, by the way?' I knew she was still just a baby so the answer had to be *one.*'

'Oh, didn't I already say? Our little treasure is going to be fabulous five.'

I was gobsmacked. How had I got it so wrong? I was sure that I had heard a baby screaming from inside the house and hadn't Janet referred to her as *babby Eleanor.* I had never seen the little girl, so it was clearly my mistake. I decided not to say anything and got stuck into work.

I jet washed all the terraces and gave the swimming pool a thorough clean. Janet gave me trays of glasses and crockery which I polished and set up in the bar area and stocked up the freezer with bags of ice and the large fridge with wine and soft drinks and covered bowls of citrus slices she had cut up ready. I mowed all the grass and checked the bouncy castle area for any sharp objects and stones and inflated and filled the new paddling pool. Janet had bought trays of brightly coloured bedding plants, so I dotted these around in planters and nearby borders.

Just before I left, John asked if I would give him a hand to raise the marquee over the wooden pillared frame he had created. With a lot of tugging, puffing and heaving we pulled the dry white skin over the skeletal structure and secured the edges with a clever, home – made guy rope system, called *Dolly Knots,* that he had learned from his Uncle Peter. It was looking very impressive and almost regal by the time we had finished.

'Thanks a lot Rob. That were a bit of a bitch, weren't it?'

I was dripping in sweat. 'No problem. Looks good doesn't it? Fit for a queen.' I was meaning the birthday girl.

He wiped his forehead and muttered, 'More like the freak show at a circus.'

I pretended not to hear him and checked my watch. 'Well, I'd better head off. I'll see you tomorrow at one.'

He was picking up his hammer and some left over stakes. 'I won't be here. Looking after the dogs and will be down on the coast. Good luck for tomorrow, mate. Rather you than me.'

As I left the garden and drove away in the van, I was still puzzled by his lack of love for his daughter. They seemed such a happy couple and yet something was just not quite right.

When I got back home to our cottage, the mood was entirely different. The sprinklers were whirring over the raised borders at the side of the house, the barbecue was smoking and Graham had laid out one of the tables with salads, breads, pasta dishes and a chilled bottle of cava with two glasses. Music was blasting from the iPod indoors, connected to our wireless speakers dotted around the garden.

'What's all this in aid of?' I asked as I entered the house.

'Go and have a quick swim and then join me on the terrace,' he said, disappearing into the kitchen to retrieve a couple of jacket potatoes.

I threw off my clothes, dashed in and out of the freezing pool shower and jumped into the refreshing water and swam a few lengths. There is nothing like cooling off in the privacy of your own pool, with no-one around, after a long day of work. I dried myself off with the *España* beach towel, wrapped it around my waist and came back down to the house.

Rich smelling, chargrilled steaks and shrimps had been added to the bounty on the table. 'Graham, what's going on?'

'Take a seat,' he said, pulling the cork out of the bottle. It exploded with an excited pop. He carefully filled the last two remaining flutes, from a set which he had been given on his fortieth birthday, and gave me a glass. 'I would like to propose a toast,' he announced.

I looked up at him, perplexed.

'Ladies and Gentlemen,' he said to an imagined audience. 'It has been one year now since the idea of becoming a gardener in Spain was first conceived. It's true to say that it has not all been plain sailing, there have been highs and lows. But now, after a lot of hard effort and determination, I am proud to declare the success of our dear Robert Nicholson. I give you, The Garden Butler.'

I was overwhelmed. Had it really been a year? I stood up, hugged and thanked him.

It was true: the dream had now become a reality.

***

It was agreed that I would continue working in the House of Lords until the next summer recess. It was a few months away but was mutually beneficial for me to find new work in Brighton and for them to advertise for a new head waiter. There were no hard feelings and to be honest, after twenty-one years, of course there were going to be changes and it was time for me to move onto something new.

An unexpected bonus for delaying my departure was that I received a reward for longevity of service, in the form of an invitation to one of The Queen's Garden Parties at Buckingham Palace. I was permitted to bring a guest; Graham and I were ecstatic to be going to such a unique venue, with the opportunity to see The Queen within her own home and gardens. I knew a few people who used to work at the House of Lords who were in service there, Luciano and Air Vice Marshall David Hawkins, so I contacted them to let them know we were coming.

Buckingham Palace has been the Royal residence for over 150 years. It was originally named Buckingham House and was built by the Duke of Buckingham in 1703. The land which now forms Green Park, St. James's Park, Hyde Park and Buckingham Palace gardens has been used by the Royals centuries before; it was the deer hunting park for Henry VIIIth in the 1500's.

As well as a place of privacy and seclusion for the reigning monarch, it has always been a place of fantasy and unusual pleasure. During the reign of James I[st], hundreds of Mulberry trees were planted with the intention of creating a Royal Silk Farm. Unfortunately the project was a disaster though many of the original trees remain which produce succulent berries used by the Royal Kitchens in desserts for Queen Elizabeth.

During the 19th Century, the house was dramatically enlarged by the architects John Nash and Edward Blore with the construction of three wings around a central courtyard. Buckingham Palace became the London residence of the British Monarch, on the accession of Queen Victoria in 1837. After her marriage to Prince Albert, the building became the site of fantastical modernisation, with the introduction of electricity and the installation of many Chinese Regency pieces transported from the Brighton Pavilion.

The last major structural additions were made in the late 19th and 20th centuries. This included the construction of the East Front, which contains the famous balcony on which the Royal Family traditionally assemble to greet the public crowds.

For our present Queen, Her Majesty Queen Elizabeth, it has been the main London residence since her father King George VI suddenly became King, after the abdication of his brother Edward VIIIth. It became a safe playground for the Princesses Elizabeth and Margaret. Although most of the original gardens became public parks, there are still 39 acres of private gardens attached to the house. This is split into three main areas: Harrisons, with its well-known main lawn and paths, The Rose Garden which extends towards Hyde Park Corner and the very private, nature reserve known as The Yard, with 3 acres of lake and its own island.

It is on this island that our present monarch has her latest flight of fantasy; in 2008, 200,000 bees were installed in hives to provide a rich source of natural honey, which is still used today in the Royal Kitchens. These have proven much more successful, than Her Majesty's private flock of flamingos on the lake which were unfortunately devoured by foxes.

During Queen Charlotte's time here, when it was known as The Queen's House, she kept many exotic specimens in the garden, including a zebra and an elephant. These were later transferred to the Tower of London, until spacious accommodation was created in the new London Zoo. Nowadays any gifts of exotic animals to the monarch are placed in London Zoo.

Her Majesty is very committed to organic farming. Horse manure, referred by the Royal household as *risings,* are blended with organic waste to make superb compost for the next year's growing season. Also green fly, which are a big problem in the Rose Garden are controlled with sprays of water infused with garlic. I've tried that one over here and it works a treat. There is a faint waft of garlic for a couple of days, but this soon disappears.

In addition to the garden party invitation, we received two tickets which were also our Personal Cards, which we needed to fill out with our full names, dates of birth and current address. Also there were details of the gate we needed to use for entry, a private car park sticker – if we were driving, a video order form (how modern) and security guidance. As well there was a leaflet detailing dress code, forms of identification we needed to bring and the timetable for the afternoon.

This read as follows:

3.00 p.m. Gates Open.

3.30 p.m. Tea is served in the Main Tea Tent throughout the afternoon.

3.40 p.m. Yeoman of the Guard hold ground.

4.00 p.m. The National Anthem announces the arrival of Her Majesty The Queen and Members of the Royal Family. Gentlemen at Arms will then form lanes for The Queen and Members of the Royal Family to move through the guests.

4.15 p.m. Tea is served in the Diplomatic Tea Tent.

4.45 p.m. Tea is served in the Royal Tea Tent.

5.10 p.m. The Queen and Members of the Royal Family take tea in the Royal Tea Tent.

5.50 p.m. The Queen and Members of the Royal Family depart.

6.00 p.m. The National Anthem.

We arrived, suited and booted, passports and documents in hand, just after three o'clock on a perfect summer's day.

'I was hoping you would get to see the Main Entrance first,' I told Graham. I was disappointed that we had been given an entrance at the rear, via Grosvenor Place Gate. However, I knew we could depart from the Main Entrance when we were ready to leave.

'Doesn't matter to me,' he said, smiling. 'Shorter queues here and we should be able to grab a glass of champers before all the other 8,000 arrive.'

That was a typical optimistic response from him. I wasn't sure there would be any champagne, but already had a back-up plan in mind.

We quickly got through security and realized that we were walking through the nature reserve in the south east corner, known as the Yard.

'Wow, look at the size of those trees,' Graham said, pointing up.

I noticed they all had metal plaques displayed at the bottom. 'Yes, and look they've all got a story. This one was given by The Queen of Denmark and this was planted as an acorn by Princess Margaret.

'Is it a whisky tree?' he teased.

As we continued along the path, behind a few glamorous ladies in enormous hats, a large cottage appeared with green houses, tool sheds and a small tractor with trailer parked by a gate.

'It must be the gardener's house,' Graham explained. 'Wouldn't that be a great job here, Beany? Just imagine.'

I was already imagining. It would be a dream to work in such a garden haven, here in the heart of London. 'The Royal Gardener,' I said, thinking aloud.

As we continued along the path, there was a row of blue port-a-loos. 'Look Rob, the Royal bogs.' We extended this theme to point out *The Royal Wheelbarrow, The Royal Litter Bins,* etc., etc.

As we turned the next corner, we were summoned into speechless silence at the imposing site of Buckingham Palace, framed by ancient yew trees, at the top of large fields of perfectly manicured lawns, with a long line of yellow and white-striped marquees which formed the refreshment tents.

'Care to join one for tea?' Graham joked.

'Yes, Lord Hamilton. It would be an honour.'

We walked up towards the tents where there were already over a hundred people sat at tables drinking and eating.

Inside were perfectly attired waiting staff, handing out plates which had three soldier slices of different sandwiches and an assortment of French fancies and eclairs. We were offered tea or coffee, served from huge, silver-guilt urns.

The tables were filling up, so we decided to find an empty patch of lawn with views of the house, away from the brass band that were playing skilfully but far too ebulliently.

'Very tasty,' Graham said, tucking into a salmon and cucumber sandwich, with his little finger out. 'And to think she made all of these herself. She must have got up early this morning.'

I looked at him and laughed. 'Don't be silly. She started making them last night, whilst she was watching *Coronation Street*. Probably Charles gave her a hand.'

'Mmm. Let's hope not,' he replied with a mouthful of bread. 'Shame there's no bubbles though.'

Our thoughts were interrupted by the Yeomen of the Guard, who were starting to usher everyone into two lines, with a clear lane of passage for The Royal Family to pass through. I spotted David Hawkins and went to talk to him, whilst Graham quickly took the plates and cups back and then re-joined us. David asked us if we wanted to speak to The Queen, as she walked through. Graham was a bit embarrassed and declined but I jumped at the chance.

At 4.00 p.m. precisely, the Royal Anthem started playing and The Queen, along with The Duke of Edinburgh, Prince Charles and Camilla, and Prince Andrew appeared at the top of the steps. David knew that The Queen would be following the right-hand side of the queue and pulled me slightly out from the perfectly straight line, so it was clear to Her Majesty whom she would be stopping to speak with. Other Yeoman had followed similar practice and there were about twenty of us, ten on either side, who had been chosen.

The Queen was wearing a bright turquoise suit and matching hat and was looking truly magnificent. As she drew closer, an overwhelming sense of awe and wonder was flowing down through the crowds, like a river of reverent respect, for a woman who had given so much of her life for her country.

I looked over at Graham, whose mouth had dropped open.

'She's just so beautiful,' he whispered, leaning out towards me. 'Her skin is like snow and her eyes are as blue as her clothes.'

It was great to see him so happy.

Just before she got to us, David reminded me that you address The Queen as her Majesty and that you give thanks to ma'am, pronounced as in *ham*. He knew I was already familiar with this, after many occasions of providing service to her, but it was his job to remind everyone, in case they forgot at that crucial, nervous moment.

He announced me to her. 'Your Majesty, this is Robert Nicholson, Head Waiter from the House of Lords' Restaurants.

She put hand her out and I gently shook it. 'What a lovely day we have Robert,' she said.

My heart was racing in my mouth. 'Yes, your Majesty,' I replied and bowed my head.

'Are you well?'

'Yes, thank you ma'am.'

'How kind of you to join us here. It is our turn to give you tea today.'

'Yes, ma'am. Thank you ma'am.'

And with that, she was gone; moving down the lawn to the give the next person their moment of magic.

'Well, it doesn't get better than that.' Graham said, as he hugged me. 'What a great finale to all your years of service.'

I thanked David and we walked up the steps of the Palace for a different view. I held his hand and we pretended to give a Royal wave.

'Let's get out of here, shall we? Fancy a glass of champagne Graham?'

'God, yes. Thought you'd never ask. But where?'

'Just follow me.' I didn't tell him where we were going but had a clear plan in mind. It was rare for us both to be up in London wearing suits and presented us with a great opportunity.

We left the palace via the Main Entrance and drifted out through the gates and into Green Park.

'Comptons?' Graham asked, expecting us to go to one of our favourite drinking dens in Soho.

'Oh, I think, we can do better than that.' I stood outside the doors of The Ritz and watched his amazed face as we entered. We took a couple of seats at the bar and ordered two glasses of champagne.

'To Her Majesty The Queen,' I announced, proposing the toast.

'And to these happy Brighton queens,' Graham added.

We clinked glasses and savoured the cold, dry, sparkling liquid.

It was a happy conclusion to the end of 21 years of service and for the two of us a wonderful celebration of all the new adventures to come.

***

It seemed strange to be putting on my morning suit and leather shoes, in place of gardening trousers, polo shirt and boots. We don't have an iron, but I managed to stretch out one of my old white shirts smoothly enough and covered most of it with my jacket and tie. I even put on my House of Lords cufflinks for good measure.

I arrived at Janet's at one o'clock. The garden was looking amazing. The red and blue bouncy castle had been inflated, colourful bunting had been added to the ropes of the marquee and covered tables harbouring a bounty of goods, delivered earlier by the caterers, had been placed near the pool bar area.

It was strange to have no dogs bounding down to greet me but it was a practical solution to allow the party to run more smoothly. I parked the van down the far side of the outside track, as I knew there would be lots of vehicles coming, presumably with more babies and buggies and stuff.

As I walked up towards the house, a fine figure appeared looking resplendent in a 1950's retro dress in turquoise and lime green, covered in pink flamingos. Her hair had been lengthened with extensions and looked a deep auburn, almost red colour. It had been gripped at the top but then fell in two long swirls of curls either side of her head, onto the thin shoulder straps. The makeover was complete with a pair of white, chunky rimmed sunglasses perched on her head and white cotton sandals. Very impressive. She was pushing an old fashioned, Victorian perambulator, with four wheels, a coral blue metal body and a white lace canopy stretched over the top.

I wasn't a hundred per cent sure that it was Janet until she spoke.

'Ey up mi duk. Come and meet our Eleanor.'

As I walked up towards them, I thought: *thank heavens, I'm not going mad!* I knew I had heard a baby crying from inside the house. But why had she said that she was turning five? As I peered inside the pram, under its cover, all became clear.

There indeed was a tiny baby figure, wearing a miniature version of the same dress as her mother. She was perfectly formed with large, almost glassy blue eyes, dark brown hair and little chubby arms and legs with flawless looking skin.

She smiled at me and cooed. And, then, it may have been my imagination, but she winked one of her heavily lashed eyelids directly at me. I looked back, up at Janet.

'Isn't she just bootiful?' she cried, proudly.

I looked back inside. 'She's amazing.'

From behind me, Janet said to her daughter, 'Eleanor, say hello to Robert.' And then to me, 'She was practicing last noit.'

After a few silent moments, the doll suddenly jolted into action. 'Hello, Robert. I am Eleanor. Pleased to make your acquaintance.' With a soft metal hum, she held out her little right hand for me to shake.

I honestly thought I had been transported into the future, through some hidden wormhole in time, but as I looked around the familiar setting I knew I was still in the here and now. I shook her tiny fingers as gently as I could. 'Nice to meet you too, Eleanor.'

She giggled and the pale-pinkish synthetic skin seemed to turn slightly redder as if she was blushing. I was speechless.

'It's my berfthday today,' she said, in a more childlike voice.

Here was my chance to set the record straight. 'I know, Eleanor. Happy Birthday to you. And how old are you today?'

'I am five today.'

I'm not sure that the confirmation did anything to appease my looping mind; I wanted to spend an hour with this miraculous toy and find out what it could do.

'Come on Eleanor,' Janet said, grabbing the handlebars. 'You've got a busy day today darling and we don't want you to get too tired before all your guests arrive.'

Before she went back inside - maybe to pop Eleanor back on charge - she thanked me for dressing up so smart, and asked if I would show people where to park and lead them over to the bar area and give them a welcome drink.

During the next hour, about thirty-five vehicles pulled up. It wasn't easy to fit them all in and some had to park across the opened gate entrance. The guests were nearly all women who were playing the role of doting mother, pouring their love and attention onto their own baby dolls, carried in prams, push chairs or colourful buggies.

There were two men there who seemed to have been summoned against their will. One was a short wiry fellow, *Stick Man,* who was complaining that he was missing his weekend walking group. The other was a large, burly skinhead, *Big Man,* who made a beeline for the bar and resolved that the only way to get through this was to get as drunk as possible.

At two o'clock, as instructed, I pressed *play* on the iPod on the bar and the speakers started to transmit, at slow tempo, the famous melody of *Happy Birthday to You.* The guests all dutifully joined in, apart from Big Man who was now stood behind the bar, and Janet appeared, with Eleanor in her arms, to receive the well-wishes.

Everyone gathered around mum and baby to wish them well and tell them how great they looked. I filled fifty flutes with champagne and took them around to the guests in readiness for Janet to give her welcome speech.

She gave me Eleanor to hold, which was a bit of a shock. I wasn't sure what the correct way was, so I just held her chest upright, with my hands under either side of her arms.

'Dear friends. Thank yous all so much for coming. I can't tell you how much these special days mean to me. It's great to be with others who understand. Peoples who have been kicked by Mother Nature but yet been given such miracles of happiness. So as well as a toast to our Eleanor and her birthday, it is a toast to all of yous as well, as we continue our journeys of parenthood with our *Blessings*.'

'To Eleanor,' someone shouted.

The crowd followed with, 'Yes, to Eleanor,' and raised their glasses.

'To all of you,' I added, perhaps out of turn, but I was caught up in the emotion.

Fortunately it was well received. 'To all of us,' they all cheered.

After the announcement, Eleanor was placed in a high chair in the shade and people placed gifts and cards around her.

As I uncovered the buffet, I saw that as well as prawn salads, cold meats, quiches and other savouries, there was a large section of children's foods including crisps, pizzas, jellies and chocolate fingers. As a centre-piece, there was a heart-shaped birthday cake with five candles. Some of the other mums had returned to their vehicles to retrieve high chairs and others were all simultaneously feeding themselves and their babies.

Janet admonished me, slightly, for neglecting to offer drinks to the children. I took around a tray of jugs with assorted juices and waters, with some plastic tumblers. All the mothers quickly accepted the drinks.

Walking around the party, I learned that, like most things in life, the quality and sophistication of the models they had purchased varied significantly, according to price. Whereas they all seemed to be able to make some kind of noises, there were great differences in their breathing and eating capabilities. Some seemed to be literally ingesting the food and drinks through tiny perfect mouths, whereas others were unable to do so and there was a steady stream of rejected juice or cake.

Eleanor was clearly a high quality specimen; she proved this when she was somehow able to blow out the five lit candles on her birthday cake.

After the food, Janet placed her daughter back into the pram to rest. 'Robert, everyone seems to have what they need. Let me take you around and introduce you to some people. Did you bring your business cards with you?'

'Some,' I replied. I had a large stack in my jacket pocket but thought it inappropriate now to hand them out.

She led me inside the marquee, where there were a few mothers manning different stalls. The light was dimmer in here and there was a stale smell of trapped air and canvas oil being heated up by the afternoon sun. There was a makeup area, where one of the Blessings was having his face painted as a tiger; a clothing stall, with all the latest new outfits and trends for the little ones; and a large area of accessories including beds, baths, toys, prams, buggies and bikes.

Janet introduced me to Carol who was painting the tiger face on the little boy.

'That looks amazing,' I said, pointing to the symmetrical stripes.

'Thank you dear. It's a bit of fun.'

'Carol does the home care work with me. We've known each other for years and met in Pediatrics in London, when we were doing our nursing training.'

It was clear this was a kind woman and a great friend of the hostess.

Janet touched her shoulder. 'She also does re-sprays for skin tones and is brilliant at skin repairs for our Blessings.'

'Janet, you're too kind. I does what I can.'

I noticed she had her own baby doll in a push chair, sleeping soundly under a blanket. I was told her name was Jessica.

As we walked through the tent, Janet explained that Carol and her husband had had a real child, Alice, but she had died in cot death and they couldn't bring themselves to go through that pain and suffering again. And that, of course, once a woman gets to a certain age, like Janet and Carol, it's quite unsafe to think about childbirth.

At last, here was a story that made a lot of sense to this incredulous situation and provided some form of hope for people who had none. The next encounter wasn't so easy to absorb.

Outside the tent, in front of the busy bouncy castle, where mothers were gently jumping up and down, holding their precious infants, was a very suave looking woman, dripping in jewels and Armani. She was pushing an expensive, double-seated stroller that looked more like a classic car than a baby carrier.

'Wow, what an amazing buggy,' I said, in full admiration.

The voice that returned was short and snap. 'It's not a buggy. It's a *Roddler.*'

I gasped, not because she had put me in my place but due to the fact I had noticed the seats were made from alligator skin. The chassis was cast in stainless steel and the red and white hood and wheel arches made it look like a Cadillac. 'It's amazing.'

'This is Maxine,' Janet announced, perhaps with a slight tone of disdain. 'She has a holiday home in Marbella.'

'Yes couldn't live here in July and August. We go back to Switzerland when it gets too hot and winter in Barbados.' Her tone was as cold and flat as her expression. She wouldn't look at me and kept her eyes hidden under the wide brim of a white, straw summer hat, with a large blue bow. The rest of her head was framed by a perfectly straight fringe and long, ebony-black hair which sheened like dark, highly-polished glass.

'And who are these two little darlings?' I crouched down to look closer at the two immaculate oriental figures, again with shiny black hair; they seemed to be making noises to each other in their adjoining seats.'

Maxine pushed the Roddler marginally forward, as if I had gotten too close.

I thought I heard one of them repeat my words to the other. Certainly I heard the reiteration of *little darlings* and *it's amazing*. The little sods were taking the piss out of me. They started laughing, uncontrollably with each other.

As I stood back up, Maxine tapped the canopy where there were two engraved name plates affixed. I read aloud, 'Phuc,' and 'Hoa.' It was so difficult not to laugh.

'It's Vietnamese. It means *lucky* and *like a flower*.' With that, the frost maiden dismissed herself, insisting she needed more shade and pushed her foreign gems out of sight. I could hear them singing, 'We are lucky, oh so lucky….'

'She's a piece of work, ain't she Rob?' Janet sighed.

'Not one of your favourites, I'm guessing.'

Janet was walking back towards the bar. 'She makes out she's so bloody righteous 'cos she's saved two orphans from Vietnam. But they're from California, like all our Blessings, and cost ten thousand dollars each.'

That would surely have bought a lot of much needed food in Vietnam, I thought.

Janet got herself a large glass of wine and a beer for me. The party was winding up, she had told the guests to help themselves and that I didn't need to serve any more. She told me to come and take a look behind the bar. Big Man had collapsed on the floor with a bottle of whisky that had spilled over his chest.

'Looks like someone's enjoying himself,' I said.

We both laughed.

As we were sat observing how happy and relaxed everyone looked, there was a scream up by the house. One of the mothers had gone inside to use the toilet and two large creatures, covered in dark fur, with huge paws and mouths had pushed past her and broken out into the garden. I recognised them immediately. It was Toby and Oscar!

I looked at Janet, puzzled. 'I thought John had taken them down on the coast.'

'He were meant to pet, but there's been a terrible gas leak at one of the houses and it wouldn't have been safe for them. He's taken Shorty, as he can keep him in the van but I shut Toby and Oscar in the utility room.' It was clear she was now regretting this decision. In a desperate attention to minimize the chaos she called them down towards her.

At first, it looked like they were being responsive. They bounded across the grass, onto the pool terrace and ran towards us. However, before we could seize them, they darted out the way and jumped up at the cold meats on the table and grabbed some mouthfuls, as if they hadn't been fed for days. The mothers were all screaming, had dropped their drinks and were holding their babies high in the air, away from the wolf-like mouths.

After finishing off the birthday cake, they lunged back onto the grass; evidently revelling in their new found freedom.

It was clear that this was the moment when the women in distress would have to be saved by a dashing masculine hero. Since Big Man was still asleep behind the bar and Stick Man was hiding behind his wife, they would have to make do with The Garden Butler.

I took some more meat off the table and planned to coax them with it and grab their collars. Before I could reach them, they suddenly parted company; Toby ran towards the bouncy castle and Oscar shot inside the tent.

I could hear Carol screaming.

It was impossible to follow both of them, so I ran into the tent.

Carol, hysterical now, stood beside an empty buggy, was pointing to a spot behind a rack of summer baby clothes.

There, lying on the floor, with a small rounded object between his front paws, was Oscar with Jessica. Her arm was inside his mouth.

Slowly, I moved towards the big dog, telling him he was a *good boy* and held out a large handful of cold beef to tempt him away. Fortunately, he fell for it; he moved away from the doll and came towards me. Carol ran over to Jessica and scooped her up in her arms. Although the tiny form was dripping in dog drool there was no serious damage.

'Thank you, Robert. Thank you so much.'

I handed Oscar over to Janet who took him back up to the house.

It was time to get Toby.

At first, there was no sign of him. I walked around all the parked cars, checked the side track, came back in and headed towards the bouncy castle, which was now empty. At the foot of the huge inflatable, I noticed the gleaming red Roddler I had seen earlier and a discarded summer hat that had been thrown onto the floor. The little girl, Hoa, who seemed to be in sleep mode, was on her own, with no sign of Maxine or Phuc. I took off my shoes and decided to check out the rubberised fortress. It looked like it had been vacated but I saw there was a small inner chamber, on the back wall. I could hear growling, roaring through the hidden enclave.

As I slowly wobbled in through the entrance, trying not to bounce too much, I saw that it was Maxine making the snarling noises and not Toby; his mouth was too full of Phuc.

'You leave my son, you disgusting mongrel or I'll fucking kill you.' She was stood three feet away from them with a silver pistol aimed at Toby. He was backed against a corner, sitting down, shaking Phuc with his mouth. It looked like one of the doll's arms had already been dismembered and was hanging off, limp at the side of the mauled body.

'Disgusting mongrel. Fucking kill you,' the robot boy was repeating in loops as it was held between the angry teeth.

'Maxine. What are you doing? That won't help.' I pleaded.

She ignored me. 'Nobody messes with my family.' She cocked

the weapon, steadied her extended arm with her free arm and took aim.

Just before the gun was fired, I jumped high in the air, thumped down on the floor and jettisoned her upwards where she discharged a single bullet, which erupted in a deafening blast, tore past me and pierced the turret of the inflated building. As air hissed out of the walls, Toby whined in distress, dropped the doll, ran out of the collapsing structure and into the arms of Janet who was waiting for him.

I clambered back out, onto the grass, and saw a dishevelled Maxine carrying the severed body out of the war zone, as if she was a general at The Somme rescuing one of her men. The victim was hanging, limp in her arms, with small blue sparks flying out of its arm. It was still speaking, telling its mother, 'I think it's time to go home now.'

Fortunately, she took his advice. She put him into sleep mode, back in the Roddler, replaced her sun hat, screamed something about legal action and casually strolled out of the garden.

After her departure, all the mothers, led by Carol, gathered around me and with her encouragement, gave *three cheers for Robert.* They then thanked me, in single file, asked me for a business card and about my availability for gardening work and serving at their parties. Janet hugged me, gave me a 100 euro tip and said she couldn't thank me enough. She told me not to worry about Maxine. She had, after all, illegally used a weapon in Spain and she was very sure that none of them would ever hear from her again.

As I finally left Eleanor's party and drove home, I was amused by my misgivings about moving to the Costa Del Sol. I was sure that I would never ever meet the colourful array of characters I had loved serving in the House of Lords and was doubtful I would find sufficient work.

I was wrong on both counts.

Moving to Spain was the best decision I ever made.

ABOUT THE AUTHOR

Graham Hamilton studied at Sussex University and has an M.A. in Creative Writing and Authorship. He has been teaching for over thirty years and runs workshops (*Your Story*) to help other ambitious writers to bring their books to life.
He has written for a number of publications and was a regular contributor and columnist for local magazines in Brighton.
He now lives and writes in Malaga, Spain.

Robert Nicholson is still gardening on the Costa del Sol and meeting a whole new range of eccentric expats.
He also gives talks and after dinner speeches on being the first waiter in the House of Lords, with entertaining anecdotes from the colourful characters he has met and served and detailed insights into the significant changes he witnessed within our House of Parliament.

Follow us on Facebook
And on twitter: Graham Hamilton@YourStory
Robert Nicholson@ServingtheLords

Printed in Great Britain
by Amazon